# Swordfighting,

for writers, game designers,
and martial artists.

This work was brought to you by

The School of European Swordsmanship

www.swordschool.com

And the patrons of this work who donated through Indiegogo and directly.

ISBN 978-952-68193-6-5 (hardback)

ISBN 978-952-67934-8-1 (paperback)

ISBN 978-952-67934-9-8 (PDF)

ISBN 978-952-68193-0-3 (EPUB)

ISBN 978-952-68193-1-0 (MOBI)

Cover image based on an original design by

Denís Fernández Cabrera of Gatonegro deseño

Book Design by Zebedee Design & Typesetting Services

(www.zebedeedesign.co.uk)

Printed by Lightning Source

# Swordfighting,

for writers, game designers, and martial artists.

## by Guy Windsor

For two sword-swinging friends:

Martin Page and Topi Mikkola.

Thanks, chaps.

# Contents

# Foreword by Neal Stephenson

More than a decade ago, while working on a historical epic called *The Baroque Cycle*, I found myself writing detailed descriptions of swordfights on a pretty regular basis. I felt a certain responsibility to get it right. The combatants were mostly using a rapier in one hand and a dagger in the other. I knew nothing about that--or any--kind of historical swordfighting, other than a vaguely remembered beginners' training session with the late, great Ed Richards, an Olympian who taught in Boston when I lived there in the 1970s. He had mentioned that foil fencers traditionally held the off hand up behind the head because, centuries ago, it had been used to grip a dagger.

Or at least that was my recollection; I probably had it wrong, and Maestro Richards may simply have been trying to hold the attention of a crowd of restless university students who had signed up for the class so that they could dispense with their physical education requirements. At any rate, it was all I had to go on when I started *The Baroque Cycle*, and so I dutifully set about trying to craft elaborate swordfighting sequences in which the combatants stood like modern foil fencers, moved like modern foil fencers, and, to make a long story short, did everything like modern foil fencers except that they were holding daggers in their off hands and would occasionally try to stab each other by lashing out over their heads "like scorpions."

When you are writing crap, as all writers do from time to time, you sometimes have to pass through the Five Stages of Grief before you can get into a place where you're not writing crap any more. These stages, as detailed by Elizabeth Kübler-Ross in another context, are Denial, Anger, Bargaining, Depression, and Acceptance. Since this is meant to be just a short preface, I'll leave it as an exercise to the reader to imagine how those played out in my soul as I stared at the pages and pages of utter swordfighting crap that I had painstakingly written based on a complete lack of valid information about historical European martial arts (HEMA). When I finally got round to Acceptance, however, I did what I should have done in the first place and went out trying to educate myself.

Part of this was looking for good books and videos on the topic. These were thin on the ground. I found some videos that, in retrospect, were geared more for stage combat than for martial arts. With some like-minded friends in Seattle I began constructing practice weapons and trying these techniques out. To tell that whole story would take a while and would delay the moment when you, the reader, begin to explore Guy Windsor's writings on the topic. So I shall fast-forward and let you know that many years' floundering around ensued. My group, which later became an organization called Lonin League LLC, experimented with many different historical styles and types of equipment before settling, circa 2007, on the longsword as our favorite weapon, steel as our favorite material, and Guy Windsor as our favorite writer of instructional manuals. I began to attend the Western Martial Arts Workshop (WMAW) in Racine, Wisconsin and there became a student, then an acquaintance, and finally a friend of Guy's. Our group has adopted

Guy's curriculum as the basis of our training. Whenever we can, we bring him to Seattle to give instructional seminars.

That's where matters stand as of the end of 2014. To conclude this preface, though, I'd like to go back to the spring of 2007, when (according to my order history on the site of a certain prominent online bookseller) I seem to have gone into a frenzy of one-clicking in an attempt to find a longsword book that was actually useful. One of the books I bought was Guy's *The Swordsman's Companion*. A month later, I seem to have ordered a second copy. Two weeks after that, I bought a copy of the companion volume, *The Duellist's Companion*. And four months later I was at WMAW in Racine, Wisconsin, sitting across the table from Guy himself in the cafeteria of the DeKoven Center.

Obviously, something happened upon my first reading of Guy's book. I remember it clearly. It was immediately obvious that this man knew what he was talking about, knew how to write, and had the rare talent for making this material accessible--not by dumbing it down, but by posing achievable challenges to the would-be swordsman. These qualities have made him a leader within the worldwide HEMA community and put him in a position to write for a broader audience. This book is the result. Whether you are a writer or game-maker seeking the kind of information I sought while writing *The Baroque Cycle*, or just a general reader with an interest in the arts to which Guy Windsor has dedicated his career, you should find much that is rewarding in these pages.

Neal Stephenson
Seattle
December 2014

# Introduction

This book has gone through a dozen title changes, ranging from the rather pompous "Principles of Swordsmanship" to the rather casual "Swordfighting for Geeks and Gamers." It is a collection of articles and essays that includes all sorts of things I wish everyone knew about swordfighting:

- how it works;
- how it can be recreated from historical sources;
- how it should be presented in books and games so that it won't make me, my students, and my colleagues wince;
- how it can enrich and enlarge your life;
- what kind of swords there are;
- what they are good for;
- what you need for training; and
- what you should look for in good technique.

The biggest challenge has been putting all this together into a coherent form and making sure that any logical gaps are filled. This book is partly new material, and partly articles and blog posts that have already made it into the wider world. It is emphatically not a "most popular blog posts" compilation: some posts included in this book got less than 100 views. I have chosen them all because I think they are important, not because they happened to do well in the Internet popularity contest.

The book is organised into the following sections:

- "What is Historical Swordsmanship?" covers some aspects of researching and recreating the Art.
- "Martial Essentials" covers some of the less-well-understood aspects of what martial arts are and how they work.
- "Lessons from the Art" covers some of the wider real-world benefits of training, especially dealing with questions of mistakes, risk, and fear.
- "Swords" describes the main classifications of the weapons we use, and includes discussion of appropriate training tools.
- "Fighting" includes historical examples of duels, and discussions about the nature of real violence.
- "Writing Swordfights" is about how swords and swordfights should be represented in fiction, with examples of fights done both well and badly.
- "Gaming" is a discussion of the ways in which swordsmanship can be adapted for game design purpose.
- "Training" is largely insights into how we train swordsmanship.

There was originally another chapter on "Teaching the Art", about how I train my students, but this book has grown to more than double the size of my next longest, and teaching is a really specific interest, so I have cut it out and worked it up into a separate volume.

Where I have included a previously published article, I have added a short description of when it was published, why I wrote it, and sometimes also the critical reception it got. I have also edited each post to bring it up to the standard expected in a published book. This has meant not only tweaking the language in places, but also deleting discussion questions, changing some links, and, where my opinion has changed since first writing, noting my current thoughts on the subject.

Let me acknowledge here that the impetus for this book came from Neal Stephenson, who suggested I write something for novelists and game designers to help them write better swordfights. With that encouragement I applied for and got a grant from the Finnish Non-Fiction Writers' Association, which kept me fed for long enough to bang out the first draft of the material on fiction and game design. I put the book on hold while my medieval combat card game, *Audatia*, was developed and brought to market, the story of which is told in the "Gaming" section. All the while I was teaching, researching, and producing articles for my blog (guywindsor.com). In March 2014 the rights to publish my long-awaited longsword book (which had been languishing in publishing limbo for two years) returned to me, and so I set up a crowdfunding campaign to raise the funds to get it laid out and printed. This went very well, and I added this book into the same campaign when we passed the 300% funded point. Those contributors to the campaign who did not wish to remain anonymous are acknowledged at the back of this book.

Swordfighting, as with any specialist field, has its jargon, and also a deep love of acronyms. Here are some of the more common ones:

- *HEMA* stands for Historical European Martial Arts. Ironically, many of the things done under that banner are neither historical, specifically European, martial, nor terribly artistic.
- *WMA* stands for Western Martial Arts, as distinct from Eastern ones.
- *WMAW* is the biannual Western Martial Arts Workshop. It's

my favorite historical swordsmanship event, and is held in Racine, Wisconsin, USA.

So without further ado, let us start with the perennial question from those that do not to those that do: why do you do swordsmanship?

# CHAPTER ONE
## What is Swordsmanship?

### WHY DO YOU DO SWORDSMANSHIP?

The following article was originally posted on February 6th 2014. It got more than seven times as many hits in the first day than the average post because, I think, many of the people who read it felt that I had managed to put into words their innermost feelings about the art they practice.

For many of us there is no need to even think about why we would train in the Art of Swordsmanship. It is simply an irreducible desire, like the way many people want to have kids. But we all know someone for whom our passion for the sword is inexplicable, just as we all know someone who does not want to be a parent. I thought I would write this rather difficult post so that you would know why I have chosen the path of the sword and, if it resonates with you, you can direct the baffled in your life here for enlightenment.

Let us begin with a wide focus: why martial arts at all? Some have practical uses, sure. Those living on meaner streets will have use for self-defense skills. But most martial arts, if they convey those skills at all, are very inefficient at it. Some martial arts, or combat sports at least, offer a career path that includes fame and riches. An Olympic gold medal, perhaps. But that is not true of ours.

I train martial arts because they can offer moments of utter transcendence. The ineffable made manifest. This is traditionally described as "beyond words" or "indescribable" but, as a martial artist and a writer, that would feel like a cop-out. I will take this feeling and wrestle it down onto the page, or at least give it my best shot.

It is a moment when every atom in your body is exactly where it should be. Every step you have taken on life's path makes sense, and is part of a coherent story. The pain of every mistake is made worthwhile by the lessons contained within. There is a feeling of physical power without limit; strength without stiffness; flow without randomness; precision without pedantry; focus without blinkers; breadth and depth; massive destructive capability, but utter gentleness; self-awareness without self-consciousness; force without fury; your body alive as it has never been, all fear and pain burned away in a moment of absolute clarity; certainty without dogma; and an overpowering love, even for your enemies, that enables you to destroy them without degrading them. For a religious person it is the breath of God within you; for an atheist it is a moment of attaining perfection as a human being.

And I can, in theory at least, get that feeling every time I pick up a sword. In practice I've only been there a dozen times, and to a lesser version of it – a breath or a hint of it – almost daily.

It is, of course, an illusion. You are not perfect or invulnerable, even in that moment of grace. And this is where the discipline of a serious art saves you from the wishy-washy, hippy shit of some other "spiritual paths." It is so easy to slip, to believe your own hype, and simply essential that reality comes crashing in like a sword to the head the moment you do so. The rigor of a true martial art contains at its heart a continual examining of your skills. This can come in all sorts of forms: I tend to use pressure drills and freeplay (explained in chapter 7), but the critical component is the existence of an objective external test. Such a test would be asking "does this work?" with a clear yes/no feedback mechanism in place. In many ways, the books from which we draw our art *are* that mechanism: the benchmark against which you measure the correctness of what you do. This academic aspect is, I think, unique to historical martial arts, and it requires that we are able to articulate in reasoned argument why we do anything a particular way. This adds a mental dimension, a way of clear, logical thinking and of making arguments supported by evidence, which is the antithesis of the "feel that energy, man" hippy shit I refer to above.

There is also the question of morality. The moral dimension to swordsmanship comes from the lethal nature of the art. It is, originally, for killing people. Some systems emphasise self-defense, but the knightly arts were for professional warriors. You kill people because that's your job. Much like a modern soldier, who must only distinguish between legal and illegal orders. If the order is legal and obeying it means killing people, well, that's what they train for. I'm not suggesting that any part of that is easy, especially distinguishing legal orders from illegal ones, but at its base level it *is* simple. Do, or do not. But for us, training exists in an artificial space that allows us to deeply examine the morality of the martial arts. (I've written elsewhere about training as a holo-deck for the philosophy of ethics. The article is on page 43.) We are training in a killing art, and so we must ask ourselves this question: in what circumstances, if any, is it acceptable to take life? This is why I have no interest in non-lethal arts. They simply lack this moral aspect. Especially combat sports where your opponent has chosen to compete with you in a fair fight, and there is no question of right or wrong at all so long as you both follow the rules.

Bodily health is also an issue. We have no choice but to live in this carcass until it stops working. There is just no way round the fact that you either figure out how yours works, and get the best out of it (it is a stunningly fabulous machine), or you ignore it until it fails. I don't train to stay healthy: I stay healthy so I can train. All of my students know that I put maintenance and conditioning at the heart of our training. I also spend about 90% of my own training time and about 40% of my teaching time working on mechanics. Most of my students come to me a bit broken in the beginning. Poor posture, bad wrists, a dodgy knee, excessive weight, or whatever. We work together to develop good habits: mostly by paying attention to posture, breathing, joint strength training, and, of course, diet. This has a way of both preparing the student for the physical training and of keeping them grounded when the magic starts to happen. The sword has hooked many students out of physical lassitude and ill-health and into a more active, healthier life. It is certainly part of the core mission of the School. Our training is healthy: our one golden rule is *everyone must finish class healthier than they started it.* And because we are interested in process, not outcome, it is literally irrelevant how fit a student is when they start. Only the attitude they bring to training matters.

This is another reason why I am not interested in combat sports. They have a pretty high threshold for physical fitness, which means that you have to start quite fit (and young!) if you wish to get really good at them. There is a genetic lottery (every sport has an ideal body type), and luck plays a huge part too. Read *Bounce*, by Matthew Syed, for more on this. Combat sports also have a very high risk of injury. So the students who need hooking off the couch and into a healthy life are barred from admission, and the ones who need it least are the only ones who can have it.

So why the sword? All of these spiritual, mental, moral, and physical benefits can be accomplished with other weapons, or with no weapons at all. There is no good reason, though I could rationalize it at length. We could talk about flow states, ala Mihaly Csikszentmihalyi: swordsmanship practice is most certainly a way to bring "order (as opposed to entropic chaos) to consciousness." We could talk about the social aspect; how good it is to find, coming to the salle, that you are not the only sword-obsessed loony out there. But fundamentally, some people are just drawn to the magic of steel. It resonates in them. Many students remember the first time they heard the clash of blade on blade, and how their heart leapt.

I train because I feel it. Oh Lord, I feel it in my very bones. But how I train is utterly rational. Together, the martial and academic truth-testing keep me from flying away with the fairies. The physical training keeps my body strong and agile. The mental training keeps my mind clear and focused. The moral aspect leads me to consider the meaning and value of every part of my life.

So, when someone asks you "why practice Swordsmanship?" perhaps the best answer is "how the hell do you manage without it?"

So, that's my reason. What's yours?

## REAL SWORDFIGHTING

There is a vexed question in historical swordsmanship circles: what is real swordfighting and how do you train for it? Only tournament bouts really count for some people; for others, there has to be a corpse by the end. This is my first stab at an answer, posted on February 6th 2013.

When I was a little boy I wanted nothing more than to learn real swordfighting. My mum told me that real swordfighting was called "fencing," and that her dad, my grandpa, was an expert. He had been a keen fencer for about 70 years at this point, and was duly prevailed upon to give his grandson an introductory lesson in the noble art. This involved him sitting in his armchair smoking a roll-up cigarette while I stood there holding a foil. When he yelled "extension!" I stuck my arm out, and when he barked "lunge!" I stepped forwards with my front foot. I was about eight years old, and this was heaven. REAL swordfighting! Unfortunately, though, he was extremely old (about 88) and my family were living in Botswana while he was in London, so I only ever got a couple of sessions with him before he died.

I made do then with what I saw on the silver screen; however, at this time sword flicks were pretty rare. *Conan the Barbarian* was my primary source, with supporting material from such legendary high-quality movies as *Hawk the Slayer*. But it was very, very hard to get my hands on movies like this because: a) the VCR had only just been invented, and b) we didn't have a TV to plug one into. But while I was home for the school holidays I went to Gaborone's one and only cinema, the Capitol, most Saturday afternoons. The kids' matinee was occasionally such a gem as *Clash of the Titans*, but usually full-length, uncut, Hong Kong kung fu movies, complete with hardcore violence and some pretty nasty porn. My friend Mark and I would gloss over the bits with naked women in (we were only 9 or 10) but treat the rest of the film as instructional; on the walk home we practiced the top-level moves we had learned. I never did quite manage to jump backwards onto a tree branch, but we waved our arms and legs with vigor and we were both adept at the sound effects.

My martial arts education took a more serious turn when a karate group started up at the local golf course. It was run by a Korean man who barely spoke, and who spent quite some time after most classes trying to break concrete paving slabs with his bare hands. He would set up a couple of slabs between some breeze blocks, put a thin towel on top, and slam his hand down. The top slab always cracked in two, but I never did see him break both at once. The class consisted of three or four students. We would start by running somewhere on the course, finding a quiet spot, and going through a set of ritualized opening moves before the punching and kicking would begin. The first command, which sounded like "chariot," had us standing up straight with our hands by our sides; then he'd yell "chumbi!" and we would drop a little with our hands fisted in front of us. This was by way of salute, I think. I didn't get a lot of training, what with commuting to the UK three times a year for school, but the buzz of doing real martial arts for the first time will never leave me.

(This still strikes me as by far the best use a golf course has ever been put to, and I would urge those of you of an activist frame of mind to set up an "occupy golf courses" movement so that these lovely spaces can serve a worthwhile function as outdoor dojos.)

My school at this time was a boys-only boarding school in rural Suffolk, not far from Ipswich. There was a general policy that the school would organize classes in something if enough boys were interested in it. So I campaigned for martial arts and, eventually, at the beginning of my final year there the powers that be allowed a karate class to start. My name was first on the sign-up sheet, and I went to the deputy head (a normally terrifying individual) and begged for a guarantee that I would be picked. The list of those doing karate was posted a week later and, thank the lord, my name was on the list.

Imagine my delight when the karate we were doing turned out to be basically the same style; chariot, chumbi, and all. But this time we also had belts and ranks, and so gradings. The club began in September 1986, which was also the beginning of my final year and the year in which we moved from Botswana to Peru. This meant that two days before my first ever karate grading

I had a load of really nasty vaccinations, and I took the test with my left arm swollen and in constant agony. There were tears running down my face for most of the exam, and I was shaking like a leaf by the end. But, and here's the lesson, I got a first-class pass. This had nothing to do with my rather feeble *ap chagis* (front kicks) and everything to do with my having got through it without quitting.

This martial arts heaven lasted only a year before I was packed off to public school and there was no karate to be had. But, joy of joys, finally there was fencing. Not only that but fencing had just been designated a "major sport" in the school, which meant that I was not obliged to do any other sport if I was taking fencing. In other words, I never had to chase after another fucking round object again. I cannot tell you how much of my life had been wasted by my being forced to pretend to care where a leather bag (football or rugby), or a solid round object (hockey or cricket), ended up relative to a white line and some posts. Hockey at least had the decency to supply me with a weapon and people to hit with it, but the rest of the sports were just so stupid. Surrounded by boys who were sports-mad, as good little Englishmen are trained to be, I had always felt like a complete alien. Sometimes I even faked a bit of enthusiasm. But hanging about outside in a muddy field, wearing shorts in winter, and being yelled at for not paying attention to a completely arbitrary set of rules is just the single least explicable human pursuit. But fencing... that made sense. Someone is trying to stab me. I'm trying to not get stabbed, and to stab them instead so that they have to stop. Makes perfect sense. I am motivated.

I loved every minute of fencing from footwork drills, to technical drills, to individual lessons with the coach, and to the actual competitive fencing. But the tournaments themselves were a pain. It meant getting up early at the weekend; going somewhere in a coach (I despise and abhor all forms of motorized transport unless

I'm driving); hanging about for endless hours waiting for it to be my turn; fiddling with stupid kit; and then, finally, getting to fence people I hadn't fenced before. Total time investment: perhaps 9 hours. Total bouts: maybe 10. Less if I got eliminated early but one of my teammates didn't, so we all had to stay. Inefficient. It was the least good bit about the whole fencing endeavor, but it had some useful aspects: mostly to do with the experience of crossing blades with new people.

I spent all five years of my secondary education doing no other sport but fencing, and I was reasonably good by the end of it; I was good enough to be captain of the team, but not good enough to get into the nationals. In September 1992 I went up to Edinburgh University to read English Literature. Naturally I joined the Fencing Society, and I showed up to my first session wondering what the level would be like. Fencing clubs are one of the few environments on Earth where it is perfectly polite, friendly even, to go up to someone you don't know and say "fancy a fight?" This I did, to a tall Chinese-looking chap who was already kitted up. He agreed, and we set to. On the first pass it was obvious to me he was out of my league, but I did okay: I even pulled off a lovely doublé in carte (he was a left hander). The score was 4–3 in his favor when I saw the opportunity for another doublé. As I took it he neatly stepped offline with his back foot and counter-attacked under my arm, and my point went sailing inches past his chest. 5–3: I lose. Then I noticed the logos on his kit; he was just back from the Barcelona Olympics, where he was on the British team. Suddenly losing was far less important than the fact that I'd got three hits! And he had set me up for the second doublé, having seen my predilection for it. Lovely.

Sad to say, though, that bout was the highlight of my University fencing; at the time a completely erroneous interpretation of the FIE rules was being applied by pretty much all tournament referees. The rule states (in foil) that the attack is determined as the extension of the sword arm with the point threatening the target. But it was interpreted as "whoever moves forward first is attacking." This led to people running forwards with their point back over their left shoulder and walking onto my extended arm while flicking their point around to touch my shoulder. According to the rules this was my attack on their preparation. In a duel it was their pierced liver versus my small bruise on the shoulder. According to the referees it was a hit against me. I was not prepared to fence like that given that my interest was in real swordfighting, so I stopped going to competitions. But around this time I fell in with some other fencers who wanted to do things for real, and I started meeting up with them to fight the way we wanted to: in a way that felt real.

One of the books in my grandfather's house was a first edition of Alfred Hutton's *The Sword and the Centuries*. It opened my eyes to the possibility of researching historical fencing styles, and even provided some details about the sources I might work from. Amazing: there were books that could tell us how real swordfighters really fought, with real swords, for real! Then, in the National Library of Scotland, I stumbled upon a little book that was to change everything: *The Expert Sword-man's Companion*, by Donald Mcbane. What a book! I wangled it onto my English Literature course, "Identity in 17th century Literature" with Dr. Jonquil Bevan, and I even managed to get course credit for it: I wrote an essay on it called *The Gallant Pander*. Best of all, from my perspective, was that the smallsword material McBane presents did not contradict my early fencing training, but allowed me to apply what I knew in a historical way. It may come as a surprise, given that these days I am best known for my work on medieval Italian swordsmanship, but my first love was 18th century French smallsword as taught by a Scottish thug.

So in 1994 my friends and I started the Dawn Duellists Society to bring together like-minded people. I quickly found that I had to teach these people first, in order for the fights to be anything like the books. So I ended up teaching historical swordsmanship in order to create opponents. The whole point of researching these historical systems was to pick up new tricks for winning fencing matches with historical weapons. I had a complete separation in my mind between stuff done with swords, and martial arts. Martial arts were about killing people; sword-activities were about fencing. Martial arts were serious; fencing was not serious. Martial arts was about the Path; swordsmanship was about scoring touches. This makes no sense now, given my interest in real swordfighting, but it was how my head worked back then.

The psychological wall I had built between swordsmanship and martial arts melted away during the summer of 2000. I won't go into the full story here. Suffice to say it involves witches and angels, sex and violence, lust, betrayal, and a mountain-top revelation. Yes, really. And, no, I'm not about to go into detail, at least not while sober. But I suddenly decided to move to Helsinki and open a school: a school devoted to historical, European, and martial swordsmanship. Devoted, above all, to restoring the arts of our ancestors and maintaining, at all costs, the martial depth of the practice. That, for me, is Real Swordfighting.

## What is Historical European Martial Arts?

Since the late 1980s there has been a surge of interest in recreating Medieval and Renaissance arts of various kinds. Perhaps the most visible example of this is Shakespeare's Globe Theatre, which was opened in 1997 close to the site of the original. Not content with recreating the physical theatre, the Globe are now offering performances with the original pronunciation (or as close to it as scholarship can develop). Similarly, contemporary musicians have recorded classical, baroque, and medieval music on reproductions of historical instruments, which sound very different to their modern counterparts. There is an entire academic field now assembled under the umbrella of "Historically Informed Performance." The process requires musicological scholarship, high-level practical skills in playing instruments, and a restoration of the ancient arts of instrument-making.

The earliest glimmerings of this trend as regards swordsmanship can be seen in Turner and Soper's 1990 book, *Methods and Practice of Elizabethan Swordplay*. It is less commonly known that a revival of the lost martial arts of Europe occurred in the late 19th century, and that it required a similar mix of academic and practical skills. With the Victorian nostalgia for the "old ways," scholars and classical fencers such as Alfred Hutton, Egerton Castle, and Cyril Matthey discovered treatises on fencing dating back to the sixteenth century. They recreated the systems of combat they found, and organized public demonstrations of the new, old, Art. A combination of factors (such as the First World War) led to this movement running out of steam, but they left behind several excellent books: Castle's *Schools and Masters of Fence*, Hutton's *The Sword and the Centuries*, Matthey's edition of George Silver's *Brief Instructions on my Paradoxes of Defence*, and others. Classical fencing remained, and developed into the modern sport.

Late in the 20th century, with the Victorians' legacy as a starting point, various groups in Europe and the Americas began to recreate these arts again. By 1992 the first publishing company dedicated to the subject was founded: Chivalry Bookshelf. It began with a quarterly magazine, but by 1996 it was producing books aimed at the historical swordsmanship practitioner. Other notable publications in the field at this time were Terry Brown's *English Martial Arts*, written in 1997, and *Medieval Swordsmanship*, written by John Clements a year later. The idea of accurately recreating historical swordsmanship styles from existing texts had hit a nerve. Groups began springing up independently of each other: when I founded the Edinburgh-based Dawn Duellist's Society in 1994, I had no idea that there were people in other countries interested in the same pursuit.Local, national, and international bodies began to form (such as the British Federation for Historical Swordplay in 1998, which is still qualifying instructors today) with the help of the newly available internet. Major conferences were organized.The first of these was the "Swordplay Symposium International" in Houston, Texas, in May 2000. This was followed by the "International Swordfighting and Martial Arts Convention" in Lansing, Michigan, in September of the same year. There has been an explosion of interest since then with literally dozens of events every year and a natural division of the field into areas of interest, preferred training foci, and methodologies.

Publications in this field come in basically four types: how-to manuals, communicating basic technical skills, translations and reproductions of the historical primary sources, and analyses of those sources.

Perhaps the most important work in the early years was Christian Tobler's *Secrets of German Medieval Swordsmanship*. It included a transcription and translation of Johannes Liechtenauer's mnemonic verses (from the Nuremberg MS 3227a, written in 1389), then translations of Sigmund Ringeck's glosses on the verses from Codex Ringeck from the early 1500s, and finally Tobler's interpretation of those glosses, sword in hand, with photos. In other words, at each stage the source is clear: first the original verses, then the later glosses, and then what Mr Tobler makes of them. This book effectively defined the process of, and set the standard for transparency in, historical swordsmanship research.

Unlike Tobler's *Secrets*, my own first book, *The Swordsman's Companion*, is a training manual for students of the longsword. It draws on the 15th-century Italian authors Fiore dei Liberi (*c.* 1350 – *c.* 1420) and Philippo Vadi (MS dated to 1482–1487, life unknown). I wrote this book at a time when my research into our medieval combat heritage was at a very basic level. I knew at the time that I, and the wider swordsmanship community, had not even begun to understand the depths of these arts. But there seemed to me to be a need for a basic primer in the use of a longsword, so that people who wanted to take up the practice of the art could do so in a useful and systematic way. My book introduced readers to the existence of the Italian sources and provided them with the means of developing certain key skills; skills such as control of body and weapon, judgement of timing and distance, power generation, and tactical awareness. At the same time Tobler produced *Fighting with the German Longsword.* It was the training manual for the German style, as it was then understood, much like my own *Companion* was for the Italian style.

Perhaps the first training manual for historical swordsmanship was William Wilson's *Arte of Defence.* It's a relatively superficial overview of the early 17th-century Italian rapier system and its 16th-century predecessor, known as the Bolognese school, with additional drills and tips for training. This work attempts to teach rapier to beginners, but it suffers from a confusing organizational style and a lack of accuracy. My second book, *The Duellist's Companion,* was written in some sense as a reply to Wilson. I also wanted to take a system that was unfamiliar to me (17th-century Italian rapier), and apply my methodology to it, to see whether I could accurately recreate a swordsmanship style I knew little about directly from the source. I chose Capoferro's 1610 work, *Gran Simulacro dell'Arte e dell'Uso della Scherma*, partly because William Wilson and Jherek Swanger had just finished a translation, which made the source more popular in the wider swordsmanship community. My book was published in 2006 and was quickly adopted by several schools as their curriculum. It has remained a standard work on training Italian rapier among practitioners of historical fencing ever since. It is an analysis of Capoferro's book: not a reproduction of it. It also partakes of the how-to manual; rapier actions are mechanically challenging for most people so it goes into detail regarding how to stand in guard, how to lunge, etc. Wilson and I do not disagree on any major points of interpretation; however, his prior work illustrates only a handful of techniques and does so without citing a specific source for them.

Since the above-mentioned books were published interest in historical swordsmanship has grown with astonishing speed: there are many events every year and new publications coming out at least quarterly. It has inevitably become much more specialized with some groups focusing on creating a historically-inspired competitive sport, others taking the work of one historical master and studying that to the exclusion of all else, and most existing somewhere in between. Academically speaking, the field includes relatively few trained researchers. Most practitioners and interpreters lack even a basic grounding in academic skills, which means that much of the work is based on very loose foundations. But at the other end of the scale we have half-a-dozen-or-so professional academics, who are setting an example for the rest to follow.

In recent years there have been dozens of translations, commentaries, training guides, and analyses made of the various sources, ranging from those in the early 1300s to 1940s military combatives. Taking only those that directly relate to my main research interests, we have

1.  Regarding Fiore's *Il Fior di Battaglia*: there are five significant secondary sources. Tom Leoni's translation, *"Fiore de' Liberi's Fior di Battaglia translation into English"*, is the standard resource for most researchers. It is a complete rendering of the Getty manuscript into clear English. *Fiore dei Liberi 1409 Wrestling and Dagger*, self-published by Colin Richards in 2007, is an attempt to instruct the reader in Fiore's wrestling and dagger plays. It is problematic

because experiment shows that Richards' interpretation does not work well against a resistant opponent. Academically, it also suffers from relying on inaccurate translations of Fiore's work (it pre-dates Leoni's translation). *Medieval And Renaissance Dagger Combat* by Jason Vail is generally considered a useful overview of the Medieval and Renaissance sources for dagger combat. It is a basic dagger-combat primer drawn from many sources: as such it is not historically precise, but it contains some sound practical advice. *The Knightly Art of Battle* by Kenneth Mondschein is a short overview of the manuscript, published through the Getty museum, which does not go into any details of interpretation. Last but not least, *Fiore dei Liberi's Armizare: The Chivalric Martial Arts System of Il Fior di Battaglia,* by Robert N. Charette, is a descriptive overview of the entire system of *Armizare* (the Art of Arms). It is generally considered a quality secondary source for Fiore scholars. My own dagger book, *Mastering the Art of Arms, volume 1: The Medieval Dagger*, is a training method for practicing the dagger combat element of Fiore's Art, and serves a different purpose. It is organized and presented for the development of practical skills (how to do these techniques) and tactical understanding (when and why to do which technique), rather than as a survey of what techniques there are. This is followed by *Mastering the Art of Arms volume 2: The Medieval Longsword*, published in 2014, which is a complete training manual for my interpretation of Fiore's longsword material.

2. Regarding Capoferro's *Gran Simulacro*: at the time of writing *The Duellist's Companion* (2006) there were only the aforementioned translations by Wilson and Swanger, Wilson's *Arte of Defence*, and Jared Kirby's *Italian Rapier Combat:*

*Ridolfo Capo Ferro's "Gran Simulacro,"* which is a translation with some commentary. This latter translation is not highly regarded as it leaves many words untranslated and in whatever grammatical form they appear at that point in the text. This makes the book basically un-usable for readers unfamiliar with Italian. Leoni produced a better translation in 2011, under the title *The Art and Practice of Fencing*. Given how many people train rapier, it is surprising that there are so few secondary sources published to date.

3.   Regarding Vadi's *De Arte Gladiatoria Dimicandi*: there are only two secondary sources. These are a full-color facsimile and translation, *De Art Gladiatoria Dimicandi*, by Greg Mele and Luca Porzio, and an Italian reproduction of the source, *L'arte cavalleresca del combattimento*, edited by Marco Rubboli and Luca Cesari. Mele and Porzio's work was the standard reference for the anglo-sphere. While it is largely excellent, the translation suffers from an attempt to reproduce the verse as verse. There are also issues with some of the interpretations of the techniques (presented in the footnotes), as one would expect from work over a decade old. My *Veni Vadi Vici* is an updated translation. It owes a debt to Porzio and Mele's work but also includes a transcription and, most importantly for most readers, a detailed summary of and commentary on its contents.

I hope it is clear that I am not working in a vacuum; there are many other scholars in this field. While I take a different approach to many of my colleagues, and we are sometimes in lively disagreement, my work adds to, replies to, expands on, or is the basis of, theirs. This field is so young and small that it is still possible to have read every book on a given source, and also possible for a single additional work to make a major contribution.

*Swordsmanship Sources from 1310 to 1610*

Given the relative specialization of my field, and medieval and Renaissance combat studies in general, an overview of the most significant historical sources may be useful. I will organise them by date and highlight those sources that the submitted works are concerned with, which will be described in more detail in the next section. The current state of manuscript studies as regards combat sources is quite under-developed. Most academics are entirely unaware of the rich vein of artistic, literary, and cultural material they represent. There are one or two PhDs granted for work on these sources and one or two publications by career academics that refer to them (notably Sydney Anglo's *The Martial Arts of Renaissance Europe*).

## Pre-1400

1320s: Our earliest source is the *Royal Armouries MS I.33* which, according to the latest scholarship, dates to about 1320. This is a beautifully illustrated manuscript detailing lessons in sword and buckler combat between a priest and his scholar. It takes the form of a series of lessons in which the priest trains the scholar in his own method, explicitly contrasted to that of the "common fencer." This was translated and published by Jeffrey Forgeng in 2003 as *The Medieval Art of Swordsmanship: A Facsimile & Translation of Europe's Oldest Personal Combat Treatise, Royal Armouries MS I.33 (Royal Armouries Monograph)*, and again in 2013 in the companion volume of the truly extraordinary *Extraordinary Editions* version.

1389: *MS 3227a* (Germanisches Nationalmuseum, Nuremberg) is a hausbuch that has sections on all sorts of things (such as fireworks, alchemy, and astrology), including several on swordsmanship, the most important of these being a record of the merkeverse (mnemonic verses) of Johannes Liechtenauer. It is the earliest reference we have for the Liechtenauer school of longsword combat, which spawned a plethora of illustrated glossa in the following century.

There are no other manuals definitively dated to the 1300s, though it is likely that the bulk of Fiore dei Liberi's treatise was written at the end of the 1300s.

## 1400–1500

1410: *Il Fior di Battaglia*: the work of the Friulian master Fiore dei Liberi, which exists in four known manuscripts. This is a complete system for all the knightly weapons (sword, dagger, spear, and pollax): on foot and on horseback, in armor and without. This is one of my primary sources and will be discussed in detail in the following section.

The majority of sources from the 1400s are German in language and origin, and they are almost all essentially glosses on Liechtenauer's verses. There are at least 40 manuscripts to choose from, and another 50 or so from the following century. The most studied of these include:

C. 1430: *Gladiatoria, MS KK5013* (Kunsthistorisches Museum, Vienna) is a treatise of knightly combat in armor with spears, longswords, and daggers, and has a section on wrestling.

1443: (and later copies from 1446 and 1459) Talhoffer's Fechtbuch (combat manual), *MS Chart.A.558* (Universitäts- und Forschungsbibliothek Erfurt/ Gotha); published in translation by Mark Rector, *Medieval Combat: A Fifteenth-Century Manual of Swordfighting and Close-Quarter Combat,* in 2000. This is a treatise of knightly combat with all sorts of weapons, both in and out of armor. It includes an array of judicial duelling techniques, including duelling shields, and duels of men against women.

1452: *Codex Danzig, Cod.44.A.8,* or *MS 1449* (Biblioteca dell'Accademia Nazionale dei Lincei e Corsiniana, Rome), is a treatise that includes but is not limited to glosses on Liechtenauer's verses. It has sections by the following authors: Peter von Danzig zum Ingolstadt, Martin Huntfeltz, Jud Lew, Johannes Liechtenauer, Andre Liegniczer, and Ott Jud.

1470 (and two slightly later versions): Paulus Kal's Fechtbuch (*Cgm 1507*, Bayerische Staatsbibliothek, Munich). This is again a wide-reaching treatise with sections on all the knightly arms and some on judicial combat.

1482–7: *De Arte Gladiatoria Dimicandi* (Biblioteca Nazionale, Rome), by Philippo Vadi from Pisa. This book is a detailed discussion of swordsmanship theory and contains illustrated plays with all the knightly weapons (sword, axe, spear, and dagger).

There is also one 15th century treatise in French on the use of the pollax: *Le Jeu de la Hache*, MS Francais 1996, (Bibliotheque Nationale Francaise, Paris). Its exact date is unknown.

## 1500s

The 1500s saw an explosion of swordsmanship treatises, driven by the twin engines of social change (i.e. the rise of the merchant classes, who demanded, and could afford, both training in the art of the sword and books on their art) and the printing press: almost all swordsmanship texts from here on are printed. The most important works of this period are

1509: *Exercitiorum Atque Artis Militaris Collectanea* by Pedro Monte, in Latin, published in Milan. Unusually, the original draft seems to have survived: it is in Spanish, and is at the Escorial. This work surveys the martial arts of the time, and as Sydney Anglo writes: "No master was more comprehensive than Pedro Monte in 1509. He not only deals with wrestling, dagger fighting, the use of long and short lance, two-handed sword and the single-sword on its own or in combination with various types of shield and buckler and cape; he also discusses the various types of pole arm such as the partisan, the ronca, spetum, and halberd. He examines in detail fencing and wrestling on horseback, along with various types of mounted lance combat; treats of physical exercises such as running, jumping, and vaulting; provides a little encyclopaedia of contemporary arms and armour; and finally places the entire corpus of material within a broader context of the art of war." Monte is also interesting because he probably knew of Vadi; Monte is mentioned (in glowing terms) in Castiglione's *Libro del Cortegiano*, which was based on the court of Guidobaldo da Montefeltro and to whom Vadi's treatise is dedicated.

1531: *Opera Nova* (Venice, unknown publisher, 1531), by Antonio Manciolino (published in translation in 2010 by Tom Leoni as *The Complete Renaissance Swordsman*). This is a thorough and readable description of the style of swordsmanship commonly referred to as "Bolognese" (as most of its author exponents hail from there). It is also the earliest source for this particular style.

1536: *Opera Nova* (Modena, unknown publisher, 1536), by Achille Marozzo: republished in 1546, 1550, 1568, and 1615. This is a very comprehensive description of the Bolognese style and is thought to have been very influential in its time, as witnessed by its many editions.

1553: *Trattato di Scientia d'Arme, con vn Dialogo di Filosofia*, by Camillo Agrippa (Rome, Antonio Blado, 1553). This was the famous architect's attempt to use geometry and reason to create a system of swordsmanship from first principles. Its influence is a matter of debate. It has been published in translation by Dr Ken Mondschein as *Fencing: A Renaissance Treatise*.

1570: *Ragione di adoprar sicuramente l'Arme,* by Giacomo di Grassi (Venice, Giordano Ziletti, 1570). This work has the distinction of being the first Italian swordsmanship treatise to be translated into English, in 1594, by "I. G." – an anonymous "gentleman."

1570: *Gründtliche Beschreibung der Kunst des Fechtens* (*A Foundational Description of the Art of Fencing*), by Joachim Meyer (Strasburg, self-published (at ruinous cost), 1570). It was republished in 1590, 1600, 1610, and 1660, and it has been published in translation by Jeffrey Forgeng in *The Art of Combat: A German Martial Arts Treatise of 1570*. This covers not only the longsword, but also the rappir (a long single-handed sword much like a rapier, though the method of use is quite different to the Italian) and the dusack (a single-edged military type sword).

1575: *Lo Schermo*, by Angelo Viggiani (Venice, Giorgio Angelieri, 1575). This book is the Rosetta Stone of Italian fencing theory. It details the function of the guards and the Aristotelean basis for the theory of tempo, and goes into detail regarding matters of mechanics that shine a necessary light on the earlier works, especially those written by Fiore.

1599: *Paradoxes of Defence*, by George Silver (London, Edward Blount, 1599). This is not the earliest work in English but it is by far the most influential, and it has a wide following of exponents. It concerns itself with two main themes: the utter wretchedness of all Italian fencing and fencers, and the solid English principles on which swordsmanship is, or should be, based. Taken with his unpublished manuscript *Brief Instructions upon my Paradoxes of Defence* (Sloane MS No.376, which was discovered and published by Cyril Matthey in 1898) we have a detailed and complete theory of fencing, based on principles such as the four grounds (judgement, distance, time, and place). Most famously though he details the True Times, determining what part of the body should move first: time of the hand; time of the hand and body; time of the hand, body, and foot; and time of the hand, body, and feet. His work has been republished and annotated in several places, notably in Paul Wagner's *Master of Defence* (2003) and Stephen Hand's *English Swordsmanship* (2006).

The late 1500s saw the emergence of treatises on the longer, thinner rapier (despised by Silver). Perhaps the first of these was Giacomo di Grassi's *Ragione*, which lead up to the "big three" rapier treatises: Fabris, Giganti, and Capoferro.

## Early 1600s

1606: Salvator Fabris published his monumental *Lo Schermo, overo Scienza d'Arme* (published in translation by Tom Leoni in 2005 as *The Art of Dueling: Salvator Fabris' rapier fencing treatise of 1606*). This was so successful it was republished in 1622, 1624, 1672, 1676, and 1713. It is a very thorough and clear explanation of the art of fencing.

1606: Nicoletto Giganti published *La Schola overo Teatro* (translated by Tom Leoni as *Venetian Rapier, Nicoletto Giganti's 1606 Rapier Fencing Curriculum*, 2010), which is a much simpler exposition of the art. Leoni calls it a curriculum, and that is close to the truth. Giganti spends much less time on theory and presents the material in a logical order. A second book published in 1608 by Giganti, thought lost for centuries, was discovered in the summer of 2012 by Piermarco Terminiello, who published it in translation in 2013.

1610: Ridolfo Capoferro published *Il Gran Simulacro dell'arte e dell'uso della scherma* (*The Great Representation of the Art and the Use of Fencing*). It is perhaps the most famous fencing treatise ever written, and in its time it went through many editions. For such a famous work, we know almost nothing about the author save that which he tells us himself: he was 52 at the time of writing and he came from Cagli, in Italy.

## 1611–1800

The production of fencing treatises continued for the next 300 years; I could fill the rest of this book with an incomplete bibliography. There are literally hundreds of primary sources to work from, in many languages, and varying hugely from military training manuals to sets of rules for wrestling, to in-depth treatises on the smallsword, rapier, staff, walking stick, knife, you name it. A brief search on the internet will bring up a cornucopia of sources. Readers that know me well would be surprised if I failed to mention the following sources, but this is very much a "Guy's top five treatises from 1620–1800", not by any means an exhaustive list.

1640 Francesco Alfieri published his *La Scherma,* which coincidentally provided the image we have had on the back of my School's t-shirts for the last 14 years.

1687 Sir William Hope published *The Scots Fencing Master,* which was one of the first treatises I ever got my hands on in the original. It is distinguished by perhaps the worst-drawn plates in fencing history, but is nonetheless a pretty thorough and clear example of the early French school of the smallsword. Sir William was quite prolific, and of his other works, the 1707 *New Short and Easy Method of Fencing* is just brilliant; it is exactly what the title promises.

1728 Donald McBane's *The Expert Sword-man's Companion* is the French School of smallsword fencing as interpreted by a Highlander, with fearsome attitude and reputation. The book is immeasurably enhanced by the rip-roaring autobiography of the author, who, it appears, fought dozens of duels as well as taking part in almost every major military action in Scotland, Ireland and the Continent between 1685 and about 1720.

1740 P. J. F. Girard's *Traite des Armes* covers not only fencing, but also vital military skills like how to throw a grenade, load and fire a musket, and so on. Highly recommended. You can download a free scan of the whole book from my website guywindsor.com/net.

1763/1787 Domenico Angelo's definitive *l'Ecole des Armes.* I use "definitive" advisedly: in Diderot's *Encyclopedie,* the first true Encyclopedia ever compiled (between 1750 and 1772), the entry on fencing is simply a complete reproduction of Angelo's book. It was translated by his son, Harry, as *The School of Fencing,* in 1787.

And I see I've left out Roworth's superb sabre manual of 1798, and Godfrey, and Liancouer, and l'Abbat...

It is at around this point in the history of duelling (1800 or so) that I start to lose interest; from the 1800s onwards, the sword fell into disuse, and ceased to be carried. Duels, if they were fought at all, tended to be with pistols. Classical fencing replaced its more martial forebears (if you can't throw your oppenent to the ground, or kick him in the nuts, it's not really a martial art any more, I think). But the point is this: there is a super-abundance of sources for swordfighting, from every period from 1300 to the present. Go, read, immerse yourself in it. It's a fundamental, and vitally important, aspect of our cultural heritage.

## *Methodology*

On the basis of the historical material discussed above, the field of historical swordsmanship has developed into a mixture of manuscript studies, cultural history, and the embodied practice of a historically contextualized art.

As Prof Andrew Lawrence-King wrote in "Links to Early Music":

"As in Historically Informed Performance of music, actions in historical swordsmanship are based on period treatises. Best practice in the teaching and performance of Historical Swordsmanship is rather ahead of today's early music, in evidence-based teaching, in uniting academic theory with practical performance, in the use of historically precise terminology, and in the detailed study of specific sources.

Where early musicians study, say, early 17th-century style in general, swordsmanship scholars will base an entire practical method on one specific source, distinguishing between fighting Capoferro-style or Fabris-style. The comparison would be to distinguish between the fundamentals of continuo-playing for Caccini and Monteverdi..."

There is still much to be done, though, to bring the profile of the study of swordsmanship up to the level of the study of early music.

There is a large amount of source material available these days, largely thanks to amateur researchers in the field scanning everything they find and putting it online for free. My work to date has focused primarily on the sources I can read in the original (English, Spanish, French, and Italian), and within that most of my work has been on 15th, 16th, and 17th century Italian sources. My intention in every case is to make the physical practice of the combat arts represented in my primary sources available to the modern student while staying as faithful to the source material as possible. The work is multi-disciplinary, as Lawrence-King points out, requiring a broad range of skills: from locating documents long forgotten in the archives, to hitting hard and accurately with four feet of sharp steel; from developing training methods for combat skills, to keeping control of a class full of armed young men high on testosterone and adrenaline.

Thus the process of historical swordsmanship has two distinct parts: working out the system itself, and teaching it. The process is not linear. Insights in reading are fed into class practice, which may yield further insights that change the reading. Since we cannot come to a definitive reading without having applied every action, and yet we require the text to determine those actions, the process grows organically with academic study and embodied practice feeding into each other.

## Working out the system

1. Find the sources. These can be as obscure as a single copy of a single manuscript, or as easily found as a simple library search. During the past 10 years much of the material located through archival methods has been made available online.

2. Manuscript study: transcription and image analysis. The usual approach to the pre-1500 manuscripts is to create a transcription so that colleagues can immediately see the

reading decisions you have made, which may affect your interpretation. The images, if any, may be intended to represent a single moment in time, a set of options, or a variation on the technique referred to in the text. They may be more or less accurate to life. All of these points must be addressed. Dating is also often an issue, and is necessary for the next step.

3.  Determine the context for the combat system being represented. There is a huge difference in the physical and psychological environment between, for example, a knightly tournament fought for prizes; a judicial duel, in which one combatant must die if he fails to prove his case; a fencing match between equals; and the training of soldiers. We need to know the social rank of the combatants and the social expectations of behavior, because they determine what the art represented is intended to accomplish.

4.  Determine the nature of the weapons, clothing, and armor in use, and acquire accurate facsimiles. This is expensive, of course, and it is the source of much debate within the field. Much of my re-creative practice is done with accurate, sharp, and modern copies of period weapons. It is necessary to test all interpretations in period clothing: especially footwear, because it can affect movement considerably.

5.  Reconstruct the techniques. This single step can take many years to get right because it is intimately connected with the next step, which is to determine the patterns of tactical choices represented by the text. The pattern can suggest how a technique is done, and how the technique is done affects the pattern (of course). Some authors do provide tactical and theoretical introductions to their work, but that is not as common as one might wish – especially prior to 1500.

6.  Pattern analysis. Determine the general rules behind the specific technical examples given, and note the consilience

between any theoretical points in the text and the technical examples.

7. Test the interpretation. This step is usually done in the following contexts: slow with blunt swords, fast and hard with blunt swords, slow with sharp swords, fast and hard with sharp swords, in set drills done competitively, and in free fencing.

8. Identify or extrapolate heuristics: rules of thumb that apply to the main body of the text, and to which specific exceptions may apply.

9. Compare the resulting interpretation with other contemporary systems for which a record exists, if any.

10. Place the system within its historical context: determine how this system fits with those that came before and after. Sometimes we see a clear step from one system to another (see my article "*Italian Longsword Guards: comparing Vadi to Fiore and Marozzo*" for an example); sometimes the system in question appears to be a complete outlier, or even the work of a crank.

At this stage we have a working interpretation of one system of combat. We must now figure out how to teach it.

### Teaching the system

1. Determine the necessary skill set. This will include control of body and weapon, judgement of timing and distance, power generation, tactical awareness, and the ability to think and act "in-system."

2. Develop training methods to impart these skills, and organize them into a coherent syllabus.

3. Test the syllabus. Do the students following it act, under stress, according to the precepts of the system?

4. Provide general physical conditioning. This is necessary given

that the students are not living a period lifestyle, and therefore tend to be physically less active.

5. Provide students with critical philosophical tools. This is necessary given our culture's attitude to violence in general, and to killing with swords in particular.. This is so that students can engage with the ethics of what we are doing, which is, from one perspective, training in murder; from another, gaining control of violent tendencies. Combat psychology, stress management (accessing your training under the stress of someone trying to kill you), and the moral justifications, if any, for duellingare all topics that fall within our purview.

It is clear, then, that a large measure of the work required falls into academic fields of study, such as cultural history and manuscript studies. Yet some is also drawn from sports coaching, sports science, traditional martial arts practices, experimental archaeology, material culture studies, classical fencing pedagogy, and other fields; all with one end in mind: to recreate as faithfully as possible the physical practice of the Art as represented by the authors. That, to my mind, is (a) historical, (b) European, (c) martial, and (d) artistic.

## A Holo-Deck for the Philosophy of Ethics

As with so many posts, and indeed with the card game *Audatia*, this one came about as a direct result of a conversation after class with one of my students. I have edited out some references. One of the core reasons I am interested in swordsmanship is the ethical dimension that training with deadly weapons requires. I recently began asking the senior students a weekly homework question, to answer by email, on such knotty subjects as "under what circumstances is it acceptable to kill someone with a sword?" The answers to this ranged from "never under any circumstances," through "in situations of legitimate self-defense or defense of others," and through to "if I'm holding one." As ever with this kind of question, how the person reads the question is as interesting as their actual answer. For instance, some read it as specifically "with a sword." Others expanded the question to include any kind of mortal violence. Others still read "acceptable" to mean "I could actually do it," and some read it as "morally defensible whether I could actually do it or not." Yes, I am planning on collating the questions and answers and publishing them in some form, at some point. Watch this space...

First posted on May 15th 2013.

I was talking to a student after class one day: someone who has been training with me off and on since the school opened. I happened to mention that, for me, one of the primary uses of the art we study is that it is a holo-deck for the philosophy of ethics. We are free of the constraint of knowing we must be willing to use our skills, because we are not expecting to use them in earnest any time soon. (This is my core moral objection to the idea of arming teachers to defend students against those sad, evil little wankers who try to compensate for their utter inadequacy by murdering the defenseless. Giving the teachers guns would not help at all without training them to use them, which would inevitably require those teachers to train to be willing and able to take life. That is a profound and utterly life-changing moral and emotional step, and it is simply not fair to ask the average teacher to make it. My practical objection is simply that kids are great at improvising; having more guns in schools will inevitably lead to more guns in childrens' hands and so more likelihood of fatal shootings, accidental or otherwise.)

For us, the salle becomes a simulator, a holo-deck if you will, in which we can examine violence and degrees of violence, and can pose questions such as

"Is this action ever justified?"

"In what circumstances would cutting off someone's head be okay?"

"How do I feel about the idea of fighting to the death over a point of honor?"

"What was it about this culture that made this response acceptable?"

It is moronic to suggest that violence never solved anything. For the entire history of life on earth it has solved the problem of hunger: I kill to eat. (Rory Miller has made this point in podcasts, and in his written works.) So the question then is, "in what circumstances is violence acceptable, and to what degree?" Current martial systems, such as police and military training, must have clearly defined answers to all such questions. In *these* circumstances, I can use a baton; in *those*, I must shoot; in *these*, I call for an airstrike; and so on. Martial arts teachers and parents both must be able to teach their students or children a moral framework in which to place violence. One interesting point of view on this, that of a mother trying to raise her son in a non-violent way and learning that violence is not intrinsically evil but has its place, can be found here http://unnecessarywisdom. wordpress.com/2013/05/02/boys-and-violence-its-not-the-problem-its-the-solution/. In short, the writer, Zoe Claire, decided on a set of rules which, if followed, would make any violence her son was a part of morally acceptable. My rules are a little different (less gender-oriented for instance), but I admire her position.

We can imagine our Art being applied in dozens of circumstances, and while many of my students use aspects of their training at the School in their work as security guards, police, and so on, most will never call on their skills outside of class. However, for the training to be of any moral use it should require the practitioner to engage with the fact that we are training in lethal techniques, and therefore must have a clear set of internal guidelines as to when their application is acceptable. We can create those guidelines for all sorts of modern or historical contexts, which, while it is not of any immediate, practical use, has the value of making us engage with these difficult questions.

It is, in my view, impossible to inflict damage on another soul without inflicting damage on your own, no matter the circumstances. But there are situations in which the better course is to inflict the physical damage and take the spiritual. Failing to act out of fear of damage, physical or spiritual, is cowardice.

Let me tell you a story:

Twenty years ago, while at University, I was walking home alone from band practice with my trumpet. I was going through a dodgy part of Edinburgh. As I was walking I saw a man, rough-looking and with a bleeding head, standing over a woman in a doorway. I was terrified of two things. Firstly that I would act, and get the shit kicked out of me or get killed. I was under no illusions as to who wins in a fight between a street-thug and a pampered kid. Secondly that I would not act, and would despise myself for the rest of my life. So I stopped, far enough away to have a running head start, and called out in my best public-school accent:

"Excuse me, but can I be of any assistance?" The subtext I was trying to imply was, "I've seen you and will call the police if you don't leave her alone."

I was astonished when the man called back:

"Yes, please, my wife is having an epileptic fit!"

So I went over and helped him get her home, and we became friends. Turns out the blood came from his trying to cushion her fall. Some weeks later I told them that I had thought he was up to no good in that doorway, and they both fell about laughing.

My point is that while we can simulate all sorts of scenarios, and come up with ideal responses to them, we cannot reasonably predict our own actions unless they have been tested under stress, nor necessarily predict the outcome of a seemingly obvious scenario. But we can use our training in violence to help us make moral choices about who we are and wish to be, and then try to live up to them, accepting that doing so can be dangerous.

## Performing Art

One of the most important requirements for this work is the presence of informed and experienced colleagues to discuss things with. Every now and then we come across irreconcilable differences of opinion, such as: my colleague stated that it was incorrect to call the primary art I teach "Fiore's." He may be right. My approach in these circumstances is to avoid sniping about on email or Facebook, but instead write up a full statement of my position, post it, and leave it at that. Let opinion fall where it may. This went up on November 2nd 2013.

It is obvious that, coming from a different time and culture, we cannot ever perfectly recreate the Art as Fiore himself did it. Not even one of his students would ever have expressed the Art exactly as Fiore himself did it. But the Art is not just the specific choreography of the set plays; it is also a set of tactical principles, a set of movement mechanics, and a body of technique, all intended to grant us victory in specific combat contexts. We have abundant exemplar techniques to work from, complete with clear instructions and before-and-after illustrations. With sufficient effort we can train ourselves to solve the swordsmanship problems that fall within this system's scope, using Fiore's techniques in accordance with his principles. Thus, we can express his Art.

As artists, though, we must apply the art according to our gifts and our natures. There is no sense in trying to be someone else; especially not if that someone else is long dead. Fiore claims Galeazzo da Mantova as one of his students. It is possible that he was, and that Fiore was proud of the way Galeazzo fought when he did so with Marshal Boucicaut: Fiore mentions it in his book. But equally it is vanishingly unlikely that, had Fiore taken Galeazzo's place, he would have fought exactly the same way. Yet Galeazzo, according to Fiore, was applying Fiore's Art.

A useful analogy here is the theatre. Shakespeare's plays, for instance, have been put on in every conceivable way: from the attempts to get it all as close as possible to the way Shakespeare would have done it, and at the Globe Theatre, to modernist interpretations. The play is not the text, it is the production; it is the combination of text, performance direction, set, stage, costumes, lighting, and audience interaction. It is possible for the same production, the same play, to run for decades with the actors changing from time to time. Of course, bringing in a new actor changes the experience of the play, but it does not become a new production. A good example of this is the Savonlinna Opera Festival's production of Aïda, which has been repeated almost every year since 1986. The cast has changed, but the physical interpretation of Verdi's music and Ghislanzoni's libretto are the same. The production is the same. It's the same opera. Every single performance will have been unique in some way, but it's still the same show.

As historical swordsmanship practitioners we are obliged, I think, to make a sincere effort to perform the art as closely as possible to the author's original intentions. Getting back to Shakespeare: The Globe Theatre is a good example of this idea in practice, especially in their "Original Pronunciation" productions. This is a movement to reproduce the accents that the actors would have had back in the day – and we thought interpreting swordsmanship texts was difficult! There is an excellent video online here http://www.youtube.com/watch?v=gPlpphT7n9s posted by the Open University, in which Prof David Crystal (a phonologist) and his son Ben Crystal (an actor at the Globe) discuss these "Original Pronunciation" productions of Shakespeare and what they reveal about the history of the English language. (Since posting this, the Crystals have published a book on accents, memorably titled *You Say Potato*, in which they also discuss Original Pronunciation. Well worth a read if you're interested.)

For examples that you can see for yourself if you wish, we can compare two film versions of Hamlet (Shakespeare wrote for the movies, didn't you know?): Franco Zeffirelli's version (1990), and Kenneth Branagh's version (1996). They are two totally different films. Gibson (despite being an anti-semitic, misogynist, and religious-fundamentalist thug whose work should be boycotted on principle, but we didn't know that when the film came out) was directed by Zeffirelli in an amazingly good, pretty much by-the-book, set-in-a-castle, and classic interpretation. But the text is heavily cut: the running time is about 130 minutes. It grossed about $20 million.

Branagh's mighty opus weighs in at 246 minutes: almost twice as long as the Zeffirelli version. It has the complete text of the play, and has been hailed by many critics as the greatest film adaptation of a Shakespeare play ever. But it grossed only $5 million. And it was set in the nineteenth century! So, while Branagh was very faithful to the script he made no attempt to make it look the way Shakespeare would have.

Nobody in their right mind would suggest that either of these movies "is not Hamlet." Of course they are. They are different takes on the same artistic vision, different bringings-to-life of the same core text, in a medium of which the original author could not have imagined. But they are Hamlet, nonetheless.

The aim of play scripts and screenplays is of course quite different to that of swordsmanship manuals, and likewise their interpreters have very different goals. Putting on a play, or making a film, is done for any number of reasons; not least among them to entertain an audience, express an artistic vision, and make money. In the theatre it is perfectly normal for actors, directors, and the rest of the crew to be deliberately expressing their own interpretations for their own reasons. Except in recreationist versions such as those at the Globe, there is no serious intent to reproduce the play exactly as the playwright saw it in his head. It is understood by all that any production is an interpretation. There is no practical limit on what constitutes a "correct" interpretation: there is really no concept of a "correct" interpretation.

The goals of Fiore's Art are simpler: kill your enemies, survive the fight and gain renown. This places a constraint on correctness. Whatever interpretation of a historical martial art we come up with must be

1. Historical. It must be a sincere attempt to accurately reproduce the art as the author intended, taking into account all the data points at our disposal.
2. Martial. The interpretation must work under the conditions initially envisioned by the author.
3. Artistic. The interpretation must be expressed according to the precepts of the art in question: principles, both tactical and moral; movement dynamics; tactics; and technique.

We are not at liberty to simply excise the portions of the text that don't suit our vision. Nor can we export the art to a foreign context and still be "doing Fiore." But within those constraints there are a pretty wide range of interpretations that still fit within the scope of "Fiore's art." There's a pretty wide range of tactical and technical choices, and of routes to renown. There's even a range of core movement dynamics, especially between versions of the text (I'm thinking of the Getty and the Pisani-Dossi here).

In conclusion, then, I have no hesitation about claiming that what I teach is Fiore's Art of Arms, in the same way that Branagh would claim his Hamlet is Shakespeare's. We have no way to know exactly how Fiore would have fought and, anyway, it would have changed over time as he learned, trained, and aged. We do have his book and what I am teaching is, as far as I can manage it, at the cutting edge of Fiore research. It is a sincere attempt to follow the Master in thought, word, and deed. I am not Fiore. If he came back to life and saw what we do the best I could hope for would be for him to shake his head sadly and say: "Guy, no. Not like that. It's like *this.*" But I am a practitioner of *his* Art of Arms, and so are my students.

## ONE PLAY, ONE DRILL, MANY QUESTIONS

I produced this as a standalone article (not a blog post), in September 2014, in response to a review of *The Medieval Longsword.* It should give you some insight into how many factors have to be taken into consideration when dealing with even a single, simple play about which there are very few dissenting opinions in the wider community.

*The Medieval Longsword* is explicitly and deliberately a representation of my interpretation of Fiore's Art of Arms as regards the longsword used out of armor, arranged so that students can acquire it as a physical skill. It is not by any stretch of the imagination an academic argument in support of my interpretation. A fair-minded and thorough – though not entirely positive – review (by Sean Manning here: "http://bookandsword.

com/2014/08/09/some-thoughts-on-guy-windsors-the-medieval-longsword/") makes the point, and also highlighted for me, that there are readers out there who are deeply interested in the research aspect. So I thought I'd take one basic technical drill and demonstrate in depth and detail *why* I do it this way. I chose for this the first two steps of "First Drill" from my basic syllabus, which is my take on the first and second plays of the master crossed at the middle of the swords in the *zogho largo,* shown here:

The drill is very specific. Written out, it looks like this (quoting from *The Medieval Longsword,* pages 97–98):

1.  "Attacker ready in right side *posta di donna*; you wait in *tutta porta di ferro.*
2.  Attacker strikes with *mandritto fendente,* aiming at your head.
3.  Parry with *frontale,* meeting the middle of the attacker's sword with the middle of your own, edge to flat.
4.  The attacker's sword is beaten wide to your left so pass away from it (to your right), striking with a *mandritto fendente* to the attacker's left arm and thrusting to the chest."

The answer to the question "why do you do it like that" must include answers to at least the following questions, and I'm sure you can think of more:

1. Why is there an attacker and defender?
2. Why would you wait in any guard?
3. Why would you wait in *tutta porta di ferro*?
4. Why is the attack coming from *posta di donna*?
5. Why is the attack a *mandritto fendente*?
6. Why is the defense a parry?
7. Why do you stand still to parry?
8. Why is the blade contact middle to middle?
9. Why is the blade contact edge-to-flat?
10. Why *frontale*?
11. Why is the attacker's blade beaten away?
12. Why is the riposte a strike to the arm followed by a thrust to the chest?
13. Why is the *passo fora di strada* done to the right?

These are all fair questions. To answer them I will use direct quotes from the treatise wherever possible, and will note any points where I have to rely on experience or other treatises. All page references are to the Getty manuscript unless otherwise noted.

Let's start with the text on f25v. Above the crowned master on the left, it says:

*Anchora me incroso qui per zogho largo a meza spada. E subito che son incrosado io lasso discorrer la mia spada sopra le soi mane, e se voglio passare cum lo pe dritta fuora de strada, io gli posso metter una punta in lo petto, come qui dredo e depento.*

My very literal translation reads like this:

"Again, I am crossed here in the wide play at middle sword. And immediately that I am crossed I let my sword run off over the arms, and if I wish to pass with my right foot out of the way, I can place a thrust in the chest, as here below is depicted."

And above the play on the right, it reads as follows:

*Lo zogho del mio magistro io lo complido, cho io ofatta la sua coverta, e subito o fatto lo suo ditto, che io oferido primo gli brazzi, e poy glo posta la punta in petto.*

Which I translate as: "The play of my master I have completed, so I have made his cover, and immediately done what he said, so I have struck first the arms, and then I put the thrust in the chest."

This begs the question, which one of the drawn figures is the "master"? We know it is the one wearing a crown because Fiore says as much in the introduction (f2r). It is worth quoting this at some length, because we will be coming back to this section later:

"The guards, or 'position,' are easy to recognize. Some guards will be set against one another and will not touch one another, studying each other to see what the opponent may do. These are called poste, or guards, or First Masters of the fight. They will be wearing a crown, meaning that the position in which they wait is optimal for defense. These guards are also the foundation for carrying arms while in guard. A posta is the same as a guard. A guard (or posta) is what you use to defend or 'guard' yourself against the opponent's attacks. A posta (or guard) is a 'posture' against the opponent, which you use to injure him without danger to yourself.

The other Master following these four guards shows the plays that come from these guards and defends against an opponent who uses the actions deriving from the four guards. This Master, who also wears a crown, we call the Second Master or Remedy Master, since (by the rules of the art) he thwarts the attacks deriving from the poste or guards shown before.

This Second (or Remedy) Master has some students under

him: these show the plays the Master or Remedy may perform after he executes the defense or grapple shown by the Remedy. These students wear an insignia below the knee. They execute all the plays of the Remedy until another Master appears who performs the counter to the Remedy and all of his students. And because he performs the counter to the Remedy and his students, this Master weans the uniform of the Remedy Master and that of his students, i.e. both the crown and the insignia below the knee. This king bears the name of Third Master or Counter, because he counters the other Masters and their plays."

(Leoni, *Fiore de' Liberi Fior di Battaglia Second English Edition*, p. 5.)

So, given that the scholar in our second pair of figures ("play") is wearing a garter (an "insignia below the knee"), it is clear that the crowned figure is a remedy master who is defending against the player. Thus, while it is obvious from the second play who is hitting whom, we can be equally sure that the crowned figure is the one defending in the first play.

It is also stated in the introduction that guards may be "positions in which [the masters] wait [that are] optimal for defense."

**1. Why is there an attacker and defender? And 2. Why would you wait in any guard?**

So our first question, why is there an attacker and defender, can be answered along the lines of because that is how the play is presented in the book. It seems that this is a defence done from a stationary guard and against an awaited attack.

Note I am not suggesting that this is the only possible, useful, or common, set-up. We do all of these drills also from a moving starting point, but we can state with confidence that it is part of Fiore's Art to wait in guard for the attack. This also answers question 2, why would you wait in any guard: because Fiore says to. So, why *tutta porta di ferro*?

### 3. Why would you wait in tutta porta di ferro?

We know that the master has "covered," which term is used elsewhere quite explicitly to mean "parry," such as in the plays of the master of the sword in one hand. The text above the master reads (f20r): *"E in quello passare mi crovo rebattendo le spade,"* which translates as, "And in that pass I cross, beating the swords." On the next page, the text above his first scholar includes, *"Quello che a ditto lo magistro io l'o ben fatto, zoe, ch'io passai fora de strada facendo bona coverta,"* or, "That which the master has said I have done well, thus, I have passed out of the way making a good cover." It seems reasonable that cover = parry.

We also know that the cover has been done from the right side because of the way the swords are drawn. It is highly impractical to parry as shown if you chamber the sword on your left. So we are looking for a guard with the sword chambered on the right, which would imply a left-foot-forwards stance; one which can parry, and in which it is good to wait.

The text above tutta porta di ferro (f23v) reads:

*Qui comminzano le guardie di spada a doy man. E sono xii guardie. La prima sie tutta porta di ferro che sta in grande forteza. Esi e bona daspetar ognarma manuale longa e curta. E pur chel habia bona spada non cura di troppa longeza. Ella passa cum coverta e va ale strette. E la scambi le punte e le soy ella mette. Anchora rebatte le punte a terra e sempre va cum passo e de ogni colpo ella fa coverta. E chi in quella gli da briga grand' deffese fa senza fadiga.*

Which I translate as: "Here begin the guards of the sword in two hands. There are 12 guards. The first is the whole iron gate, that stands in great strength. And she is good to await every manual weapon, long and short, and for which it has a good sword, that is not too long. And she passes with a cover and goes to the close [plays]. She exchanges the thrust and places her own. She also beats the thrusts to the ground and always goes with a pass and against all blows she makes a cover. And standing in this guard, one may easily make a defense against anyone who bothers him."

So left foot forwards, "good to await every manual weapon," "passes with the cover," "against all blows she makes a cover," and "one may easily make defense." Seems like a reasonable choice.

### 4. Why is the attack coming from posta di donna?

It appears to me from the image of the player that the attack is a descending blow from the right (*mandritto fendente*), done with a pass forwards, because the player is right foot forwards. It is generally accepted, Though Fiore never says so, that longsword blows are usually struck with a passing step from the side the blow comes. Experience shows that you can strike more easily when cutting from the right if your right foot is forwards; it is necessary to initiate the attack with the motion of the sword, to prevent exposing yourself as you step forwards. This results in most mandritto attacks from one step out of measure being executed with the pass of the right foot. (This could use better supporting evidence; a full and detailed academic study of cutting mechanics is long overdue. My next article project, perhaps.)

Whatever guard we choose should therefore be left foot forwards, to allow the passing step, and with the sword chambered on the right. *Posta di donna destra* is one such guard. The text above it reads:

*Questa sie posta di donna che po fare tutti gli setti colpi de la spada. E de tutti colpi ella se po crovrire. E rompe le altre guardie per grandi colpi che po fare. E per scambiar una punta ella e sempre presta. Lo pe che denanzi acresse fora di strada e quello di driedo passa ala traversa. E lo compagno fa remagner discoverto, e quello fe ferir subito per certo.*

Which I translate as: "This is the woman's guard, that can make all seven blows of the sword. And she can cover against all blows. And she breaks the other guards with the great blows she can make. And she is always quick to exchange a thrust. The foot which is in front advances out of the way, and that which is behind passes across. And she makes the companion remain uncovered and can immediately strike him for certain."

So there is nothing there to suggest it would be a bad choice. And let us refer back to the introduction: "Some guards will be set against one another and will not touch one another, studying each other to see what the opponent may do." It seems fitting to me to begin the paired longsword drills in our syllabus with one such pair: the first two guards of the sword in two hands.

### 5. Why is the attack a mandritto fendente?

Firstly, it is a very common and natural blow: an instinctive strike. Secondly, the image of the player has the sword approximately where it would be when a mandritto fendente is parried. He is right foot forwards, the swords are crossed clearly on each others' left, and his point is high.

### 6. Why is the defence a parry?

As we have seen, it is because the text above the scholar says it was ("*coverta*"). And because parrying is what most people naturally do when attacked.

### 7. Why do you stand still to parry?

In the first place, Fiore does not specify any footwork to be done during the parry. This is in contrast to other plays where footwork (such as an *accrescere fora di strada* and *passo ala traversa*) is specified during the defense, as it is in the *colpo di villano* (f26r), exchange of thrust and breaking the thrust (f26v), the plays of the sword in one hand (f20r-f21v), and the play of the sword from *dente di zenghiaro,* or in any other left-side guard (f31r). Standing still fits with the "waiting" associated with our chosen guard and is academically supportable in the absence of any other data. However, there may be good reason to step back (and offline) while parrying: especially if put under time pressure by the attacker (stepping away buys more time to act). I discard the possibility of passing in with the left foot here because it makes no mechanical sense given the parry that is clearly shown from the right, and the measure as illustrated does not support it. It makes sense to start with the simplest possible set-up given that this drill is taught to beginners.

### 8. Why is the blade contact middle to middle?

The blade contact is middle-to-middle because the text explicitly refers to "meza spada," which we understand to mean about halfway down the blade. This is in context with the previous master, crossed at the *punta di spada*, here: the text states, "*Questo magistro che qui incrosado cum questo zugadore in punta de spada*" or "This master that is here crossed with this player at the point of the sword."

Furthermore, we can refer to the *Morgan MS*, here:

Which describes three crossings of the sword:

*Quista doi magista sono aq incrosadi a tuta spada. Ezoche po far uno po far l'altro zoe che po fare tuti zoghi de spada cham lo incrosar. Ma lo incrosar sia de tre rasone, Zoe a tuta spada e punta de spada. Echi e incrosado a tuta spada pocho gle po starre. Echie mezo ?sado? a meza spada meno gle po stare. Echi a punta de spada niente gle po stare. Si che la spada si ha in si tre cose. zoe pocho, meno e niente.*

Which I translate as: "These two masters are here crossed [in] a tuta spada. And what one can do the other can do, thus they can do all the plays of the sword from the crossing. But the crossing is of three types, thus a tuta spada and a punta de spada. And the crossing a tuta spada little can it withstand. And mezo spada less can it withstand. And a punta de spada nothing can it withstand. And so the sword has in it three things, thus: little, less and nothing."

Comparing these three images, it is incontrovertible that the reference "meza spada" here means "at the middle of the blades."

In practical terms, we also find that with an open-hilted sword like a longsword it is dangerous to parry close to the hands (for extra leverage); to make the beating parry that Fiore describes (*rebattando*), the optimum balance between power and leverage – and the optimum place to aim for on the opponent's weapon – is indeed the middle of each.

### 9. Why is the blade contact edge-to-flat?

It is obvious from the description that this parry is a blow of some sort. It is clear from the illustration that it is done from the right, which means it can only reasonably be done with the true edge of the sword. The illustration clearly shows this, in my view. When striking at the opponent's sword, it makes mechanical and practical sense to aim at his flat. This is because (a) it is the weakest line of the sword itself, (b) it is unlikely to be supported by the opponent (see *Finding Bicorno* for details on this), and (c) it reduces damage to your sword by spreading the contact over a larger surface than an edge-to-edge parry.

### 10. Why frontale?

The blow you use when parrying up from a low guard is effectively a *mandritto sottano* (a rising forehand blow).This could be done with either edge, but for mechanical reasons I prefer the true edge. The natural ending point of a true-edge sottano aimed at the sword (as opposed to the opponent) is either a fenestra or frontale-type position. For the argument regarding blows beginning and ending in guards see both Angelo Viggiani's *Lo Schermo* and also Fiore's statements on f23r regarding fendenti: *"E ogni guardia che si fa terrena, Duna guardia in laltra andamo senza pena;"* "And all guards that are made low, from one guard to the other we go easily." Likewise, *sottani* can *"remanemo in posta longa"* or "remain [i.e. end] in *posta longa*." It is a bonus that Fiore provides us with the guard *frontale*, and says that *"per la incrosar ella e bona"* or "she is good for crossing."

Of course, if you are parrying from a high guard then you would be parrying with a *fendente*, and will not arrive in *frontale*, so the instruction would change.

### 11. Why is the attacker's blade beaten away?

The instruction that immediately follows the parry is to let your sword run off over the opponent's arms. If his sword is still coming towards you, or indeed is stationary but close to your face, you just can't do that without getting hit. One of the functions of the parry, as we see from the text, is to leave the opponent "uncovered." If his sword is in the way then he is clearly covered. The treatise abounds with alternative actions after the parry, which deal with other contexts (such as the opponent's sword being grabbed); it seems clear that, in this case, the sword has simply been beaten away by the parry as the defender intended. You see a similar situation in the second play of the sword in one hand, f20v.

This also goes to the definition of *"zogho largo"* as I understand the terms. Please refer to *The Medieval Longsword* pages 43–45 for this, and also to my earliest stab at a definition, the article *"Crossing Swords,"* available here: http://guywindsor.net/blog/wp-content/uploads/2014/06/Crossing-Swords.pdf

### 12. Why is the riposte a strike to the arm followed by a thrust to the chest?

Let's start with the text, which I'll repeat here to save you scanning back for it:

Above the crowned master it says

*Anchora me incroso qui per zogho largo a meza spada. E subito che son incrosado io lasso discorrer la mia spada sopra le soi mane, e se voglio passare cum lo pe dritta fuora de strada, io gli posso metter una punta in lo petto, come qui dredo e depento.*

Which I translate as: "Again, I am crossed here in the wide play at middle sword. And immediately that I am crossed I let my sword run off over the arms, and if I wish to pass with my right foot out of the way, I can place a thrust in the chest, as here below is depicted."

And above the play on the right, it reads

*Lo zogho del mio magistro io lo complido, cho io ofatta la sua coverta, e subito o fatto lo suo ditto, che io oferido primo gli brazzi, e poy glo posta la punta in petto.*

Which I translate as, "The play of my master I have completed, so I have made his cover, and immediately done what he said, so I have struck first the arms, and then I put the thrust in the chest."

This makes the issue of where to riposte to pretty clear, I think.

## 13. Why is the passo fora di strada done to the right?

The pass out of the way can in theory be done in any direction. I do it to the right because (a) it makes sense given the motion of the opponent's sword to the left as I see it; (b) it fits with the instruction to pass "out of the way," because I am literally getting out of the way of the attacker; (c) I am also getting out of the way of the sword; (d) it takes me to a place where I can reach with a strike, but my opponent has to step to strike; and (e) by doing it this way I end up looking like the illustration.

The image could support the idea of a step done diagonally to the left, instead of to the right as I do it. However, in my experience that would put me much closer to the opponent than is shown here.

So, there we have it. Over 3500 words written to support my interpretation that lies behind the basic execution of one drill in the book. I hope two things are clear from this:

1.  In the training manual I set out to write, there just isn't room to provide support in this depth for every detail of interpretation.

2.  I *can* support every aspect of every drill in this way. Feel free to ask me to do so. I don't have time to write one of these every week, but I stand by my interpretation and will back it up with evidence from the text at any time. Ask for the supporting evidence if something in the book seems off to you!

Please also bear in mind that, even with all this evidence, I may still be doing it wrong. That's historical swordsmanship for you.

# Chapter Two
## Lessons from the Art

"We are so accustomed to disguise ourselves to others that
in the end we become disguised to ourselves."

Francois de La Rochefoucauld


## Self-Reliance

I believe that the practice of swordsmanship has the capacity to
greatly improve the quality of people's lives and, indeed, the quality
of the people themselves.

One of the key things that we do is to develop autotelic
personalities. This means that we train people to set their own
goals, work towards their own ends, and find meaning and value
in everything that they do. Swordsmanship is, as I constantly tell
my students, about the finer things in life. Love, friendship, self-
discipline, bravery, and finding beauty and value in things that
may be overlooked by others. For how many centuries did our
sources lay gathering dust, uncared for and unappreciated? It is
easier to develop this ability to focus in an environment where

focus comes naturally. Just think of all those kids who can't focus in Geography class but have no trouble playing *Assassin's Creed* for hours at a time. Games demand focus, and they naturally induce the flow state. So does training, but the barriers to entry are higher. By finding an Art to fall in love with we can learn to find the flow, and having found it once, without the artificial stimuli of a screen and sound system, we can apply the same state of mind to any other endeavor. I think for many practitioners this is the single biggest benefit outside the salle. Bigger, even, than improved strength and fitness.

George Silver put it well, in his *Paradoxes of Defence*, back in 1599. He wrote

> "I speake not against Maisters of Defence indeed, they are to be honoured, nor against the Science, it is noble, and in mine opiniõ to be preferred next to Diuinitie; for as Diuinitie preserveth the soule from hell and the diuell, so doth this noble Science defend the bodie from wounds & slaughter. And moreouer, the exercising of weapons putteth away aches, griefes, and diseases, it increaseth strength, and sharpneth the wits. It giueth a perfect iudgement, it expelleth melancholy, cholericke and euill conceits, it keepeth a man in breath, perfect health, and long life. It is unto him that hath the perfection thereof, a most friendly and comfortable companion when he is alone, having but only his weapon about him. It putteth him out of feare, & in the warres and places of most danger, it maketh him bold, hardie and valiant."

I think we could all use less disease, more strength, sharper wits, better judgement, less depression, and less anger; and to be kept in breath, health, and long life. And we could use less fear. Every martial art is, at its root, a way to handle the terror that comes with someone trying to kill you. So let's look at that.

## Handling Fear

The key skill is to control your autonomic responses: the ability to choose all your actions from a position of confidence and strength, rather than just react out of fear and dread.

Let me give you a deeply personal and painful example.

My wife was about to give birth to our second child. Two years previously she had had pre-eclampsia with our first child, which is fatal to both mother and child if the baby is not immediately extracted. So Grace's birth was induced a month early. This time everything had been fine (except for morning sickness that had my wife vomiting every day for the full nine months; ah, the joy of pregnancy), but on the Friday she was admitted to hospital because it looked like she might be developing pre-eclampsia again. The doctors began chemically inducing labor on Saturday (as they had with Grace), and it looked like Sunday was D-day. I took Grace to see her on Sunday afternoon, took Grace home and left her with her godfather, and took a taxi back to the hospital at about 6 p.m. When I was sat in the car I had a sudden, overwhelming sense of dread, quite unlike how a prospective father should feel. Something was wrong, and there was nothing I could do about it.

I got to the hospital, went to my wife's ward, opened the door, and saw a bunch of machines, arranged with a clear path to the door, and her bed gone. Oh fuck. This is not good. A deep in-breath through the nostrils to a count of five got the rising panic back down, and I turned to go find someone to tell me what was going on.

There was a nurse standing behind me.

"Are you Mr Windsor?"

"Yes. Where is my wife?"

"She is in surgery, they are doing an emergency c-section. Come, I'll take you to the waiting room."

"Can I be there in the operating room?"

"No, that's not possible."

I didn't know it then, but that was a mercy. Naturally I wanted to be standing over the surgeons with a sword, making damn sure they knew that failure = death, but on sober reflection that would not have actually helped at all. Failure would equal death anyway.

She took me to a room I already knew, just down the hall from the delivery room where Grace was born. She told me to wait: they'd come with any news. I knew an emergency c-section takes about 20 minutes. It had already been at least half an hour since surgery began, and no news. Things must be very wrong.

So I sat down and figured out what to do. I needed plans for all contingencies so that I could stop thinking. Higher-level functions such as planning are deeply draining and hard to do under stress, so the point of having made plans in this situation was to allow me to shut down and conserve energy. Here is what I came up with.

(1) Worst case scenario: wife and child both dead. This will entail two related problems: (a) coping with the loss, and (b) mitigating the loss for Grace. Practical problems (funerals, etc.) are not relevant at this point, so discard. Real problem is emotional. So solution must be about emotional survival. Plan: every night for the rest of my life I will tell Grace that her mother loved her very much. Note that this required that I survive also (suicide not an option, however attractive it may be in the short term). I formed an image in my mind of Grace, having left home, being exasperated (she was doing exasperation very well already at age nearly-2) by her bloody father (me) ringing her up at bedtime every damn night to tell her something she already knew because she'd heard it thousands of times already. So I could project a future for us both, which included Grace being emotionally stable and happy, and it would be okay. This was not much of a plan, really, but more than enough to get me through the current crisis.

(2) Wife dies; baby lives. Plan: devote rest of life to raising two

happy children. Possible, likely even, that baby will be damaged. Recall examples of friends with disabled siblings. This is totally survivable, and is a chance for Grace to grow as a person.

(3) Baby dies; wife lives. Plan: look after wife and Grace. Devote 100% of available resources to handling grief, mine and wife's; especially make sure Grace is not neglected or overly cosseted as a result.

(4) Both live. Best case scenario, regardless of disabilities, trauma, etc. Two beating hearts. Plan: 100% of resources applied to whatever healing needed.

Short-term problem: maintain fitness-for-purpose during this situation of unknown duration (purpose = guard wife and child's interests; Grace is okay for at least 24 hours, so can be ignored in this situation). Assume duration 24 hours. Requirements: hydration, maintain energy levels (so rest from emotional distress), and minimal alertness. Plan: drink one glass of water every hour, do five minutes' light calisthenics every hour, and shut down all non-essential functions and avoid thinking about the situation until I have more data.

So I went into an odd mental state where I focused on reading the novel I had brought with me for about 40 minutes at a time, stopping only to drink water, go to the bathroom, go ask the nurses again if there was any news, do light exercise, and most importantly do my breath-control exercises. These were a lifesaver; every time my mind rebelliously went to dwell on the situation my heart rate would climb, and I risked becoming exhausted to no purpose if I let it continue, so I'd bring my heart rate back down to sustainable levels (about 70–90 BPM, well over my usual resting BPM of between 55 and 60, but low enough for endurance work).

After the first round of this, so about an hour after I'd gotten to the room, a midwife came in and said: "congratulations Mr Windsor, you have a daughter."

My mind shrieked: "I know I have a daughter, she's at home

with her godfather, NOW TELL ME ABOUT MY WIFE!"
Fortunately, my wits gathered in time to realize I had another one.
But this news, momentous in any other circumstances, barely
registered.

"Oh, lovely. How's my wife?"

"She's still in surgery. But your daughter was born with an
APGAR score of 1."

Oh shit. Oh shitty shitty shit. 0 is dead. Healthy babies score
8–10.

"She was blue, with her eyes open, and only a faint heartbeat.
She's in the intensive care unit now. We think your wife had a
placental abruption, and so both she and your baby were bleeding
out. The concern is brain damage, from being starved of oxygen."

"OK. Understood. Can I see her?"

"Not yet. I came as soon as she was stable, but they are running
tests now. We'll come get you when you can see her."

So, she may be completely fine. Or she may be a vegetable. Or
something in between. That's a long-term problem. File it and
come back to it later.

Plan: advocate for my daughter. (This is usually unnecessary in
Finland: she was getting 100% of the doctors' best efforts and 100%
of the medical support available to modern science. This plan was
for *me*: I had to have a plan so that I didn't have to think too
much.) This little scrap, bound in wires and tubes, had a paladin
on her side. No matter what. Forever.

I resumed my holding pattern. About two cycles later the
doctor in charge came to get me, and we went over to the
children's hospital next door, via an underground tunnel. He
couldn't give me any *numbers*. I wanted probabilities and
scenarios, but all he could say was, "we'll see." He mentioned a
chilling procedure that they were thinking of doing; it reduces
brain damage if the body is cooled by a few degrees for long
enough. I looked at him.

Me: "Why are we talking about this? Just do it! And thank God for the Falklands war!"

Him: "Huh?"

Me: "This procedure was developed thanks to the difference in survival rates between soldiers with the same injuries in Vietnam and the Falklands." [The colder climate meant that injured soldiers got hypothermia, and that led to a paradoxical improvement in survival rates. The body is a weird thing.]

Him: "So you know about this then."

Me: "Yes. Now what are we waiting for? Time is of the essence!"

We got to the ICU and there she was, festooned in wires. A little girl with a very uncertain future, but who was now my complete responsibility. I stroked her tummy, the only bit of her I could really get at, and told her that I was there, that I loved her, that her mother loved her, that she had a sister who would love her, and that everything was going to be all right; no matter what happened.

I stayed with her for a while, then went back to wait for news of my wife.

A couple more cycles passed. No news is good news, sort of.

Then finally, sometime after 11 p.m., a surgeon came in dressed for the street. She said that the team now thought that my wife would live. She didn't have more details, but someone would be in soon to tell me what was going on. I thanked her, perfectly calmly, and she left. My phone rang about half an hour later: it was my mother-in-law. I told her that the doctors said that Michaela would live.

"Oh, as bad as that?" She'd had no idea. One thing I had not done was call everyone so that they could worry too. What would be the point?

It turned out that my wife had bled out completely, losing 7 liters of blood (she started with about 4), because her clotting factors were all used up. So they had to do an emergency hysterectomy and keep filling her up with more blood, while she leaked it out of everywhere. The next day I heard that doctors were referring to her as "the woman who lived."

I got home about 1 a.m., had a stiff whisky, and managed to sleep for about four hours. Then I was up and back at the hospital at about 9 a.m. They wouldn't let me in until she was awake so I went to check on the baby, and the staff there told me to come back at 12. So I had a couple of hours. I spent it purging. The humongous terror and relief were impacting my ability to function, and so I rang several of my friends in turn and told them the story. After each call I leaned against a tree and howled my eyes out. I had it under control after the fifth or sixth call. The last thing my charges needed was a basket-case looking after them.

It took my wife more than two years to fully recover: first a hard pregnancy, then an emergency c-section, then complete exsanguination, then an emergency hysterectomy, and then a small child and a newborn baby to care for; all the while also dealing with sudden-onset menopause. The baby, chilled to 33°C for 72 hours, was in the ICU for a week, and has since made a complete recovery. She is now six, and she likes reading and writing and ballet. A miracle child. We named her Katriina, after the doctor who pulled her out.

Many people go through far worse things than this and are fine. Many people, with no training at all, could have held it together as well, or better, than I did. But I attribute my ability to maintain function and take proper care of my family during this time entirely to my swordsmanship training. The Art is all about pre-determining your responses under extreme pressure. It's about making rational decisions beforehand, to be executed under stress. Controlling the effects of stress, such as heart-rate, is a component of that. So is the ability to plan under pressure, and so is dealing with issues that affect your emotional control.

This section is all about those aspects of training that have little to do with hitting people with swords and much to do with why practicing swordsmanship in this modern age is nonetheless hugely worthwhile.

Let us continue with the theme of fear...

## I am fearful. So I study boldness.

This article was originally intended as part of a group of four, based on Fiore's four virtues; boldness, strength, speed, and foresight. Strength and speed are dealt with in the next section on martial arts, so here we have boldness. Or rather, fear. In the end it cut too close to the bone for a blog post, and so I have sequestered it here in an actual book. I cannot say why that seems more private or less exposing.

I have spent large chunks of my life afraid, but these days I almost never act purely out of fear. My decisions are not driven by it, and shaking off the fear was one of the most profoundly liberating and empowering experiences of my life. So I thought I'd share with you how I did it, or, more accurately, how I continue to do it. Fear comes in many shapes and forms: from the soul-destroying attrition of chronic anxiety; to the "oh shit" moment where you realise things are about to go wrong; and to the mad, screaming terror that takes over your whole body and over which there is no control because your conscious mind is, for all intents and purposes, switched off. You have seen above how planning and heart-rate management helped me when my wife and child were on the brink.

Fear is a response to the perception of threat. The solution is similar in all cases: defiance, boldness, courage. Audatia. And it has the following components

1. Regaining control over your physiology, which is accomplished by breathing exercises.
2. Assessing the threat dispassionately.
3. Responding to the threat in a deliberate manner. Either ignore it, deal with it, or run like hell; whatever makes most sense.

One of the key purposes of training is to make steps one and two instinctive and thus very fast, and to build in reactions that, after the fact, are logically sound. The key distinction between trained and untrained combatants is the level of stress they are under in the same situation, and so their ability to act intelligently in those circumstances. Point a gun at the average civilian and they will likely gibber in terror. Point a gun at a highly trained and experienced police officer, for whom this is perhaps the hundredth such occurrence, and the response is very different.

Let's start with chronic anxiety and work our way up to gibbering terror.

## Anxiety

I was sent off to boarding school in England when I was eight years old. England was familiar, but it was not home. We first left England for Argentina when I was five, then returned for six months or so when I was seven, and we had been in Botswana for about a year when the time came. Africa was home. I was taken out of the little, local school run by my best friend's mum, and brought back to England with my mum. I was then taken to this gigantic house in the middle of nowhere and left in the care of strangers. My older brother was there too. This actually made things worse: not only was he a constant reminder of home but he was also a complete and utter shit, as the rest of this post will relate. (Please note that he was 12 at the time, and thus not entirely responsible for his actions.)

The school itself was well run by caring staff, and in general there was none of the Nicholas Nickleby stuff most people seem to imagine whenever they find out I spent ten years in boarding schools. No savage beatings (except from my brother), no buggery of any kind, and nothing that would actually constitute abuse. But it was utterly terrifying to be locked up in an institution, entirely at the mercy of the staff and the other boys. So much so that I didn't take a dump for eight days, because I was way too scared to risk dropping my trousers. You are uniquely vulnerable when sat on the bog. So I couldn't do it. In the end nature took its course and I shat my pants.

At its root, this fear is based on the question, "can I cope with this new environment?" As I learned the rules (of which the unwritten were vastly more important than the written), got to know the people, and found safe places to hide, I eventually settled in and actually enjoyed some of it. I learned to cope. More importantly, I learned that I *could* cope. The experience of surviving it, though it had far more to do with the luck of there being no sadists on staff, nonetheless makes it a trivial matter for me to fly to a foreign country and be surrounded by the unfamiliar.

So, the solution is to recognize that the threat is not as real as you at first thought. Isolate what is worrying you, assess it through experience, and adapt to it.

## Shame

Shame is worse than anxiety. It is a cancer that will eat your heart out, as it did mine. Shame is often about social exclusion. We are ashamed of the things that we think will make other people not want us in their group. A criminal past, for instance. I know all about that one. I once committed a crime so heinous that I was convinced my own mother wouldn't love me any more if she found out.

I was eight years old and scared shitless (literally. See above). My instinct told me that I needed allies to survive in this strange environment, and the best way to get them is to identify with a specific group.

Let me say at this point that I loathe all forms of sport. Especially team sports. I really have no interest at all in football teams, or in any of that ghastly tribalism that seems to go with them.

But one day, early in my first term, I found a pen on the floor in the bogs at school (cubicles that were so covered in graffiti that you could scarcely discern their original color). I picked it up and wrote the following immortal lines:

"Up the Spurs." (Ed. note: a British football team, in which I had zero interest.)

And, most stupidly:

"Windsor was here."

My brother was a Spurs supporter. I figured that the flock might take me in if I could adopt the plumage. Big mistake. My brother saw the graffiti, obviously, and knew it was me, obviously. And he told me that I might be expelled if anyone ever found out I was such a degenerate that I would vandalize the school like that.

Expulsion, as any 8-year-old at boarding school knows, means that your life is over. No proper school will ever take you again. So no university, and no job; you end up a vagrant, shunned by decent society forever. It's over. Finding out, years later, that Stephen Fry, David Niven, and other luminaries had themselves been expelled from school was amazing. Their autobiographies ought to be read by any kid about to be packed off to boarding school.

Worse than expulsion: if Mum found out, I might never get to go home again. After all, why would our parents want me back? I was a vandal! The lowest of the low! But so long as I did what I was told, of course, no-one need know.

There is a special hell for blackmailers. Next to them, there is a refreshing honesty in a simple murderer. Blackmail murders the soul.

What I should have done is pick up a hockey stick and beat the shit out of him, but what I did was cave in. I folded. And a piece of me died; by not calling his bluff I was implicitly accepting that I was so degenerate, so degraded, that literally my own parents wouldn't want me back home. Let me say here that if I had called his bluff and he had told on me then the teachers would have made me clean the wall, and my parents would have told my brother not to tell tales on me; and that would have been it. Everyone concerned would have forgotten about it in short order. Instead I became my brother's personal slave, staying behind after games to take off his muddy boots and sweaty socks, and other humiliations too mundane to bother you with. I'm lucky he wasn't a pervert. The saving grace was that he was so much older that we only had three awful terms in the same school before he moved on.

But I had learned that I was unworthy. Corrupt. And that had to be hidden. It tainted the next twenty years of my life, because it meant I had real difficulty forming proper friendships based on honesty and respect. Just exactly the wrong build-up to the ordinary hell of adolescence where healthy, normal urges and body changes can be made to feel unimaginably shameful. It took some radical intervention in the form of kundalini madness to get me out of it completely.

This long-term shame is about fear of exposure. Fear of what will happen when people find out who you really are: a bog-wall-writing degraded and defiled piece of shit. But you know what? Being hated for who you are is bad, but there is nothing worse than being loved for who you're not.

Blackmailers live on shame, and shame depends on secrets. The only solution is to have no secrets. There is much in my life that is private, but nothing at all that is secret. If you went through my life with a fine-tooth comb and exposed all the human oddities, foibles, weirdness, and baroque bizarreness that constitutes my privacy, you wouldn't find anything that my wife doesn't already know. And some of my friends, too. Sure, it would be embarrassing, but I'd get over it and you'd look like a fool. Publish and be damned!

When you screw up as you inevitably will, being human, hiding it is worse for you than 'fessing up. I have nothing to be ashamed of. And neither do you. How do I know this? It's because if whatever you may have done is actually wrong then contrition, confession, and restitution lead inevitably to absolution. They are the only solution to shame.

Getting forgiveness from others is usually impossible or easy. For many of us, forgiving ourselves is the real problem. Here is a top tip that I got from a friend of mine when I was dealing with another source of shame: "Imagine your best friend has the same secret. How do you now feel about them? If you can forgive them, why not yourself?" This worked for me.

## Stage Fright

Stage fright is an acute form of fear of ostracism. They will despise you if you do badly; fail, and they will hate you. All that. I used to get so scared doing solos on the trumpet in the school's Big Band that I would nearly vomit beforehand, and I would shake so much even the soles of my feet were vibrating. Playing the trumpet requires exquisite fine-motor control (in the lips, tongue, and fingers) and large amounts of force (in the diaphragm and abs). Both are very hard to achieve when you are trembling like a leaf. There are two main solutions for this kind of thing: getting control of yourself, by bringing down your heart rate through breathing, and getting the right response from the audience.

When I opened my school I began with a free demonstration in a small room at the Olympic stadium, here in Helsinki. The place was so packed that I had to abandon my original plan of running a taster class, and instead I had them sit on the floor while I talked and demonstrated for about 45 minutes. Then we did some very basic pair exercises. I was utterly terrified: I had moved from Edinburgh to Finland for this audience. If this failed, my whole school idea might fail. Stage fright – with teeth.

So I picked up a gigantic sword and stood still, while looking at the audience until they realized we were about to start and the talking tailed off. There is nothing quite so reassuring as a 5 foot longsword in your hands. I opened with humor: something along the lines of, "it's amazing how everyone quiets down when I pick up an ENORMOUS sword!" They chuckled, I relaxed, and it went well from there.

But, oh my, it was a scary moment. You can't always carry an enormous sword with you to defend yourself against the audience. But you can use a talisman, or even a mantra; something to hold onto, just in case. There are all sorts of specific programs to help you get over stage fright. My solutions are: breathing to bring down the heart-rate; an honest assessment of the threat (i.e. they may not like me. It happens. My wife and kids will not leave me over this though, so I can live with this crowd hating me); and habituation: I routinely try to schedule opportunities to get over this fear in my schedule. Need a lecture? Let me know...

## Fear of Injury

Fear of injury is a bit different. Injury is physically real, and potentially permanent, in a way that people not liking you isn't real. But, again, the root of the fear isn't usually the pain. It's "can I cope with the pain?," or the fear of living with the injury – "can I cope with only one eye?" – or whatever.

My job is dangerous, and I am quite scared of getting injured. This makes me careful. But I vividly recall the time when my wrists were so bad from RSI from my cabinet-making job that a few clangs of sword-on-sword would have them swell up and I'd lose a day of work, and so a day's pay. At a time when I was making about £6000 *a year*. Trainee cabinet-makers do not drive Rolls Royces, or indeed any kind of car. Really, every penny mattered. I was on the point of quitting swordsmanship altogether. Then one day I was at a DDS meet-up and sword-bash at Craigmillar Castle, near Edinburgh. I was watching everyone else having fun, and I simply decided that swords were too important. Fuck it; wrists be damned. I'll fight anyway and, if needs be, hold my chisel in my teeth tomorrow.

So I picked up my sword and fenced my friends, knowing that it would do me an injury but not caring. That was one of the key moments in my life, though I didn't realize it at the time. Through this increased commitment to swordsmanship I met a kung fu instructor who, in 20 agonizing minutes, did what the doctors of Edinburgh had failed to do: he fixed my wrists. Like most things, the fix is not permanent. I have to keep up my maintenance or I am swollen-wristed again after a week-or-so of writing and teaching. But I can fix it in minutes when that happens, and simply getting back into my maintenance routine keeps the problem away. My wrists have never been stronger than they are now thanks to the injury, and thanks to its cure.

## Acute Terror

Acute terror is different in terms of how it works in the body, and in how it should be handled. A recent example is from my first trip to Australia. The thing about Australia is that all of the most poisonous animals in the world live there. It's remote for a reason: you're not supposed to go there! Take the funnel-web spider. It looks like it can kill you, and it can. I was staying at my friend Paul Wagner's house, and he calmly informed me that there are certainly funnel-webs in his garden (so where's the fucking napalm, Paul?). We visited the museum, and in the gift shop he picked up a plastic model of a funnel-web to show me what they look like. Walking home from the pub after a seminar the following day, just strolling down the pavement, I walked between someone's garden hedge and a tree; I got a faceful of spiderweb. "Oh shit," I thought. Then I looked down, and there was a fucking funnel-web on my shoulder! A moment later I realized I was running like hell and screaming in terror. I was running away from the spider on my shoulder: not a carefully-thought-out strategy. A part of my mind was taken by the irony of being one of the very, very few tourists who die from Australian wildlife. I started unzipping my jacket, but my hands were shaking too much. My legs carried on running, and I started combat-breathing (in for 4, hold for 4, out for 4, hold for 4) to get my heart rate down; in a moment I could get the zip open and the jacket off. After about another 50 yards my legs were mine again, and I stopped.

Paul was doubled up in paroxysms of hysterical laughter; meanwhile, rational thought was returning to me. I explained about the spider, how a funnel-web was on my shoulder, and how I knew I was going to die stupidly. "Oh, don't worry, funnel-webs live in the ground. That was probably a little huntsman. Very unlikely to kill you. Unless you happen to be allergic."

"No, Paul, it was a fucking great Ozzy spider and I was going to die."

Paul kindly picked up my jacket and shook it out. I refused to put it on until he had gone through all the pockets. By this time my heart rate was back below 100, I had full use of my faculties, and was having just the occasional full-body shudder.

There is nothing to be done about this kind of terror except to bring your heart rate down and eliminate the threat. Spiders are not impressed by your defiance, though, so either stamp on them or run away. There is no way to win that fight.

The next day, at the end of my seminar, Paul told the attendees all about my utterly stoical and phlegmatic response to the spider incident, producing a full and quite accurate impression of my high-pitched screaming. He presented me with a Barbie Princess bag, inside which was a book on Australian poisonous creatures. I bask in the respect and admiration of my colleagues!

## Subconscious fear

I don't go out of my way to find scary situations. There are plenty of those at work! But when I find that one of my decisions is fear-based I immediately review it, and I usually overturn it. To give an example that every fencer can probably relate to, let me tell you about how I chickened out of fencing someone.

There is an unnecessary but oh-so-human schism in European swordsmanship between those that like tournaments and those that don't. Or, to be more accurate: those that organise competitive tournaments and make them the center of their training, and those that don't. It's more complicated than that, of course, but I was recently referred to as "one of the anti-tournament crowd" (despite the fact that I organize at least one tournament per year, and many of my students are active participants in the wider tournament scene). If we accept the binary schism for a minute, WMAW is very much "non-tournament" (though last year's event had at least three tournaments running). We had Jake Norwood – Captain America himself, and one of the "leaders of the opposition" – attending as an instructor at the 2011 event. Of course, I had to fence him. But he is tall, fast, strong, very good, and, in community terms, one of them: not one of us. Or so I thought at the time. High stakes, then. So I dillied and dallied, and was too busy or too tired, until right before he was due to leave. I was fiddling with my kit bag when I realized that I was stalling, and that I was afraid to fence him. I honestly hadn't realized it until then. I think it was a combination of "he might hurt me," and "he might totally own me." So I grabbed my gear, ran as fast as I could to where he was, and we fenced. It was lovely. Not either of our best-ever bouts perhaps, but a pleasure. (I should point out that there was no reason at all to think of Jake as more likely to injure me than any other fencer. More likely to hammer me, perhaps. But, even then, totally unlikely to be mean about it. The fear was utterly irrational.)

On principle, the things you fear are either legitimate threats to be avoided or growth opportunities to be embraced. Distinguishing them is the trick. A martial artist must err on the side of boldness, just as a driver should err on the side of caution.

## Training for fear

In addition to fear management strategies, it is also useful to actively practice handling fear. For this you will need one irrational-fear-inducing activity, ideally one that requires little cash or preparation, and a commitment to daily practice. One easy option is cold showers. It's not ideal because most people are not actively afraid of cold water, they just don't like it. But having the nerve to turn the tap all the way to cold and let it hit you is a good start.

I personally have a wildly irrational fear of hanging off things, especially upside down. I'm okay hanging off a pull-up bar by my hands, but jumping up to catch hold of it in the first place gives me a heart attack. In the back of my mind, I am completely certain that if I miss my catch the contact of my fingers on the bar will flip me upside down, and I'll fall on my head. Yes, really.

But I *know* that it isn't so. The forces at work just cannot make that happen. My rational mind overrules my irrational body, in this case. So I jump and catch the bar every day, and I nearly die of fright every day. But it is much easier to handle now than it was a year ago. I can feel the dread building as I approach the bar, and I steel myself to jump and catch. It's horrible but useful, and it's good practice.

Hanging upside down by my knees is another one. For the longest time, I could not do it. I knew, in my heart of hearts, that if I let go with my hands my legs would straighten and I would fall, as if my legs were not under my control at all; as if the teeny, little muscles in my grip were somehow able to generate more force than the relatively large (in comparison to my forearms at least) muscles in my thighs.

My cousin is a professional aerialist (she organised the Mary Poppins's at the London Olympics opening ceremony), and way back in 2005 she was performing in Berlin, doing scary-as-hell rope tricks. I flew over to see her and while I was there she invited me along to their training hall, to have a go on ropes and trapezes. It was fantastic good fun. While she was teaching me to get onto a trapeze I managed to get my legs over the bar, but I *could not* let go with my hands and hang down. No way. Instant fall onto head. So she shinned up the rope next to me, laid her arm on my shins, and said, "don't worry, I won't let you fall." (The physics do not work, of course. She was about half my weight and hanging off a rope. But irrational fears do not require rational solutions.) I let go, and after a moment she could take her arm away. There I was, hanging by my knees upside down, for the first time ever.

Unfortunately, trapezes are quite tricky to find round here: I didn't do it again until this summer. We have a climbing frame in our yard. My eldest daughter and I were playing on it, and I did Katherine's trick of holding her shins (though in this case the reassurance was backed up by physics!). In short order my 7-year-old turned into a monkey, as regards hanging off stuff at least. So I decided to join her; I had my wife hold my shins, and I let go with my hands. After a few reps of that I could do it without her. And now it's easy. Scary, but easy. I still feel like I'm about to fall, but I still do it. I'll have to find something else to be frightened of when that stops being scary enough, because the benefits of daily-overcoming-terror are way too great.

So, give it a go. What are you afraid of?

To conclude, then:

I'd rather be injured than be afraid of injury. I'd rather be ridiculed than afraid of ridicule. I'd rather be ostracized than afraid of ostracism. I'd rather you knew the stuff I don't want you to know about me than be afraid of you finding it out.

Bring it on!

## THE MYTH OF TALENT

First posted on December 3rd, 2012, as "Complexity". This drew some active disagreement, mostly, I think, from people who felt threatened by the idea that they could be held directly responsible for their successes or failures. Personally, I feel *less* threatened by things that I can exercise some control over.

I don't believe in innate talent. I've never seen it in a student, and I have noticed no correlation between early successes in training and long-term achievement. But you can draw a linear relationship between hours spent in class and acknowledged skill. Perhaps the most obvious example of this is my sort-of-ex-student (in that he has gone on to set up his own independent school) Ilkka Hartikainen. Round about the time he was developing an international reputation for his Bolognese research we, coincidentally, did a review of attendance data. Turns out that my star student had 50% more class time logged than the next-keenest student. This is a clear indication that his effort, not some genetic predisposition to historical swordsmanship, was the underlying cause of his success. This is as it should be. I see no point in engaging in any sort of activity where genetic factors are the prime determinant of success. Everybody now knows (or should do!) about the 10,000 hour rule, which indicates that ten thousand hours of dedicated practice (not just going through the motions) is needed for mastery in any complex field. A major component of my job is to ensure that the time students spend in class is actually *dedicated practice*, not just swinging a sword about.

This always begs the question, though, *what is complexity?* In which areas does this rule apply, and in which does it not? In one lecture I gave on this subject someone clearly felt threatened by the idea that it's effort, not talent, that generates expertise. They asked me if it took 10,000 hours to master blinking. The best definition I have so far come across for complexity in this context is in Matthew Syed's *Bounce*, the subtitle of which is bang on the money: *the myth of talent and the power of practice*. He says (on p. 48 of the 2011 Fourth Estate paperback edition):

"...complexity... describes those tasks characterised by combinatorial explosion; tasks where success is determined, first and foremost, by superiority in software (pattern recognition and sophisticated motor programs) rather than hardware (simple speed or strength)."

Chess is the usual example of a pursuit characterised by combinatorial explosion. Thirty two men on sixty four squares leads to more possible game permutations than there are atoms in the universe but, from our perspective, chess is *simple!* It doesn't matter *how* you place your knight on the board: it only matters where. Likewise, there is only one desired result: checkmate. There are no nuances or degrees. You can win, lose, or draw. We can learn much from the paths to mastery that top chess players have used (e.g. in Josh Waitzkin's *The Art of Learning*), but chess is sadly lacking in terms of breadth. In addition to the complexities of tactics that chess players use, in swordsmanship we can add depth and breadth of research; skills of motor execution (performing the physical movements of the art); levels of control allowing a choice of outcomes; (such as kill, wound, capture, evade); and so on. Even if someone suffers from severe physical disability there is nothing stopping them from mastering an area of this art to a degree that puts them at the top of their part of this giant field.

There are many insights in Syed's book that will no doubt make their way into my other writings at some point (he has a lovely section on double-think, for instance, and another on the necessity of consistent execution of basic actions, for another instance). For now I'll leave you with this thought: the *only* thing that stands between you and mastery of the art of arms, or any other art, is the amount of dedicated practice you are willing to put into it.

## Five barriers to success and my solutions to them

Posted on 19th June, 2013

This is one of my most popular posts: I think people have found it useful.

There are many reasons why people are afraid to begin training swordsmanship, or indeed are afraid to follow any path, and many reasons why those who have begun the journey may quit. What follows is by no means an exhaustive list, but it contains some of the more common problems that I have encountered and my own solutions to them. These worked for me (so far); your mileage may vary.

(1) Fear of failure. Perhaps the biggest step I have ever taken in which fear of failure was a major issue was opening the school. My friends at the time could tell you that I projected two possible outcomes for my mad move to Finland. Outcome one: I'd be back in six months with my tail between my legs. Outcome two: it would fly. I chose to view the whole thing as a lesson. In other words, I was going to Finland to learn something. I did not know what the lesson would be. If the school failed, if I failed, then that was the lesson. I comforted myself with the knowledge that no matter how badly it failed, so long as I was honest and gave it all that I had, the worst possible outcome (other than serious injury) was bankruptcy and embarrassment. The culture and time I was

lucky enough to be born into would not allow me to starve, nor would I be hauled off to debtors prison. Really, there was nothing to fear except my own incompetence.

(2) Fear of success. At its root, this is a fear of change. If I succeed in the thing I am setting out to do, what then? What if I actually become the person I wish to become? Who am I? My solution to this was to set up my school and my training in such a way that success was impossible. There is no end goal or end result. There is only process. My mission in life is deliberately unattainable: to restore our European martial heritage to its rightful place at the heart of European culture. Of course that cannot be achieved alone, and there is no reasonable expectation of it being accomplished in my lifetime. There is no question that European martial arts have come a long way in the last decade or so, and my work has been a part of that, but another excellent aspect to this goal is that nobody would ever suggest that I did it, even if we could say it was accomplished in my lifetime. So fear of success is not a problem because success is impossible.

(3) Outcome or process? The most common problem I have had in my career choices to date is putting outcome before process. I was more interested in training martial arts than in studying English literature when I went to university to get my degree; though I got my degree, I didn't get that much out of it at the time. I wanted the outcome, and not the process. Then when I went to be a cabinetmaker, again, I was more interested in *having made* the furniture than in *actually making it*. Sure, I enjoyed parts of the process very much. But I did not have that dedication to perfection-in-process that marks a really good cabinetmaker. Ironically, I enjoy the process of it a lot more now that I do it for a hobby. In a similar vein to step two – fear of success – teaching swordsmanship is the only thing I have ever done where I have truly been more concerned with process than with outcome. Which is why I am a much better swordsmanship instructor than

I ever was a cabinetmaker. Writing books is another process/ outcome issue. I enjoy writing books quite a bit. I absolutely hate the editing, polishing, and publication process. By that point outcome is everything: I just want that bloody book done and out. This is why I don't think of myself as a writer. When I write, good enough is good enough. In my swordsmanship, though, good enough is shit; perfection is the minimum standard. Never got there and never will. Don't care. Get it perfect anyway. It truly bugs me when my left little toe is not in quite the right place when I am waiting in guard. So far, in the thousands and thousands of hours I have put into it, there have been perhaps three whole minutes where my swordsmanship felt perfect. But those minutes are only because my faculties of judgement were not developed enough to spot the imperfections. So, while I am deeply dissatisfied with the outcome (i.e. my current level), I am actually quite pleased with how far I have come: with the process so far.

(4) External validation. This is related to the outcome/process problem. External validation tends to come from outcomes rather than processes. People bringing me one of my books to sign is hugely gratifying, and it validates the outcome of all that work. But the books are likely to be crap if you only write them in the hope of people asking you for autographs, and who wants an autograph on a crap book? I get around this problem by thinking of my books as steps towards the overall goal of establishing European martial arts at the heart of European culture. This makes even the production of books part of a larger process. And because they are mission-oriented I have the emotional energy reserves to demand a certain standard in them, if not quite the standard I demand of my basic strikes. The external validation trap is one reason why I tend to prefer martial arts that have no belts or ranks, because it is too easy for me to care about the next belt rather than actually mastering the art. Ironically, the best outcomes are usually the result of the best processes. The best way to get

great outcomes is to forget about them and focus on the process.

(5) Time and attention. It is not enough to want to want it. I only have a certain amount of energy to give, and it is what I actually choose to do that indicates what is truly important to me. The only currencies that actually matter are the ones you can't make more of: time and attention. How one spends these vital currencies is of course influenced by the problems outlined above. My priorities are: family first, school second, and then everything else. Within "school" it goes: teaching, research/writing, training, and then admin. As I see it, the school is the emergent property of the students, the teachers, and the syllabus coming together in a suitable space. My students make it all possible, they are the base, so their needs come first. The research and writing are for them, so that we have an art to train. The training I do is so that I have something to show them. Admin, running the business side of things, is so far down the list it's pathetic. I only do it so the school can keep running, because it's the school (students, research, and syllabus) that actually furthers the mission. As has happened more than once, though, if the shit hits the fan at home I abandon the school to take care of itself and put all my attention on the family. Of course. My mission as husband and father outranks my personal mission in life.

## CONSUMING RISK

Risk management is a key skill in life. How do you know what insurance to buy, what dangers to ward against, and so on? And just how dangerous is the practice of swordsmanship anyway? Risk management is a critical skill: especially for working out a fear-training program. For the program to be sensible the fear must be irrational; the perceived risk must be much higher than the actual risk. If you are afraid of wrestling crocodiles then don't do it, because it's really dangerous. House spiders? Not so much. (Unless you live in Australia. Or certain parts of the USA. Or

Africa.) My point is not that you should go out and do dangerous things; probability will catch up with you and bad things will happen. My point is that you should practice handling fear in a safe environment, and that you should know how dangerous something really is. Your fear is an unsteady guide to both of these.

Posted on 29th August, 2012

The study of risk has been developed to the nth degree over the last five hundred years or so. For an excellent overview, see *Against the Gods: the remarkable story of risk*, by Peter Bernstein. (Thanks to my friend Lenard Voelker for sending me a copy!) The assessment of risk may be described as assigning probabilities to events that have not yet occurred. If they have happened before then we can see how many times over a given period, and can use that data to evaluate the likelihood of it happening again. For example, if it has snowed at Christmas 20 times in the last 100 years you can state with some confidence that there is about a 1 in 5 chance of it happening again this year. But many of the events we fear have no measurable risk. This is either because they have not happened (yet) or we have an insufficient pool of data from which to draw meaningful probabilities. So they are uncertain, but they have no definite probability. This distinction was drawn by Milton Keynes (and explained by Niall Ferguson on p. 343 of his book *The Ascent of Money*).

Swordsmanship practice is inherently dangerous. The risk we all fear is a training accident leading to serious injury or death. In the wider world of swordsmanship practice, all of the serious accidents (which I define as "requiring hospitalization") have occurred in either competitive freeplay or outside the bounds of a formal school (such as on the re-enactment field). So we know that there is a possibility of such accidents occurring in the salle, yet they have no definable risk as the incidence is so low. They are instead uncertain. Given the thousands of hours spent in swordsmanship training worldwide every year and how few accidents occur, it is reasonable to assign a low probability of serious injury or death. Assuming that we do not relax our safety standards in response to this we can assure prospective scholars of the art that "this is dangerous, but pretty safe."

Cars are also pretty safe these days. Airbags, crumple zones, safety glass, and seat belts, all reduce the likelihood of serious injury or death in the case of a collision. But they do nothing to prevent collisions in the first place, and they encourage a false sense of security. Cocooned in hi-tech armor, we ride invulnerable to our deaths. I think a shiny, steel spike sticking out of the steering wheel to impale the driver at the merest fender-bender would do wonders to improve road safety.

When a risky activity becomes safer human beings tend to consume that risk. Safer cars are driven faster. Better healthcare encourages unhealthy lifestyles. The Munich taxi experiment (you'll have to google it: The original article I linked to has been taken down) is an excellent example. Drivers went faster when given better brakes. Likewise, protective equipment in swordsmanship offers the comforting illusion of safety. We take more risks when given good protective equipment. Yes armor works, but tell that to the French knights at Agincourt.

So, a balanced approach to swordsmanship training requires at least some time spent face-to-face with the naked possibility of your own death: such as a sharp sword aimed at your unprotected face, in careful pair drills with a trusted, highly-trained partner under competent supervision. There is nothing like a sharp, steel point inches from your eyes to cut through the illusory safety of a fencing mask.

My favorite quote on this comes from Viggiani's *Lo Schermo* from

1575 (as translated by Jherek Swanger: note he does not translate "spada da marra," which is a kind of blunt steel practice sword):

"ROD:... but now it is time that we begin to practice, before the hour grows later: take up your sword, Conte.

CON: How so, my sword? Isn't it better to take one meant for practice?

ROD: Not now, because with those practice weapons it is not possible to acquire valor or prowess of the heart, nor ever to learn a perfect schermo.

CON: I believe the former, but the latter I doubt. What is the reason, Rodomonte, that it is not possible to learn (so you say) a perfect schermo with that sort of weapon? Can't you deliver the same blows with that, as with one which is edged?

ROD: I would not say now that you cannot do all those ways of striking, of warding, and of guards, with those weapons, and equally with these, but you will do them imperfectly with those, and most perfectly with these edged ones, because if (for example) you ward a thrust put to you by the enemy, beating aside his sword with a mandritto, so that that thrust did not face your breast, while playing with spada da marra, it will suffice you to beat it only a little, indeed, for you to learn the schermo; but if they were spade da filo, you would drive that mandritto with all of your strength in order to push well aside the enemy's thrust. Behold that this would be a perfect blow, done with wisdom, and with promptness, unleashed with more length, and thrown with more force, that it would have been with those other arms. How will you fare, Conte, if you take perfect arms in your hand, and not stand with all your spirit, and with all your intent judgment?

CON: Yes, but it is a great danger to train with arms that puncture; if I were to make the slightest mistake, I could do enormous harm. Nonetheless we will indeed do as is more pleasing to you, because you will be on guard not to harm me, and I will be certain to parry, and I will pay constant attention to your point in order to know which blow may come forth from your hand, which is necessary in a good warrior."

This says it all!

In case it is not obvious from the small sample here, Rodomonte/ Viggiani's student, the Conte, is clearly an accomplished swordsman already. There is no suggestion of equipping beginners with sharps. As Manciolino (an ardent proponent of using blunt steel swords, as am I) put it in Book Six of his *Opera Nova* (as translated by Tom Leoni):

> "I now wish to show how wrong those are who insist that good swordsmanship can never proceed from practice with blunted weapons, but only from training with sharp swords. ...
>
> It is far preferable to learn to strike with bated blades then with sharp ones; and it would not be fair to arm untrained students with sharp swords or with other weapons that can inflict injury for the purpose of training new students to defend themselves."
>
> (With thanks to Ilkka Hartikainen for digging out and typing up the reference.)

Quite. "Untrained students" find blunt steel sufficiently threatening that there is no need to make the swords sharp, and indeed it would be grossly irresponsible to do so. Highly trained and experienced students tend, over time, to take the blunt steel less and less seriously, and they need to be reminded that swords are weapons. Likewise, the more armor you wear the less vulnerable you are, and the less vulnerable you *feel*. This tends, in most people, to actually increase the risk of injury as this safety margin – plus a bit more – is consumed.

## Six Lessons from my Favorite Mistake

It may seem odd to you that I have a favorite mistake. After all, I make so many of them that they tend to get lost in the crowd. But this one had major positive consequences, and it was the first proper test of my character after taking up swordsmanship for a living. Some readers got the impression that I was in some way blaming the charlatan mentioned below for my mistake; this is not so. Blaming others doesn't help, because it places the power to correct errors outside of your own domain and into theirs. Being a charlatan is not a mistake, anyway; it's a sustained and deliberate lie, which is quite different.

Posted on 13th June, 2013.

Way back in the dawn of time – when I came to Finland to open my school – my research into historical swordsmanship was at a very early stage, but we all have to start somewhere. I wasn't sure whether to focus on Vadi or Fiore so I included elements of both systems in the material I taught my students. After a couple of years we dropped Vadi to focus on Fiore. It took about nine years to get that system solid enough to build upon. So, then I returned to Vadi (as most of you will probably know). Instead of a messy hodgepodge of material we have a solid base and an expansion pack. Mixing the systems is a mistake, but it's not the one this post is about. To be sure, these days that approach is completely unnecessary and counter-productive, but I don't think anybody knew that then.

No, the mistake I made was to take an outlier, an apparent exception to the norm, and make it part of the core training simply on the word of a native-speaker. Yes, I am referring to the infamous rising *fendente* blow. A quick look at the segno of blows in Vadi might lead one to believe that the *rota* blows descend and the *fendente* blows rise.

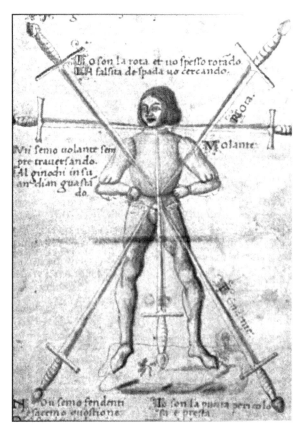

But you only have to actually read the book to know that the image is misleading; a quick cross-reference to Fiore, and indeed to every other Italian sword fighting system in the history of the world, will simply put that mistake right. But no, I took the word of a charismatic, self-proclaimed "master" who happened to be a native speaker of Italian, and I cheerily taught my trusting students that in Vadi's system the fendente is a rising blow.

I had kept this bizarre misreading in my first book, the *Swordsman's Companion*. One of the editors picked up on it when the book was in the editing phase. Unlike the "masters" of my acquaintance at the time, this editor (Greg Mele) did not simply say "No Guy, that's wrong, it's like this." He sent me a page of explanation supported by quotations from the actual source to establish why Vadi's fendente is a descending blow. The truth, the evidence, was incontrovertible.

So then I was faced with the first proper character test of my new career. Half of me thought that my students would quit if I admitted such a basic mistake to them. The other half of me thought that this would be an excellent teaching opportunity to set the example that changing research leads to changing interpretations, and of the truth being infinitely more important than ego or embarrassment. But oh, God, it was scary. I candidly admitted my mistake to my students. I don't think a single person quit in disgust at my making the error. And I know for damn sure that some were actually reassured or impressed that I could admit it so openly. Some of them are still training with me 11 years later; some even, with enough beer in them, still rib me about it. So, the lessons learned:

1. Students worth teaching understand that their teacher is human and will make mistakes. What makes a good teacher is not infallibility, but transparency and integrity. How you deal with mistakes is crucial; that you will make them is a given.
2. If a point of interpretation is an outlier, and appears to contradict the normal usage of the term, check it, check it, and check it before relying on it.
3. It is perilous to mix treatises and systems. Study one system deeply and broadly before attempting to blend two potentially incompatible systems. Create a base of one master's work before adding to it.
4. Always check the whole book. The usage of a given term will tend to be consistent. If it appears to mean something weird in one place then check that it means the same weird thing

everywhere else. This is basically point 3 again, but it's worth repeating!

5. Being a native speaker does not automatically make you an expert. When I was studying , the professor of English Language at Edinburgh University was German. His speciality was phonology. Although his own pronunciation was decidedly Germanic, he knew more about how English words are created in the mouth than anybody else I have ever met. But finding out that the professor of English Language was German was something of a shock. Yes, there are nuances of understanding a language that only native speakers can attain, but most do not. I have certainly met non-native speakers of English who use and understand English better than the average native speaker.

6. "Don't pull that Maestro shit on me:" be very, very wary of anybody expressing an opinion on the research or practice of this Art (or indeed any art) whose authority rests on a title, or who seems to believe that the fact that it is *their* opinion should be sufficient to convince you. Expect supporting evidence: true experts will always (a) have it, and (b) be happy to supply it. Listen to those who will provide it, and avoid – like the plague – those who will not. In case it isn't clear: as the great Quiller-Couch once wrote, "Murder your darlings." He meant that when writing you should be prepared to cut even your favorite sentences, words, or phrases. For us involved in researching our Art it translates as being ready to sacrifice any opinion, way of doing things, or interpretation if the evidence demands it.

## Mindful practice

There has been a raft of proponents for and against the idea of 10,000 hours of dedicated practice being required for success in any field ever since Malcolm Gladwell popularized the idea. I am making no claim here other than that mastery cannot be attained without the ability to do focused, dedicated, and mindful practice.

26th April 2013

This week's intermediate class yielded some interesting insights. I began by asking my students what they thought my job was. As far as I see it, at their level, my job is mainly to keep their practice mindful, and to provide solutions to any problem that crops up and they cannot solve themselves. We started by having each student identify for themselves a specific problem they were having, and then articulate it clearly to the class. These included difficulty in closing the line after the first action in a bout, difficulty in controlling measure in dynamic situations, and difficulty in maintaining flow under pressure.

We began with the cutting drill as usual, and then we discussed how it could be used or adapted to address their specific needs. We concluded that for their purposes right now it was of limited use in its basic form. So we went to the X-drill, with the pell in the middle of the salle, and the students divided into two groups. One individual from each group crossed the space in style and struck the pell couple of times. One group's aim was to arrive first, and the other group's aim was to arrive at the same time. This brought in dynamic control of measure and timing.

The next exercise was first drill, with the variations that the attacker may feint and the defendant may counter-attack instead of parrying. This highlighted specific difficulties, such as vulnerability to a counter-attack or difficulty in distinguishing between a feint and a real attack. After a few minutes of this each student had a super-specific example of a specific weakness related to the more general problems they had highlighted at the beginning of class.The next exercise was to articulate exactly the problem they were having to their partner, who then coached them through that specific issue. For example, your partner would coach you in getting that second parry in time if you found that you were vulnerable to a feint. This required the coaching partner be able to control elements of the fight in real time so that their student was training at the optimum level of difficulty. After five minutes the roles were reversed and then, each student having had a lesson, we returned to the particular variation on first drill, with the same original partner, to see whether the corrections had taken.

Next up we have to establish whether the corrections, having worked (because each student reported an improvement), were general or specific; in other words, whether an improved ability to defend against a feint of *mandritto fendente* followed by a *roverso fendente* led to an improved ability to deal with feints in general. So I had the students change the drill so that they could defend from any right-side guard, and the attack to be of any kind – real or feint – from any side. As it turned out, most of the improvement was quite specific. This meant that what we ought to have done next would have been developing that more general skill, but given the problems declared at the beginning of class it was necessary to move on to address the issue of controlling measure. I pointed out that they could follow this thread in free training. By this stage they were all sweating hard and out of breath. This is one of the hallmarks of mindful practice. *It is tiring.*

We started our addressing the issue of measure with a drill that I invented back in 2001. One student establishes a measure with their partner then the students move around freely with the partner initiating change to that measure. When I clapped at random intervals they were to check whether they were still in measure. There may have been push-ups involved. Then we used wooden bucklers like focus mitts, with one student coaching another. This prepared them for giving a specific lesson on measure. I gave a specific example for them to copy, given that the students present were not trained coaches. In this case it was simply a variation on first drill in which the coach is defending; if he ends up close after his parry then the student should pommel strike, but if he ends up further away then the student should cut on the other side. This allowed them, in a very simple set-up, to take one specific aspect of the art and develop measurable improvement.

There is absolutely nothing wrong with gathering together with some swordy friends and having a bash. Neither is there anything wrong in playing around with some aspects of swordsmanship. I would actually go so far as to say that not all practice should be mindful, because you can become *too* goal-oriented: it's the journey that matters, not the destination. But you don't need a professional instructor for those activities, and without goals there is no progress; thus, no journey. So when I am running the class, there is no point my being there unless I am making it possible for my students to really improve. Mindful practice is without doubt the most efficient approach for that.

The basic pattern is this:

1. Practice something that you know at a pace and level that generates error.
2. Articulate the error in the clearest possible terms. Fixing this becomes your goal.
3. Select the training tools that you think will most efficiently address your goal. Apply them with rigor.
4. Test to see whether your goal has been reached by returning to the original set-up in which the error occurred. If yes then return to step 1 to find a new error; if no then either select new tools or apply the same ones better.

If you're not sure what skill it is that you're trying to develop then you're not practicing mindfully. If it does not demand the absolute limit of your concentration and physical skill, you're not practicing mindfully. If it does not generate measurable improvement, you're not practicing mindfully. If it's not tiring, frustrating, or painful, you're probably not practicing mindfully. If your practice highlights your every weakness and makes you strengthen it, efficiently and deeply, then it is – must be – mindful.

## Switching between Systems

First published on the Chivalric Fighting Arts Association Blog, September 21st 2012. This article has ramifications for learning any skill.

One of the benefits to having produced things like my books and the syllabus wiki is that they provide a service to a vastly wider range of students than I can possibly train in person. Those students consequently ask me a wider range of questions, forcing me to think about things differently. One such example is this from Javier Andrés Chamorro Bernal, in Chile.

> "I would like to ask you about something that troubles me now that I started to study I.33. Do you have problems with your footwork and technique when you practice with another sword or another fencing master? I know that you practice Capoferro's rapier, does that cause trouble for you when you go back to Fiore?"

This, on the face of it, has a simple answer: "no, I keep them separate." But that demands an explanation: how? And that leads me off on this rambling perambulation through what it is like to have these systems cheerfully cohabiting in my spine.

My approach to understanding and applying these arts is largely mechanical. Every system has its own mechanical preferences that are based on the handling characteristics of the weapon, the context of the fight, and the aesthetic preferences of the author (e.g. Fiore or Capoferro). But all of them (and I include every martial art I've ever studied, and sport fencing, and walking down the street) have at root the following fundamentals:

1.  Power generation, through tasking large muscle groups to do the work and small muscle groups to stabilize and direct.
2.  Structural support for the power – i.e. a delivery system. This includes the weapon, and it is intimately linked to grounding, (the route by which energy reflected from the target into the weapon is safely dispersed into the ground, or put to good use), and to the route by which energy is put into the weapon.
3.  The overall strategy: strike without being struck.
4.  The overall tactics to apply that strategy: keep your defensive arm (the first half of your sword blade, your buckler, your armor, your dagger, or whatever) in the way of his sword (or other offensive weapon). Hit him with your sword (whichever part seems appropriate).
5.  Differences between systems then resolve into a change in the handling characteristics of the weapons and a change in what constitutes a strike. These are easily adopted. The weapon is there in your hand, constantly feeding information into it, and the target is right there in front of you, begging to be hit.

Keeping Fiore's mechanics separate from Capoferro's is especially easy as they are very, very different. Fiore has us in a very easy stance of weight on either the front or the back foot and moving with somewhat-improved-upon natural steps. The longsword will naturally draw those mechanics out of you if you can simply establish a proper ground path, and can accelerate the weapon with little effort. Capoferro has us hiding behind the sword (not very knightly!) with the right shoulder forwards to get the sword-point in the opponent's face and the left shoulder back to (a) push the right shoulder forwards, and (b) profile your chest to minimize your opponent's available target area. From here, keeping your weight on your back foot is very natural if your opponent is similarly threatening your face with his point. All systems operate some kind of compromise, emphasizing some key benefits at the expense of others. As an obvious example, students starting rapier after learning our basic Fiore syllabus all agree that rapier is much more physically demanding. Any beginner can be put into a longsword guard position, but most are physically incapable of a correct rapier guard position without months of specific training. Rapier mechanics are optimized for a short, sharp, and illegal duel. Longsword mechanics are optimized for a longer and public tournament, duel, or battle.

Keeping two such distinct systems separate is easy. Things get a little more complicated when the systems are mechanically or tactically closer, when the weapons are more similar, or when the source for the system is more vague about mechanics. So there is a much longer period of figuring out what works rather than just following the treatise. I.33 is a good example. If you look carefully at the I.33 videos on the wiki you'll see me sometimes chambering the sword on my right shoulder much too far around, away from the Priest's second ward, and into Fiore's posta di donna. This is also partly due to the fact that I spend way more time with longsword and rapier than I do with sword and buckler. Oddly, I never get my backsword (18th century) confused with my smallsword, nor my smallsword confused with rapier or backsword. They live in totally separate compartments because the weapon in hand feels nothing like a longsword or a rapier, nor each other.

One of the advantages of teaching many different systems is that my students can usually find the one that suits them best, both emotionally and physically. This requires me to frequently switch between weapons and styles from day to day, and often within a single evening. I have noticed that whatever weapon I am holding becomes, until I put it down, just the best, most natural, why-would-you-waste-time-on-any-other-system, and top favorite. When holding a smallsword, rapier is just a long, clumsy, stupid, and out-of-date, obsolete horse and cart to my nimble, modern, and up-to-the-minute smallsword Ferrari 458. I think this is part of the skill of switching between styles: the one you're doing must be the one you want to do. I am often asked by students when they should start a second system. My advice is, as usual, an analogy. Swordsmanship styles are like languages. If you can speak Spanish fluently then learning Italian is easy. The former supports the latter. But if you try to learn them both from scratch, side-by-side, you'll run into trouble because they will interfere with each other. Your native language probably does not interfere much, because it is clearly separated in your mind from the foreign language you are acquiring, and the closer it is to the new language the easier acquiring the new one will be. Given that nobody has a native swordsmanship language (if you've been taught since birth, then forgive me; you're the exception), we must first learn one style until we are fluent in it. It doesn't matter which, though in my school it's easiest to start with Fiore just because most people do, so there are the most training opportunities. Once you have a solid base and can conceive of any combat situation in terms of that style, because you understand the mechanical and tactical compromises in play, you will find the acquisition of a second style is much faster.

Frustration occurs when a beginner takes up a second style too early for optimum speed of acquisition. That is not really a problem in that there is no hurry to master this Art; however, if you are finding that the style you know is contaminating the style you want to learn it is probably because the style you know has not been fully mastered yet. Either drop the old for the new, or the new for the old until the old is fully absorbed, or live with a slower pace of learning and with some confusion.

## ONE WAY TO SEE WHAT IS REALLY THERE, WHEN FENCING.

This was posted on May 21st 2013.

The essential skill behind the application of swordsmanship is to see what is really there, not what you think is there. This is a profound and difficult skill to master, because we are all subject to all sorts of cognitive illusions and biases. Daniel Kahneman's *Thinking, Fast and Slow* is perhaps the best single resource on the subject.

For us, in practice, we have to pay attention to what the opponent is doing all the time, but refrain from telling ourselves stories about what we see. "His sword is coming towards me" is meaningful. "He is attacking" is not meaningful: it prevents us from realizing his action may be a feint. Ascribing motives to his motions is to be avoided. Likewise, we must not tell ourselves stories about what we are doing. "I am parrying that attack" is a lie because you don't know whether the parry will work, whether the attack is real, or anything. "I am moving to intercept his motion" is better, because the movement is real. Its intention is clear, and if the interception fails to occur then there is nothing in that statement to prevent the motion changing to find his weapon.

If we are telling ourselves a story and the action changes then rewriting the story to fit the new data is hard. So we tend to ignore the data that doesn't fit: we prioritize the story over the facts. This is normal, but it will get you hit. I don't think we can truly prevent the story-writing process, but we can cast the story in terms that permit endless, easy rewrites as the situation changes.

Of course, the fight happens faster than conscious thought can keep up with. This makes story-telling that much worse because the data is not just incomplete: it's out of date. Better then to give yourself a set of instructions that fit the goals of the bout, such as "control his sword and hit him," and let your training do all the hard work of actually issuing specific commands to the sword.

My own solution to the distractions of the conscious mind is to quietly sing a little song to myself. That keeps my conscious, story-telling mind gently occupied, leaving my adaptive unconscious relatively unfettered and able to see what is happening. It also freaks the hell out of my opponent if they get close enough to hear it. A win-win situation.

Postscript: In real life I find that this skill has endless applications, but the trick is to train yourself such that your instinct is a reliable guide to your actual environment and to watch out vigilantly for when you are being seduced by a story, rather than the actual facts.

## Artists and Slugs. Typing too.

Learning skills is a skill. Here is how I applied my swordsmanship training skills to mastering another useful skill: touch-typing.

Posted on December 12th 2012

I am typing this very slowly and without looking at the keyboard (much). This may seem trivial to those of you that learned to touch-type young, but I have twenty years of bad habits to overcome: five published books and God knows how-many-thousand emails, all written by poke-and-pray. I got pretty quick with my bad habits. But a chance exchange on Facebook led me to think that time spent learning to type properly might be a good investment.

Martin: "you are a professional writer, by the way. You should damn well learn to touch-type.

Me: "Typing hurts..."

So Martin (a professional writer, swordsman, and long-time good friend) put me on to the BBC Schools typing course. And, if you can see past the dancing hippos with questionable Middle Eastern accents, it is *brilliant*. The course starts at the very beginning, with the home row:

asdf jkl;

And then it adds one pair of keys at a time. First it adds g and h, and then r and u; it builds up over 12 levels until the whole keyboard is covered (sans the numbers, tabs, etc.). Most importantly, every step is clearly taught and every error is apparent but not dwelt on; you just can't get to the celebratory turtle dance until the correct keys have been hit. The way the authors have structured the course is an essay in perfect pedagogy. Every new level begins with revision of the previous material, and there is constant praise and encouragement. I applied the same sort of discipline that I use for learning other skills (such as, oh I don't know, swordfighting perhaps?) and worked through the levels at my own pace. I repeated most of them several times before moving on, and often went back to repeat previous levels. In under a week I can find any key without looking, though my current pace is a dilatory 12 words per minute with a mere 97% accuracy rate.

It is costing me ALL of my self-discipline not to switch back; right now this is WAY slower and VERY frustrating. But all the evidence suggests that, in the end, this dip in speed will be as a run-up to hitherto undreamed heights of productivity – if I can just stick with it. (I just deleted a correct letter because I used the wrong finger to type it.)

This is of course an excellent analogue for the perils of too much freeplay, or sparring, too early. One gets into terrible habits that, while they work for a while, set a lower cap on ultimate performance and make it harder to attain deep competence, because going back to basics and getting it right entails a temporary but frustrating drop in performance.

Mastery of any skill is largely a process of taking a rational construct, a product of the slow, conscious mind (Kahneman's System 2), and installing it in the super-fast adaptive unconscious (Kahneman's System 1). This inevitably leads to a period of adjustment where the techniques and theories of the art in question get in the way of the artist's natural expression, and this leads us to a moment of choice: do we truly believe in this art?

If we do then we accept a short-term dip in ability for a hoped-for long-term increase in skill. If we do not then we should maintain our current skills. The artist, one who follows the art, should find dips in performance heartening. They suggest an improvement is coming.

One of the pitfalls of evolution in nature is that once an organism is adapted for its niche it cannot accept a dip in reproductive success for the sake of a long-term gain. Adaptations that convey disadvantage in the short term are ruthlessly selected against. So we have slugs, masters of their tiny, leafy pinnacle, genetically oblivious to the possibilities of scaling further evolutionary heights. Only human beings, artists, can deliberately seek higher ground via a descent into an abyss.

So, in terms of your training, are you an artist or a slug?

Update: I now touch-type on a Dvorak layout without thinking about it. My current rate is about 54 WPM. That may not sound like much, but it is a huge improvement. In the real world (i.e. not a touch-typing speed test) I can now generate about 1,200 words of usable prose in an hour. Typing speed may still be slowing down production a bit, but not nearly as much as it did.

## BEGIN AGAIN

Posted on October 17th 2014.

As I slowly progress towards mastery in my chosen Art I get further and further ahead of my beginners. I also get accustomed to a certain routine: a set way of doing things. Both of these things are death to a good teacher. So I have made it a deliberate habit to be a beginner at something all the time. From early 2001 to the end of 2003 I was a private student of an instructor in a very traditional kung fu style; the same chap that fixed my wrists (see page 158 "I am Weak" for more on this). He belongs to the sort of traditional school where you have to be legally adopted by the grandmaster to learn the inner secrets of the Art. "Old School," indeed. So much so that I will not identify the school here, because its internal politics are so damn Confucian that it may cause all sorts of trouble if I do. The training was not just profoundly uncomfortable: it was hellishly painful because this school included serious hardening training in its core curriculum. I would not normally touch hardening with a stick because it is often a short-term, unhealthy strategy, but in this case it went hand-in-hand with serious health-care: specifically massage, breathing, and herbal medicine. So I ended up much healthier than I started. Also, and this is the point, I was an absolute beginner from 7 a.m. to 9 a.m. three mornings a week. This meant that I had some sympathy for, and insight into, what my students were experiencing when I was standing up in front of my class that evening.

As I started to get emotionally comfortable with the kung fu, and so it lost some of its beginneriness (if you'll allow me to coin a term), I took up something I'd wanted to learn since I was a little kid: bullwhip cracking. I loved loved *loved* Indiana Jones, and I could think of no more apposite multi-purpose tool than a bullwhip. You can fend off baddies *and* swing across ravines with these things. Really, why doesn't everyone carry one? I met a professional performer, Ari Lauanne, at Hämeenlinna medieval market in 2002, and she taught me some basics. In half an hour I striped myself from knee to shoulder and found out why they are not so commonly carried. They are *damn* hard to use! So I got a beauty made by Alex Cobra of *Cobra Whips*, just a six-footer to start with, and practiced most nights before class. I got quite good compared to a beginner (though I'm not in the same class as Alex or Ari) and so, while I keep up my skills every now and then, I needed to find something else. The essence of beginneriness is having no frames of reference with which to make difficulties approachable. The same is basically true for everything else; I'm no longer really in the true beginner state once people ask me what I'm doing and I can explain it properly.

Around this time I started to study Finnish seriously. Now there is a language in which you can stay a beginner for a very long time. I put in two years of real effort and got to a very basic level of competence. Then my first daughter was born, and I had to make a decision; spend my now much more restricted time putting in another thousand hours or so getting to fluency, or spend that time writing a couple of books. I chose books. While there are negative consequences to not being comfortable in Finnish, there are about five million people who can speak Finnish but perhaps only fifty people who can write books like mine on European swordsmanship. The world needs my books more than it needs me to speak Finnish. Another side-benefit, of course, is that I can step outside my comfort zone (I literally break into a cold sweat) by simply engaging a neighbor in basic conversation.

Being a parent is also a state of being a constant beginner. Just as you get competent at taking care of a baby you're suddenly running round after a toddler. They develop faster than you do. Excellent, long-term beginneriness. But it gets easier, like everything you do day-in and day-out.

In 2012 I was given a flying lesson in a light aircraft by a friend of mine. Oh. My. God. It was terrifying, exhilarating, very, very challenging (like learning to drive a car in three dimensions instead of two, then multiplied by about a million), and I was literally giddy with it for days afterwards. But it will cost about €6000 to get my license, so that will have to wait until one of my books goes all *Fifty Shades* on me and I am rolling in cash. (No, I will NOT be adding tepid BDSM scenes to my next book.) So in 2013 I took up the yo-yo. Yes, really. It's very cheap and really, really hard. There are some excellent tutorial videos online (go to André Boulay's site yoyoexpert.com; there he has arranged a complete curriculum from beginner to master level, and explains every trick in detail. Check it out online to get some idea of what expertise in that field actually looks like). So for a thousandth of the cost of learning to fly I was constantly working at, and failing at, something. And it was really fun.

Then *Audatia* came along, and what a learning curve that was. I knew nothing about game design or producing card games, and not much about any of the nitty-gritty of getting a project like that done with several different experts all working on it at the same time. However, now that the first decks are out and the rest are on their way, while it remains challenging, I'm not a proper beginner any more.

Of course, from the inside, I am a beginner whenever I pick up a sword. My errors of form and technique are as obvious to me as those of the clumsiest beginner, but I have a large store of experience to draw from when figuring out how to improve. The art is deeply familiar to me, and huge chunks of the relevant sources are just there in my head for me to read at leisure. So even though my skills are sadly lacking, from my perspective, it doesn't give me a true insight into the beginner because the problems are well known to me, not confusingly new. I know exactly how to fix them; I just have to get on and do it.

Right now I am looking for the next activity to be a beginner in. It needs to be (a) ethical; (b) affordable; (c) have a physical component other than using a computer; (d) have clearly defined basics (success/failure states. Is the yoyo tangled? Fail. Did the whip crack? Success. Is the plane still in one piece? Success. Is the whip wrapped round my own face? Fail. And so on.); and (e) not require formal classes unless they happen in the mornings. I welcome your suggestions!

# Chapter Three
## On Martial Arts

### Doctrine

Martial arts are about systematically increasing your likelihood of surviving combat and achieving your goals. The layperson tends to see martial arts as sets of kicks, punches, weapons strikes, and so on, but the specific techniques of a given art are in some respects its least important factor. Much more critical are the *goals* of the art in question because these are at the heart of why the art is as it is, and why the popular image of a martial arts master being someone incapable of giving a straight answer to a straight question is so prevalent. Yes, there is some Yoda-esque stuff which is just true and irreducible: some questions to which the only honest answer can appear to be mumbo-jumbo or deliberate avoidance of the topic. But by and large it has been my experience that many martial artists don't know what their art is for, nor why they do things a particular way. Let me quote from *The Medieval Longsword:*

> "Every martial art, from T'ai Chi Chuan to the nuclear deterrent, is based on a doctrine—an idea of how combat

works. The actions and tactics of a given art reflect the conscious and unconscious assumptions of its founder. If we compare two combat sports, boxing and Greco-Roman wrestling, we can see a basically similar situation: two antagonists, without weapons, in a controlled environment, with a specified fighting area and a referee. But they are acting in completely different ways. One pair punches each other, the other rolls around on the ground. In both cases, if the fighters switched tactics, they would be barred from competition. The source of these different approaches is in the minds of the founders of the sports—what constitutes the best way for two fighters to determine who is better? The rules of the contest are then developed to encourage the desired fighting behaviour, and the techniques most likely to achieve victory are then determined by those rules. So, to contrast these sports, we have:

|  | Wrestling | Boxing |
|---|---|---|
| **Doctrine** | Grapples and throws are best | Hitting with hands is best |
| **Strategy** | Immobilise opponent | Damage opponent with punches |
| **Tactics** | Choose best throws and locks | Combinations of strikes |

There is no way to say which is better; both work well in their contexts. But which is better for you? Much depends on your nature, and your body type. This process is exactly the same in a lethal environment. There is no one 'best' way for a gun to be carried—or even one 'best' gun to carry."

(For an in-depth discussion of doctrine, strategy, and tactics see Forrest E. Morgan, *Living the Martial Way*.)

Rory Miller, in his seminal *Meditations on Violence* (p. 7), suggests that martial arts have many conflicting possible goals or ideals: self-defense, the duel, sport, combat (i.e. military), assault, spiritual growth, and fitness. To this list I would add display (such as stage combat). Knowing which one your art is adapted for is critically important, because that is the only thing it is likely to be efficient at delivering. There are few things sadder than seeing someone whose art is optimized for spiritual growth trying to spar with someone whose art is optimized for sparring. Miller goes on to list 11 aspects of martial arts: the reality of the event; the reality of the event to the person; the real goal; the best goal; distractors (fake goal or illusions); the optimal mindset; the best asset; strategy; training focus; the real danger; and the perceived danger. He goes on to list what each of those is, in seven different arenas: self defense, duel, sport, combat, assault, spiritual growth, and fitness.

This table (next page), reproduced by kind permission, is one of the most important documents for any martial artist because if you understand it correctly it will save you a world of confusion and hurt. The term "martial art" is way too broad; this table allows you to define exactly what any martial art is for, and what you can reasonably expect from it.

Most of the swordsmanship sources I study assume that you know the context in which you will fight. I go into Fiore's contexts in some detail in *The Medieval Longsword* but, in short, the arts I study are mostly adapted for success in the duel: two people fighting at an agreed time and place, with agreed weapons, to death or incapacity, and doing so for social advancement.

| | Self Defence | Duel | Sport | Combat | Assault | Spiritual Growth | Fitness |
|---|---|---|---|---|---|---|---|
| **Reality of Event** | Recovery from bad luck or stupidity. | Glorified Monkey Dance | Contest of the Similar | Monkey Dance between groups | Neutralize threat/ enemy | Mostly stumbling in the dark | Physical training |
| **Reality to Person** | Absolute threat to health, survival and identity | Voluntary physical danger for social gain | Test of self | Boredom, confusion, busywork and occasional terror | Job | Reality doesn't go here | Part of life |
| **Real Goal** | Survive | Maintain or increase social standing | Ego validation | Please supervisors and peers | Mission and survive | Achieve and maintain satori | Varies, improve appearance |
| **Best goal** | Prevent, if too late, escape | Win with style | Prove/test oneself | Defeat opposing group, preferably by display | Mission and survive | Understand self | Improve health |
| **Distracters/ fake goals, illusions** | Maintain social illusions, deny reality | No choice | Fear of losing, belief that X=Y | Personal meaning or mission, freelancing | Fear of liability, crusade, ego, admin interference | Understand the world, ego | Appearance equals ability |
| **Optimal mindset** | None or rage | Arrogance w/o overconfidence | Athletic focus, "the zone" | obedience | Implacable predator | Percieve | Everyday- habit |
| **Best Asset** | Aggressive reactions | Cunning? | Skill? Cunning? | Teamwork and discipline | Planning and preparation | Bullshit detector (or openness?) | Perseverance |
| **Strategy** | Beat the freeze | Dazzle the opponent | Psych the opponent out | Control individuality, make troops predictable | Shock and Awe | Listen, watch, feel | Stick to training plan |
| **Training focus** | Contact, response | Skill, fitness, and conventions; showmanship | Skill and fitness | Obedience and rote specific skills | Teamwork, skills, threat analysis | Letting distractions go | Training, nutrition, recuperation |
| **Real danger** | Loss of life, identity | Death | Injury | Stupid leaders | Luck | Being defrauded, otherwise very safe | Overtraning, training for the wrong thing |
| **Perceived danger** | Same | Dishonor, loss of face, embarrassment | Damage to identity | Enemy | Enemy | Inability to see the world "in light" | None |

## The Perfect Strike

Correct technique requires correct mechanics, timing, and measure.

Mechanics are the means by which we deliver force into the opponent and deal with force coming in from the opponent. Newton demands that every action has an equal and opposite reaction. Generating a lot of power to hit with is great, but it's not very useful if the equal and opposite reaction when we strike is used to move our sword around involuntarily or shock our joints. Pure and correct form either allows that force to move the sword in a useful way, decoupled from our body (such as in ballistic strikes); creates a pathway for the force to dissipate harmlessly into the ground; or moves us in a useful way (such as chambering the next strike). My preferred approach is to teach students to direct the force into the ground, because it's the safest starting point. We do this by slow and careful pressure-testing of the end point of the strike, establishing a pathway, and striking inanimate targets (such as tyres) to put that pathway to use. Read more on this in "I am Weak" on page 158.

Timing exists only in measure: if you cannot strike or be struck, the motions with which we define time are irrelevant. Measure is when you can reach to strike without further footwork. Usually, you enter into striking measure with an attack (which is in measure when it arrives), or you allow your opponent to enter measure with his own attack. Either way, the attack can be seen as the process of entering measure offensively. I.33 sword and buckler uses a modified form of attack, the *obsessio*, to enter safely and draw the opponent out from his guard; with the rapier we normally enter carefully into measure with little steps, finding the opponent's sword. With the longsword, used in a public context, we bravely and flashily enter with committed attacks. Judging measure allows us to control the time in which we can be struck.

Both mechanics and measure can (up to a point at least) be practiced alone.

Timing is proportional. It is rarely relevant how much real time (seconds, milliseconds, etc.) an action takes: what matters is how long it takes in relation to what the other person is doing. If my sword takes less time to get to the target than his sword takes to parry then my attack *must* succeed. So, timing is the process of assessing the proportional lengths of motions. Starting with your sword well back, to give it a nice long path to accelerate down to hit with more absolute speed and therefore more power, is a great idea if your opponent's defense or counter-offense must travel further and take more time. Practicing timing requires a partner, or a really superb (and accurate) imagination.

So a correct strike is mechanically perfect, and is done at the perfect measure in the perfect time. Not too much to ask is it?

## I am Weak

This was published on November 22nd 2012, and in many ways this post, and the one that follows it here (I am Weak) encapsulate the root of my martial arts approach. It is all about finding the optimum way to do something, rather than creating the optimum body to do it with.

I am weak. So I study strength. In martial arts strength has little to do with the usual measures of muscular performance and everything to do with grounding, structure, power generation, and joint maintenance.

I am blessed with a pretty crap skeleton, given my choice of profession. My 12 year-old niece has wrists about the same size as mine, I've had neck issues since I was 14, and I will generally get injured at the slightest provocation. This means I have always been looking for ways to win fights that did not rely on robustness, and that I have always been working through health issues of my own.

120

So I am able to help my students, most of whom have some kind of physical imperfection. Indeed, about half my time in private lessons with them is spent fixing postural issues, knee or wrist problems, or similar.

My wrists, for example, have suffered from tendonitis since the early nineties. It got so bad when I was working as a cabinet-maker that I literally had to choose between swinging a sword and working the next day. Then I met a kung fu instructor who, in 20 agonizing minutes, did what the combined medical profession of Edinburgh had failed to do in five years: he fixed my wrists. The treatment involved massage (the agonizing bit), very specific exercises with very light weights, and breathing exercises. I had gone a year without touching a sword and five years without push-ups and then, suddenly, my wrists worked again. I can now do push-ups on the *backs* of my hands. So it is no wonder that I place massage, targeted weight training, and breathing exercises at the core of the conditioning syllabus. You can't use your body if it doesn't work, and striking targets, and being one, requires that your joints can handle the impact of hitting and being hit.

Simply building up the joints is not enough: we have to minimize the impact to which they are subjected. Every action has an equal and opposite reaction: when you hit the target, the target hits back. That energy has to go somewhere, and it may very well go into shocking your joints if it is not carefully directed. So it is necessary to establish a safe route for the kinetic energy coming back from the target. Either it should move the weapon (not ideal, usually), or it should be routed down into the ground through the passive structure of your skeleton. This skill can be refined for decades but I find that even beginners can generate major improvements if we simply create the position of the moment of impact (the lunge, for instance), and then apply very gentle pressure in the reciprocal direction to the strike. The student can feel the place where it takes most effort to hold the position (the lead shoulder, for instance), and then create a correction to the position that allows the same pressure to be absorbed with less effort. Then we can apply the pressure at the beginning of the movement and establish that the entire movement is properly grounded. (This is much easier with thrusts than cuts, obviously.) Ultimately, we are looking for a structure that does not need to change at all to route the energy; a structure in which there is no need for any kind of muscular reaction, or any increase in effort or tension, when we add the pressure.

This sort of practice leads to all sorts of gains in efficiency. The starting position, the movement, and the end position all become naturally grounded, and so all the muscular effort being made is directly applying force to the strike. Muscles that are not working to hold the position are available for generating power. So, a deeply relaxed guard and a deeply relaxed movement allow for massive increases in power generation.

Power is generated by muscular contraction: the difference between the relaxed state of the muscle and the contracted state. It pays to work both ends of the differential. Increasing the raw strength of the muscle is an obvious way to go. Creating more efficient positions and movement is less obvious, but it generates much faster gains because it doesn't require opening up new nerve channels or building muscle mass. The stability drill is a good example of this kind of training.

In many students the weak link in the chain between sword-point and ground is their grip on the sword. I don't think I have ever come across a student in any seminar, regardless of experience, whose grip could not be improved. In most cases, the interface between the sword and their hand does not allow a clean flow of energy up the arm from the blade. The modern tendency towards chunky grips exacerbates this; most antiques I have handled have very slim grips, which makes perfect sense when you understand grounding. Indeed, after coming to a seminar on this topic, many students end up having their sword grip modified. The human hand is an incredibly complex and sensitive machine, but all too often folk hold onto their swords like they are carrying a suitcase.

I usually demonstrate the proper interface by hitting a tyre with a longsword with both my hands open and by hitting the wall target with my rapier: again, with my hand open. Simple beer-can-crushing grip strength has almost nothing to do with striking power with the sword. The role of the fingers is to direct the energy in the sword into the lifeline of the palm, and thence up the arm.

Having established a safe and efficient route for the energy to travel down we can use the same pathway for energy to travel out. With a rapier, for instance, once the lunge position is grounded we can find the same pathway in the guard position, too. While the lunge creates a straight diagonal line from the point of the sword to the back foot, in guard that line goes horizontally along the arm and curves in the upper back to go down through the hips and into (usually) the back leg. If you can feel this line clearly then lunging is simply a matter of taking that curve and snapping it straight. A more sophisticated version of this works for cuts too (with any weapon). It is much easier to maintain the ground path than to break and re-form it in motion so establish it in guard, and let the strike be a resistance-free extension of it.

As you become more efficient, so you hit much harder, so there is more energy coming back down into your body; and so you need to improve your grounding, so that you can hit harder and so there is more energy coming back, and so on. Given that you can walk up six flights of stairs but not jump down them in one go it is obvious that you can generate far more power than that of which you can withstand the impact. So gains in power generation come from increases in your ability to handle the power, more than increases in the power itself.

When you practice like this, it swiftly becomes obvious that general carry-a-TV-up-the-stairs, real-word strength has little bearing on the outcome of a sword fight. So it is necessary (because real-world, TV-carrying strength is *useful*: just not so much in the salle) to do a bunch of not-sword-training to develop it. Push-ups, kettlebells, and the like. This is not to help us hit harder. It's more an insurance policy against errors in technique, and also for general health and fitness. Likewise, joint-strength training and massage should ideally be a matter of maintenance, not cure.

## I am Slow

One of the more baffling moments of my fencing career was when a colleague, after fencing together with me, remarked that I was very fast. This was odd because on that particular day I was moving quite slowly, thanks to a strained lower back and lots of sitting in aeroplanes. What he had seen as speed was just efficiency and economy of movement. It dawned on me that most people don't really know the difference. Nearly a decade later, on October 11th 2012, I wrote this post to explain it.

I am slow. So I study speed.

The first advanced Fiore class every month is a freeplay-based session in which we use freeplay and related exercises to expose specific weaknesses in individual students, for them to work on, and general weaknesses in the group as a whole. This sets the theme for the next month of classes. This month we are working on speed. The first indication that this would be necessary was that almost none of the students present could get their freeplay kit on in under 120 seconds.

Speed, *celeritas*, is one of Fiore's four key virtues that a swordsman must possess. The others, for non-Fioreista readers, are *audatia* (boldness), *forteza* (strength), and *avvisamento* (foresight). There are two key models available to us for developing speed. These are the sporting approach, and the musical.

The most obviously applicable is that of sports. High-level sportsmen, in games like tennis and fencing, must be quick. This is trained mostly by repeating explosive movements to task the correct muscles with the motion desired. In this model actions should pretty much only ever be trained at speed. If you do the action slowly too often you end up training to use the wrong muscles, and the maximum speed of the action is diminished. This sort of thing tends to emphasize gross motor movements, such as extending the arm, rather than fine motor movements, such as manipulating with the fingers. As Johan Harmenberg writes on page 28 of his must-read book *Epee 2.0*, "only simple movements are used (even an action like a disengage is not very common in a World Championship final)." He attributes this to the stress that the fencers are experiencing. At this level, "the pressure is so intense it is impossible to describe." (p. 43.) Harmenberg won the Epee World Championship in 1977 and Olympic gold in 1980, so may reasonably be assumed to know his stuff.

In music, though, speed of execution is attained through getting it right at slow speeds first, and then letting the phrase get faster and faster. Wynton Marsalis playing the *Carnival of Venice* by Jean-Baptiste Arban is a good example of astonishing speed of execution (you can find it on YouTube). If music's not your thing, just scroll ahead to 2:40 where he plays the 8th variation so fast it sounds like there are two cornets being blown: one for the tune, and one for the accompaniment. The fine motor control is just dazzling. I have been taught to play this (though I never got close to this level of execution) and can attest that it is simply appallingly difficult to do, and that it's even worse under the stress of the performance. But the advice I was given (and every musician I have ever met would agree) was to get it absolutely accurate slowly first, and then speed it up. As my teacher Mr Foster wrote on my sheet music, "go at the speed of NO mistakes."

We find a remarkable similarity between training to play a musical instrument and combat shooting. All actions in shooting are trained slowly first, to become smooth and efficient, and are then sped up. I've been shooting pistols since I moved to Finland in 2001 and I have never, ever heard an instructor tell a shooting student to hurry up. This is not only because mistakes can cost lives (just like in a sword fight) but also because shooting requires fine motor control, which becomes inaccurate if sped up too soon. In both areas, music and shooting, the goal is to enable the practitioner to execute complex motor skills under high levels of stress.

I can attest to the stress of performance: I played the trumpet at school and developed an absolute phobia of playing solos, despite being a member of several bands and orchestras. Though I was never under any direct physical threat (there were no beatings for splitting a note, nor would anyone have shot me for fluffing a phrase), I was at times incapacitated by fear when a solo was coming up. I never actually vomited, but it was pretty damn close. Yet I still did solos. While they were never perfect, and I could always play a lot better in practice than performance, I was able to produce a passable result. The training worked. The level of stress is probably much higher for a professional musician, because not only his ego but also his career rides on the quality of the performance, and much higher still for a soldier or policeman facing an armed assailant. Yet the process is the same.

In both these areas you'll hear the phrase, "slow is smooth, smooth is fast." In other words, get the action right slowly and let it speed up as you practice. Keeping it smooth will allow it to become fast.

We can summarize then by saying that if you think of swordsmanship as a fine-motor-control skill then the musical/shooting model is best. If you think of it as a gross-motor-control skill then the sporting approach will work best. In my experience, students training to win tournaments should emphasize the sporting approach; students training to recreate historical duelling arts should emphasize the musical approach.

It is, of course, possible – often desirable – to do both. Swordsmanship for sport or murder (duelling) have some overlap. Use the slow-smooth approach for those elements of the sporting game that are improved by fine motor control; use the sporting model for those elements of the martial art that involve improving explosive power. If a student is having difficulty lunging with sufficient speed to take advantage of tempi that he ought to be able to strike in, for example, the critical skill for the instructor is to diagnose the problem. Are the mechanics of the lunge at fault? If so then slow it down and smooth it out. If the mechanics are okay then apply drills that develop the raw speed of the lunge. Just don't try this with a disengage; it's so much a fine motor skill that trying to speed it up by making the student go faster will just make it clumsier and slower. Get it smoother and smaller to make it faster.

Speed serves two functions in swordsmanship: damage and timing.

Damage first; the speed of the sword determines how hard it hits. $E=mv^2$, so the energy available for damaging the target is proportional to the striking mass and to the square of its velocity. Double the mass of the sword and you double the impact; double the speed and you quadruple the impact. This assumes of course that to make the sword go faster you haven't made the motion less efficient, so energy is wasted on impact. There is a huge difference in practice between the amount of energy technically available, and the amount actually delivered into the target.

I believe that the sword should act as a labor-saving device. Its function is to destroy certain types of target, and it should require less effort to do so with the sword than without. So there is limited virtue in simply making the sword go faster and faster to hit harder and harder; at some point there is sufficient energy to do the desired damage, so additional speed is wasted effort. Timing: the purpose of speed is to ensure that your strike arrives before your opponent's parry, and your parry arrives before his strike. It is therefore proportional to the motions of your opponent. The key skill here is to be able to adjust the acceleration of the weapon, rather than attain a specific top speed. There is a lovely section on this in Karl Friday's excellent book *Legacies of the Sword*, on pages 74–5. The graphs showing the different rates of power applied to the weapon by beginners versus experts are especially good. The graphs look like this:

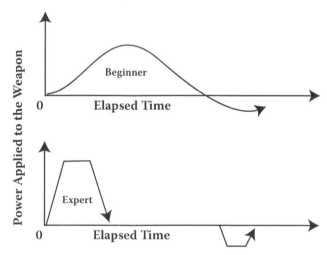

The key point is that the expert can accelerate the weapon quickly; the total force exerted is actually a lot less, but the weapon is moving fast enough when it needs to be. The key to this kind of skill is to eliminate inefficiencies in the starting position, minimize the tension in the muscles about to act, and develop perfect mechanics for the strike itself. The importance of early rate of acceleration over final speed attained is elegantly demonstrated by this exhibition at the Heureka Science Museum in Vantaa, in which two tennis balls are rolled down two slopes. One slope is straight, and the other curved. Though both balls are moving at the same velocity when they get to the end, the ball on the curved slope always arrives first because it has a higher rate of acceleration at the beginning of its movement compared to the other. They would both hit with the same force, but one would arrive long before the other.

The easiest way to reduce the time in which an action is done is to make the action shorter. So, a great deal of speed training, training to do an action in less time, is to eliminate any extraneous motion – to pare the movement down to its absolute minimum. To take a beginner's marathon and create an expert's 100 m. There are several ways to do this from the obvious (select a starting point that is closer to the end point) to the more sophisticated (tuning the path taken between those two points). In general, the sword-hand should move in the straight line from A to B. But sometimes it's the middle of the blade that does that, and sometimes it's other parts of the weapon or wielder.

In practice, it is useful to be able to adjust the path and the rate of acceleration at various points on the path for best effect. To simply hit hard, make sure the sword is at maximum velocity at the moment of impact. To make the hit more likely to land, though, adjust the acceleration pattern and the path taken to best fit the tactical circumstances. Easier said than done. It is always slower to lift a heavy weight than a light one. So speed training is also about reducing unnecessary tension, making the action as smooth and efficient as possible, and expending the least possible force to get the job done.

So, as we would expect with a medieval virtue, cultivating speed for its own sake – simply going as fast as possible – is a route to ruin. It takes an essential quality that should exist in equilibrium with others and makes a vice out of it. This is a common theme in medieval thought (and should be still today); that which is virtuous when in balance becomes vicious when done to excess. Excessive courage leads to foolhardiness, excessive strength leads to stiffness and slowness, excessive speed leads to weakness and over-extension, and excessive judgement leads to cowardice.

In the case of speed, emphasizing raw speed over speed in proportion to your opponent's movements leads to getting hit through being over-committed and over-extended. It is also hell on the body because explosive force applied to the joints is only safe when the motion is being done perfectly.

In every discipline there is usually an optimum balance between youthful vigor and the experience of long practice that can only come with age. A sportsman usually peaks between the ages of 20 and 40, a concert soloist peaks somewhere between 35 and 60, and a martial arts instructor normally peaks somewhere between 50 and 70. Fiore said he was about 60 when he wrote his book. So cultivate speed carefully, getting the mechanics absolutely right before you put a lot of force through them, and make sure you develop the muscular support of your joints to absorb any slight errors. Muscles and bones last forever; the weak spot in any mechanical system is the joints. The syllabus wiki has some of the school's joint-care curriculum uploaded, including wrist and elbow exercises, knee exercises, and joint massage. I do these a lot because I intend to hit my peak in about 15 years, and I need to make sure my joints can handle all that force.

# Chapter Four
## Swords

### The Tools of my Trade

Posted on April 3rd, 2014. This was inspired by posts from writers going on about their hardware and software toolboxes. To think, back in the good old days, a writer needed paper, pen, and ink; these days, eight screens, six computers, twenty-seven special programs, nineteen websites, and so on.

I am often asked for equipment recommendations, and people seem to be interested in the sort of equipment professionals use. So this is the first of a series of blog posts about the tools I use at work. I spend most of my time teaching Fiore's Art of Arms so let's start there. In the photo you can see four longswords, a mask, a stopwatch, and a stick.

The longsword on the left is an *Arms and Armor* fechterspiele, and it's my most-used sword. It's light, very durable, and it handles beautifully. I've been using it now for about 8 years and have replaced the handle leather once or twice, and it's still going strong. Note the rapier blunt on the point.

Then the stick. It is a really useful teaching tool that I use for "the stick game":

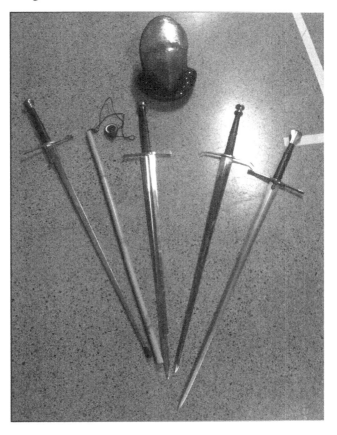

"Once the static forms of the footwork are comfortable it is a good idea to develop your ability to apply it unconsciously. In practice, I introduce this kind of playful exercise before most students have mastered the static forms then point out that the steps they just did naturally were the same as the ones they were learning as as static drill. Feel free to do likewise. For this we have several exercises, my favorite of which is the stick game. Played in pairs, it looks like this:

One player (A) has a stick, and the other (B) doesn't. B stands
  on guard;

(A) gently swings the stick at him;

(B) steps as necessary to avoid the stick and get behind (A),
  tapping him on the back; and

(A) moves away, and strikes again.

You can also add penalties for getting hit, such as three
push-ups.

Played in class, one student or the teacher has the stick.
They charge about trying to tap people, who have to get out
of the way and touch his back. This works best if everyone
is obliged – on pain of push-ups – to keep moving (we usually
start with everyone practicing the step-and-three-passes drill
before bringing out the stick), and if the stick wielder is
careful to only hit people who are making mistakes, like
flinching or losing their guard positions. With a bit of practice,
this is a good workout for everyone and teaches the most
important lesson of footwork: footwork is how you get to
the right place at the right time to strike safely."

(From *The Medieval Longsword*, page 72.)

I also use the stick for non-verbal correction. No, not savage
beatings. When a student knows what they need to fix, but doesn't
know when to fix it, a tap on the relevant body part is sufficient
to let them know and does not interfere by engaging the language
centers of their brains.

The stopwatch is brilliant for telling the truth. It cannot lie. We
use it for the Syllabus Form Applications Drill, the Stability Drill,
and for all sorts of conditioning, such as: how many push-ups can
you do in 60 seconds? Or worse: can you do one push up that
lasts for 60 seconds? In each direction? None of my students fear
the stick. I think most tremble at the sight of the stopwatch.

The mask is from Terry Tindill. It includes the optional-but-you-must-buy-it-it-makes-all-the-difference suspension system. It also has a removable back plate. These are the absolute best solutions for unarmored longsword training that money can buy. Light, but very good protection. You only have one head (I assume) so look after it! I get hit in the head a lot at work. When I'm coaching a student they strike if they get the thing we are training right enough. It's my job to keep them working in the zone where they are struggling but succeeding to get it right. So I might get a couple of hundred hits to the head in a single lesson. "This explains much," I hear you say. Yes, not least why I think these masks are well worth the price!

The pair-drill sharps are both from Angus Trim, and they are reasonably priced and easy to maintain (these are not the Christian Fletcher pimped-up versions!). While they work just fine as test-cutting weapons, or similar, I have tasked these two for pair-drills work. This means that they get badly beaten up and have to be sharpened often, and also re-ground every now and then. Yes folks, sharps wear out. For more on pair drills with sharps, see p. 186: "Why you should train with sharp swords, and how to go about it without killing anyone."

Finally, there's my longsword of DOOM from JT Pälikkö. This thing of beauty, this poem in steel, is his idea of a joke. Yes chaps, a witty remark. Prepare to roll on the floor laughing. It is a medieval-style longsword, based on an original in the Wallace Collection – but it has a pattern-welded blade like a Viking sword! Hahahahahahaha! See! Funniest thing you ever heard, right? Five bars of layered and twisted steel, the outer two of which form the cutting edges and come together at the point. This sword cuts like a lightsaber and is one scary beast to handle.

## PLASTIC SWORDS ARE FOR CHILDREN

The post below is still generating hits two years after I wrote it.

It really struck a nerve. Unfortunately, some people did read it as an attack on their training methods (which I suppose it was) and thus an attack on them and their character (which it was not). This post should be read as a completely personal, utterly unscientific, non-practical, emotional, and historical-fundamentalist tirade against something I find offensive. On this matter I am an unreconstructed fundamentalist. You have been warned.

20th August 2012

About eight years ago I was appalled to find, at a WMA event in America, the majority of practitioners using aluminium swords. When I returned home I drew a line in the sand by posting this on SFI, under the heading *Aluminium Wasters: NO!*

> Aluminium wasters are becoming more and more popular as longsword training tools. Two main reasons are put forward for their use:
>
> (1) Price: at about \$120–\$150, they are half the price of steel blunts.
> (2) Safety: given their thicker edge and lower mass they impart less energy to the target on impact, and so they are safer to fence with at high speed.
>
> I find this development alarming, and not in the best interests of the Art of Swordsmanship. Here are my reasons:
>
> (1) Aluminium wasters are unhistorical. There is abundant record of the use of wooden wasters and some extant

examples of blunt steel training longswords, but (obviously) no aluminium swords were used in period. That said, I use protective equipment like fencing masks and hockey pads, which are equally unhistorical, but in my view have far less negative impact on how techniques may be executed.

(2) They do not behave like steel swords. Their handling characteristics are totally different, they weigh less, and the heft is just wrong. You can spot an aluminium sword being used from across the room, simply by the way it moves. Aluminium planks resonate quite differently to tempered steel blades (blunt or sharp), so when the weapons collide they behave totally differently (this is true for all wasters: wooden, aluminium, padded, bamboo, or whatever). Many of the more sophisticated techniques rely on the feeling of the blade contact in your hands (often called sentimento di ferro). Think of *mutieren* or *duplieren* in the German school (see page 184 of Tobler's excellent *Fighting with the German Longsword*); think of the difference between yielding through frontale to get to the outside, or holding your opponent in frontale for an instant while you grasp his blade and kick him in the kneecap (as one sees in *Il Fior Battaglia*). You simply do not get the same level of information coming through aluminium.

In addition, steel swords spring away from each other, or stick, depending on how they meet. This is a vital consideration when working on deflections. Aluminium wasters just do not behave the same, and so they do not adequately prepare you for the conditions of a real fight. (Though none of us intend to fight for real, all our training must work as preparation for the real thing in order for it to be valid. Otherwise we can give up our pretensions to Western Martial Arts, and start developing western combat sports. Nothing wrong with that – so long as the terms are not confused. The sporting approach is death to the Art, as the history of fencing clearly demonstrates.)

(3) Safety in free sparring is an illusion. Your equipment cannot keep you safe. Granted, it is less easy to hurt someone with an aluminium waster than with a steel blunt, but the risk is there. This is a wasteful shortcut to learning control, and is symptomatic of the "I wanna be a knight, NOW" attitude that infects a lamentable minority of practitioners. It takes thousands of hours of hard training to learn to control a steel sword so that one may freeplay with an acceptable degree of safety. Any compromise that gets people sparring too soon is inappropriate.

(4) My students all buy steel swords, and they do so relatively soon after they start training. If they can afford it so can you. If you need a very cheap starter weapon a wooden waster is the way to go. It's historically accurate and very cheap. Aluminium wasters are three or four times the price of a wooden waster, and half the price of a blunt. As such they form an economic barrier to purchasing a steel sword, which wooden wasters do not. Save up a bit longer while training with a wooden waster and you can have a proper sword.

I have discussed this issue at length with many of my colleagues in the United States, and so far I have only heard one valid argument for the use of aluminium. In a litigious culture, where horrendous punitive damages may apply, a school or teacher must be seen to be making every possible safety concession just in case there is an accident. I live in a country where any judge would say, "you swing swords at people's heads and then come crying to me when you get hurt? Get out of my courtroom!" So I have no good answer to the argument of litigation, except education of the jury-forming general public.

This is a particularly difficult topic as many equipment manufacturers, particularly the small-time producers, have no facilities for making steel blunts but can churn out aluminium wasters with ease. I hate to undermine their business, because these are decent people doing the community a good service. However, they will hopefully not lose if they turn their talented hands to wooden wasters and safety equipment.

It is up to us as a community to always seek the best way, the highest way, to pursue our Art: not just the most convenient way. Aluminium wasters are a convenience, a compromise, and a step on the slippery slope towards sporting interpretations. They have no place in my salle, and I wish they had never been invented.

I look forward to hearing your opinions...

This post generated something of a storm, and the whole six pages of wild opinion can be found here: http://www.swordforum.com/forums/showthread.php?40940-Aluminium-Wasters-NO!

Going back across the pond as I do once or twice a year, I have seen a steady diminution of aluminium. By WMAW 2011, I think there were still one or two knocking around, and everyone had steel. My primary goal at that event was to introduce students to the difference between blunt and sharp steel. Blunt steel behaves differently to sharp steel, just as aluminium behaves differently to steel. Sharp swords stick, and an awful lot of period technique becomes a lot easier and more natural to do when the blades are sharp. As I said a hundred times that weekend alone, "if you haven't done it with sharps, you haven't done it at all."

While this general improvement (as I would see it) has been going on in the part of our WMA community that I spend most of my time in, there has been a simultaneous shift in the opposite direction. It's mostly amongst those elements of the community who are most interested in creating tournaments. This has led to the development and widespread adoption of the only training tool that is more aesthetically offensive to me than an aluminium sword: plastic, sword-like objects. Are we children, that we want to play with toy swords?

Other than simple disgust, my objections are the following:

1. They in no way simulate the behavior of steel swords when they meet.
2. They in no way encourage students to treat the swords as if they were sharp.
3. They in no way reproduce the handling characteristics of steel swords (they tend to be too light).
4. They encourage foolish freeplay.

It is, of course, possible for two experts to use these things like swords; but they are generally used by beginners who are then lulled into a totally false sense of security, and a delusion of competence, that can only do them harm.

If you cannot afford a steel training sword, and want something a bit better than a stick to practice with, there is always the wooden waster. It's widely available and about the same price as the plastic monstrosity. To take those offered by Purpleheart Armoury as an example: Their plastic "longsword" costs $73, is 124 cm (48.5") long, and weighs 785 g (1.73 lb) (according to their website. I don't have any of these things in my possession. You can also pay $125 for their type III). Their (excellent) wooden wasters are $70, are 120 cm (48") long, and weigh about 950 g (2.1 lb). There is not a lot to choose between them in terms of mass and dimensions. In terms of usefulness as a training tool one has millennia of pedigree, and the other does not. One has been used by many of the greatest swordsmen in history at some stage in their training; the other, only by a few modern practitioners.

I am well aware that serious living-history buffs may find my plastic-soled training shoes, modern-pattern mask, and t-shirt-based training uniform equally appalling. I wear historical clothing and footwear for research purposes, but it is not practical for class or teaching when on any given night I may teach five different systems from five different centuries. I apologize for their suffering, and I understand it. But, at the end of the day, I care about the swords. I just don't care about the clothes.

What the argument for plastic boils down to is lowering the short-term barriers to entry, especially those to freeplay entry. They are an apparent shortcut but, as my grandma used to say, "Short cuts make long delays!" Proponents of the plastic sword argue along the lines of cost, durability, safety, etc. *But there is nothing inherently practical about the Art of Swordsmanship today.* Go train with Rory Miller, Marc MacYoung, or someone of that ilk if you want self-defense. None of them will recommend studying medieval combat treatises to learn modern self defense. Join the army if you want a practical battlefield art. The art and practice of historical swordsmanship should not be confused with any kind of modern combat, nor should it ever be reduced to simply playing with swords. It is not easy. It is not for everyone. It certainly demands a much higher standard of aesthetics and risk management that you can possibly attain to by following the Tupperware path. Blunt steel is already a huge compromise, which is why I test all interpretations and most drills with sharps. Plastic is just lazy, offensive, and disgusting.

## — Swords —

### Why you should train with sharp swords, and how to go about it without killing anyone.

This was originally a guest post on the Chivalric Fighting Arts Association blog, and I wrote it to help serious students of swordsmanship arts get over the problem of how to incorporate sharp swords into their training.

February 18th 2014

Swords are, by definition, sharp. Anything sword-like that is not sharp is either a foil or a percussive weapon like a club. I am a swordsman, and so I use sharp swords. Do I let my beginner students fight each other (or even handle) sharps? No, of course not. But my senior students have done all the basic drills in our longsword syllabus sharp-on-sharp.

I would go so far as to say that if you haven't done it with sharps you haven't done it at all. The arts that I practice were all intended for combat with sharp swords. There are two main differences between training with blunts and training with sharps: the way the weapons behave on contact, and the psychological factor. Sharp swords tend to stick together when they meet; blunt swords slide off each other. This makes binds, winds, transports, and other blade-on-blade actions more difficult with blunts. Also, there is nothing that demands your attention quite like a sharp sword pointed at your face. You behave differently when the swords are sharp; you're more attentive, more alert, more focused, and more careful. More alive. The conservative tactical choices that the treatises tend to favor make much more sense.

It is well to remember that you are compromising your swordsmanship when you practice safely and are not attempting to harm your partner. So we do lots of practice with blunts and sharps, at every degree of freedom and level of intent. (I've written extensively on this concept in the chapter "Bullshit" on page 259.) Sharpening the sword does not eliminate the compromise, it just moves it from the tool to the level of intent. Blunt swords and wooden wasters have their place in swordsmanship training, and always have done. With sharps you can practice full-intent actions alone or against inanimate targets, and careful actions, up to and including light freeplay, with a partner. You can do all of that with blunts too, and also more vigorous actions such as full-speed freeplay. It is also possible to use a sword-simulator that is sharp in the middle of the blade and blunted at the tip, which gives you most of the binding and handling characteristics of a true sharp with much less risk, and so much less of the psychological characteristics. This can form a bridge between blunt-only and full-sharp training, and can also allow you to freeplay with a tool that binds properly.

The question "should we train with sharps" simply does not arise in many other blade-oriented martial arts. In Escrima, for instance, drills are usually done with sticks or sharps. On every one of Kaj Westersund's knife courses I've attended, we have done drills with sharps; only on some of them did we use blunt training knives at all. In a ten-weekend seminar series there was, I think, one minor cut that was not self-inflicted. (The balisong weekend was a bloodbath! Thirteen self-inflicted minor cuts in the first hour. It was hilarious.) Traditional Japanese sword arts are similar. If you read Dave Lowry's *Autumn Lightning*, a memoir of his childhood spent mostly training martial arts, you find that after many months of using a bokken (wooden sword) he, while still in high school, started using a sharp:

"But unleashing a yard-long, wickedly sharp sword out of a scabbard inches from my belly, slashing with it, and then sliding it back into its sheath, again only a finger's distance from my abdomen, was one of the most frightening things I had ever done. It was worse by far than the time my best friend and I went canoeing on a flooded river and nearly drowned... It was the only distraction that could occupy more of my attention than Linda Smith's legs, stretched out two rows in front of me. Teachers who saw me walking to classes with a fretful look about me probably concluded I was worried about acne, or a relationship with a girl like Linda Smith. It's a safe bet they never suspected I was really wondering how many stitches it would take to close the gash opened by a carelessly handled samurai katana." (p. 106.)

Sure, it's frightening. It should be. But isn't swordsmanship all about behaving well in scary situations?

Our treatises from before the 1500s don't seem to address the issue. As far as I know, the earliest reference is in the introduction to Book Six of Manciolino's *Opera Nova* (1531), which begins as follows:

"I now wish to show how wrong those are who insist that good swordsmanship can never proceed from practice with blunted weapons, but only from training with sharp swords. ... It is far preferable to learn to strike with bated blades then with sharp ones; and it would not be fair to arm untrained students with sharp swords or with other weapons that can inflict injury for the purpose of training new students to defend themselves."

I couldn't agree more. I start all my students with blunt steel swords, and I introduce sharps when they are ready for them.

So the questions are: when, how, and how much?

## (1) "When should sharps be incorporated in a student's training?"

When students are thoroughly able to control a longsword simulator and have a solid grounding in basic technique they should start incorporating work with sharps as soon as possible. In my school we have a set basic syllabus, which allows us to track student progress quite precisely. I would say that once the student has passed our four basic levels she should, while she begins to add freeplay into her practice, go back to the beginning and do it all again with sharps; at first she should only do this with me, and then under the guidance of an experienced senior.[1]

## (2) "How do I incorporate sharps safely?"

Incorporating sharps in training is totally dependent on local conditions. It is unworkable for some and straightforward for others. Local experience levels and local legal conditions vary wildly. Just bear in mind that all physical activities have injury rates, and an accident does not necessarily kill the club. Obviously, my solutions are adapted for a formal school. Other groups may not be able to implement them, but I suggest talking to other martial arts clubs in your area that do use sharps (there are bound to be some) before dismissing the possibility as an insurance nightmare.

Normally in my classes, a student's first time handling a sharp sword happens when I take a person individually, put a sword in her hand, and take her through a basic pair drill. This is not reproducible, though, so here are other options for instructors. Let us assume that whoever is leading the class has sufficient experience with sharps to do this:

---

1 My use of "she" here caused some speculation about political correctness and other such tomfoolery. At the time of writing the last student I had done this exercise with was female, and so she was the person in my head when I was writing this up. Make of this what you will.

- Cutting seminars; let everyone have a go. Run properly, there is no real risk at all, and they learn much about how sharps work. In this context you can even take people who have never handled any kind of sword before and get them to safely cut a tatami mat, or similar. I've done this in public demonstrations with members of the audience.

- In our syllabus we introduce doing drills with sharps at level 5. This is after the student has completed the basic levels and is beginning freeplay, too. Usually in their first advanced class (which are scheduled separately: beginners can watch but not train), I take them one at a time through a couple of basic drills that they know really well. No protection for the student. I may wear a mask if they are really worried. (Almost every student I've done this with was more worried about injuring than getting injured.) You can do this in protective kit if you want, but that tends to generate a false sense of security.

- At this level of their training I also encourage my students to do all solo training with sharps, if they can buy or borrow one.

- Once they are habituated they can do any drill with sharps at any time. My senior students are always working on a specific training issue. If their issue is best addressed with sharps then that's the tool they will choose.

It is more difficult with thrust-oriented weapons like rapier and smallsword because thrusts to the face or body are much harder to control than cuts, and they are more likely to cause permanent damage. I think all students of any system should practice test-cutting and test-thrusting, and I normally demonstrate rapier drills with the one "winning" that step of the drill holding a blunt and the one who won holding a sharp. That way you are really careful to get the opponent's sword out of the way before lunging forwards.

And exercises like "Hunt the Debole," which do not involve striking, can easily and usefully be done with sharps. So it takes a bit of thinking about, but it can be done.

### (3) "How much training should be done with sharps?"

Angelo Viggiani (in *Lo Schermo*, 1575, page 52v–53r) was insistent that all training be done with sharps. Note, though, that his student in the book is already an experienced swordsman. This is one of my favorite passages in all of swordsmanship literature; so much so that I'll repeat it again, even though it's reproduced already in this book on page 93. ROD is Rodomonte, Viggiani's character in the book; CON is Conte, the Count that Rodomonte is giving a lesson to.

"ROD: ... take up your sword, Conte.

CON: How so, my sword? Isn't it better to take one meant for practice?

ROD: Not now, because with those practice weapons it is not possible to acquire valor or prowess of the heart, nor ever to learn a perfect *schermo*.

CON: I believe the former, but the latter I doubt. What is the reason, Rodomonte, that it is not possible to learn (so you say) a perfect schermo with that sort of weapon? Can't you deliver the same blows with that, as with one which is edged?

ROD: I would not say now that you cannot do all those ways of striking, of warding, and of guards, with those weapons, and equally with these, but you will do them imperfectly with those, and most perfectly with these edged ones, because if (for example) you ward a thrust put to you by the enemy, beating aside his sword with a mandritto, so that that thrust did not face your breast, while playing with *spade da marra*, it will suffice you to beat it only a little,

146

indeed, for you to learn the *schermo*; but if they were *spade da filo*, you would drive that mandritto with all of your strength in order to push well aside the enemy's thrust. Behold that this would be a perfect blow, done with wisdom, and with promptness, unleashed with more length, and thrown with more force, that it would have been with those other arms. How will you fare, Conte, if you take perfect arms in your hand, and not stand with all your spirit, and with all your intent judgment?

CON: Yes, but it is a great danger to train with arms that puncture; if I were to make the slightest mistake, I could do enormous harm. Nonetheless we will indeed do as is more pleasing to you, because you will be on guard not to harm me, and I will be certain to parry, and I will pay constant attention to your point in order to know which blow may come forth from your hand, which is necessary in a good warrior."

While I adore this book I don't think that all training should be done with sharps, even for experienced swordsmen. Competitive sparring, for instance, is best done using a tool you feel able to really strike with. But in my ideal world all solo drills and set drills would be done with sharps, once a certain level of competence has been reached. You may note that, in the excerpt above, Viggiani is teaching an experienced swordsman a set drill.

If you are thinking to yourself "this is all very well, but I am not experienced enough to do pair drills with sharps yet," then firstly, you're probably right; secondly, you may instead be ready to do the solo drills and test-cutting with sharps. You may also want to go to a professional to train you past this hurdle. I routinely do unprotected sharps drills with students I don't know at seminars. WMAW 2011 is a good example. There, I offered the class the opportunity to do some basic drill (often the breaking of the thrust, which is much easier to do with sharps than with blunts, and a variant on the Four Crossings drill) sharp-on-sharp with me, with no masks or other protection. All of the 40-or-so students took me up on it (I was expecting about 10!). Many of them came up to me afterwards and said it was one of the most important training experiences of their lives. This encouraged me to risk losing my sharps at Customs when I went to Melbourne in 2013; they have very strict sword laws in the state of Victoria. (I declared them, and there was no problem getting them through with the right paperwork.) It was worth the risk. On that trip, almost everyone at the seminar got to experience pair work with sharps; again, it opened their eyes and minds to an amazing degree. As Shannon Walker wrote in his review of that seminar:

"Guy Windsor is known for saying 'if you haven't trained with a sharp sword, you haven't trained to fight with a sword at all.'

Like others in the HEMA community, I always took that with a grain of salt. After all, I've been training with the Melbourne Swordplay Guild and the Glen Lachlann Estate College of Arms in Melbourne for over four years, using blunt weapons, and I think I have a reasonable grasp of what it would be like with actual swords.

And then Guy stood in Posta Longa in front of me with a sharp longsword to explain a technique and I realised, quite simply, I was wrong. Sharps make a world of difference. There was no way – NO WAY – I was going to attempt techniques against a sharp I would normally have been happy to try against a blunt."

Most frightening was a demonstration I did last summer at Ropecon, a major roleplaying convention here in Helsinki. The theme of the demonstration was sharps v. blunts and I allowed members of the audience, whom I did not know, to have a go. This is wildly different to doing it in a seminar, where I've had an hour or more to assess and prepare the students beforehand.

The way I set it up was really important. It came at the end of the demo, and so they were habituated to listening to me. They did a slow drill, using blunts and wearing masks, with a senior student so that they would get some experience with a longsword first, and would get used to following directions. Also, it was a filter for undesirables (there were none).

The set-up had the attendees with their backs to the audience, and I had five students in uniform and the senior assistant behind me. Literally, they had my back. So those having a go were clearly in MY space. They were handed each sword in turn by another assistant. They were primed, psychologically, to follow directions before we faced each other with sharps.

Most of them had some background in weapons martial arts, but not all of them. Everybody (especially me) learned something. And nobody got hurt.

I did this for three reasons:

1.  It was a really useful experience for most of the participants, especially the martial artists, and was memorable for all.
2.  It clearly differentiated what we do from the Boffer Tournament, and from other events.
3.  It was a useful training experience for me. I was utterly focused on the person I was training with, while keeping half an eye on the crowd. It was an exercise in awareness and control.

In my experience about 1 in 3 students do something suicidal while facing a sharp so, really, it's me keeping us both alive. That's okay. And if I fail, one day, that's okay too. I think the risk is worth it. It is an unparalleled learning experience, and is simply essential when working on an interpretation. If you haven't tested it with sharps then you haven't tested it at all. I would not tell a class outside of my school "now go do this with sharps," the way I will with my senior students. But as a service to the students present, I accept the risks of sharp-on-sharp with people I don't know. I just prepare them – one way or another – really carefully beforehand, create a safe environment, and make the assumption that they will try to stab me and try to run onto my point, before we cross swords. This is my job. I would not expect any amateur to take that kind of risk; the cost-benefit analysis would not work out.

A decade of injury-free sharps training suggests that even without masks the risks aren't that high, because they are so obvious: more obvious than the risks when driving. In fact, almost all the training injuries I've seen happened during freeplay with blunts. This is because of the human tendency to apply risk homeostasis: you are intuitively comfortable with a certain level of perceived risk, and will take more risks in what you think is a safer environment. See "Consuming Risk" for a discussion of this, on page 116. Ironically, based on our injury record, I would say that training with sharps is safer than training with blunts!

I hope that this article demonstrates that training with sharps is a necessary and achievable aspect of learning the art of swordsmanship. Let me finish on this note though: if you feel totally competent and comfortable to train with sharp swords, that is a good indication that you are either a master swordsman way beyond my level, or that you are dangerously deluded. Much of the value of the sharps comes from the clear and present danger they embody. Please make sure that you can see it and feel it before you draw your sword from its scabbard.

## Cutting with Sharps

First published in *Western Martial Arts Illustrated Magazine*, Issue 2, fall 2007. I am ruthlessly goal-oriented in all training environments. You can get a feel for that in this article; there is no element of "let's just cut stuff" about it.

Cutting objects with a sharp sword is a vital research and training method for practitioners of historical (or any other kind of) swordsmanship. It is usually referred to as "test cutting." This is because in the traditional Japanese sword arts new swords would be tested by an expert swordsman who would cut through soaked rice-straw targets, or prisoners, and would grade the sword accordingly (a process known as tameshigiri). The soaked straw was chosen because it apparently closely simulated the muscle and connective tissue in the human body. There are in fact three subjects to be tested with cutting practice: 1)The cut itself: how changes in cutting style can alter the effectiveness of the cut. 2) The sword: how changes in sharpness, blade geometry, or length affect the cut. 3)The substrate: how well different materials stand up to a sword.

In any cutting session it is very important to limit the variables above to one. If you wish to examine different cutting styles, for example, use the same sword and the same targets so that you know for sure what is causing the changes. There are many distinct sword types in the European arsenal, and many different styles of using any given type, so for convenience I will henceforth refer only to longswords of the early fifteenth century used in the style of Fiore dei Liberi's *Il Fior di Battaglia*.

It is almost impossible to simulate a combat situation when doing cutting practice: opponents do not stand still.

Neither is it easy to exactly simulate a human body in the

normal fencing protection of the style in question. The best simulation from that perspective (given that we can't use people) is almost certainly to cover a large bit of dead pig with a gambeson and/or chain mail or plate, take an accurately-reconstructed period sword, and see what kind of damage occurs when striking the pig with various types of blow. Unfortunately, there are no metallurgically accurate reproductions on the market that I know of. Even the cheapest modern longsword is usually made of far better steel than that available in the period. So already, our research is hampered by having too good a sword.

However, we do know that swords of this period could cut very effectively; perhaps the most famous example comes from the Chronicle of Pero Niño, started in 1431 and concluded sometime after 1449. In it, the chronicler Gutierre Diaz de Gamez records that in 1396 Pero Niño was aboard King Enrique II of Spain's galley and was being rowed up the Guadalquivir river to Seville. Some fishermen, unaware of the King's progress, had strung a hawser "as thick as a man's knee" across the river, supporting a net for catching shad. The rope would have swept the galley deck and overturned the vessel had our hero not "leapt briskly to the prow, drew his sword and gave it such a blow that he broke the hawser...wherefore all were amazed."[2] This feat argues for two things; those are a good sword and an excellent swordsman, one who has probably practiced cutting targets a fair bit. The skeletons dug up from medieval battlefields (of which Wisby is perhaps the best known example) also show horrific instances of the damage done by swords against the human body.

The question for us researchers is this: how do we simulate the

---

2 *The Unconquered Knight*, by Gutierre Diaz de Gamez. Translated and selected by Joan Evans, published 1928 by Routledge, and reprinted 2004 by Boydell Press.

target, and how do we assess the effect of the cutting actions we learn from the treatises?

When designing the target we need to take into account the following things:

- Verisimilitude: how well does it simulate the "real" target?
- Cost: how much money and time does it take to prepare?
- Consistency: how similar can we make each target piece, to ensure minimum variations that might affect the resistance to cutting?
- Damage: will the target materials damage the sword, and if so is that acceptable? Blood and water rust steel, bones can chip blades, straw scratches, etc.

The following targets seem popular in current WMA circles: Japanese-style mats made from soft rush material (tatami omote); beach mats (used the same way as tatami; they're cheaper, but do more damage to the sword and are less consistent); animal parts; cardboard tubes; carpet rolls; dangling rope; plastic bottles filled with water; rolls of newspaper; and newspaper rolled around a plastic tube to simulate bone (this last comes from David Lindholm's *Knightly Art of the Longsword*, page 225). (Paper products such as newsprint or cardboard can carry the abrasive grit used in the pulping process, which will scratch and may dull your sword.) Given the range available, it makes sense to try out the ones suitable for your training environment. In each case the targets vary according to their weight, density, hardness, how much resistance the materials give to the blade (mats, rope, and paper are usually soaked to lubricate the cut and soften the fibers; this also more closely simulates the conditions in the human body), and how stable they are on impact. A dangling rope is much harder to cut than one held taut because it can move away from the cut. Likewise, the same rope is easier to cut with a downwards blow than a rising one. An empty plastic bottle standing on a level surface is harder to cut than the same bottle filled with water, because the weight of the water holds the bottle in place at the moment of impact. It is necessary that the target be cut-able by the sword in question: no sword should be used to cut down a tree (that's why loggers used axes). Where armor is placed over the target (such as putting a gambeson sleeve over a leg of pork), it is important to be clear whether it is the armor, the sword, or the cut being tested.

I have found that the tatami omote, though laborious to prepare and relatively expensive to obtain, are the most consistent and hence most useful cutting substrate. WMA practitioners in America may be familiar with tatami from cutting seminars held by Jim Alvarez and Dave Wilson (who also kindly reviewed this article) at the Schola St. George Swordplay Symposium, Benecia 2003, and at WMAW Dallas 2006. They also supply Europe through Emil Strenge in Sweden (this was true in 2007; I think it is no longer the case).

The sharpness of the sword is also an issue. People who specialize in test cutting tend to prefer a very sharp edge because it cuts better. However, practicing technical drills with sharp swords teaches you first and foremost that during a sword fight a very sharp edge gets damaged worse and faster than a slightly dull one, and that any sword that can be considered sharp will incur damage to the edge on contact with another sword. Medieval combat styles often include half-sword technique, whereby the sword is grasped by handle and blade; a super-sharp edge makes this very dangerous, but an ordinarily sharp sword will not cut the hand unless the blade is drawn across it. For cutting practice it is perfectly acceptable to use an over-sharp sword, provided that we take the excessive sharpness into account when estimating the blow's effectiveness in combat.

It is not actually necessary to simulate a body part at all for the purposes of testing the effect of different styles of cut or changes to your cutting technique: any consistent target that is appropriate for cutting will do to start with. Careful examination of the target and the blow should tell you whether your cut is hitting (but not cutting), whether it's slicing through easily, how accurate the blow was, what part of the edge cuts best, how your footwork (if any) affects the blow, and how much effort the effect is costing you. Video taping the cutting session is extremely useful for these purposes, as is the presence of a competent instructor.

The cut is affected by the following factors:

**(1) The sword sharpness;**
blade geometry (edge straight or curved, edge profile, and distribution of mass);
steel used (affects primarily how quickly the blade gets blunt, but also laminations cause micro-serrations on the edge, which make slicing more effective); and
blade harmonics (how the blade vibrates when swung and on impact).

**(2) The target**
resistance of the material, and
stability.

**(3) The mechanics of the cut, in**
blade speed and mass (faster blades cut better, and heavier ones are more stable);
blade alignment (the edge angle must be in line with the swing angle; different cutting angles have different effects); and
blade stability (how well the blade is supported by the cutter, and how much the blade vibrates on impact).

155

The biggest problem faced by most practitioners of swordsmanship when doing sharp cutting practice is the lack of tactical feedback from the target. It is an unfortunate fact of swordsmanship life that the most effective cut on a static target is usually wildly untactical but incredibly satisfying to do. We feel rewarded when the sword hisses through the target with no apparent effort, and so we naturally change our cutting style to make it happen. This often leads to cuts that are initiated in the hips, with the sword trailing. Done in combat, this is clearly one of Silver's false times. By exposing ourselves to a counter-attack our lovely, powerful cut never actually lands, because we stop the opponent's sword with our face first. Setting up a video camera behind the target allows us to examine this; also, a competent instructor will spot it and tell you to stop.

It is important at this point to understand that test cutting is only one part of a swordsman's training. Since we are training with edged weapons it is important to make sure that we know how to make the best use of that edge, in the context of our Art. Test cutting is common to most swordsmanship styles worldwide. So it affords an excellent opportunity for cross-training with martial artists from other disciplines, and also a chance to dispel myths about our weapons and styles.

So, for research purposes, we can idealize the sword (making it unreasonably sharp), idealize the target (making it stand still), and then vary the mechanics of the cut to see what hits hard and what cuts. The two are not the same, and it is as well to remember that being hit hard on the head by a long piece of steel is always going to have some effect. Whether you completely sever his head or just slice halfway through his neck is unlikely to make much difference in combat. There are many different ways to cut correctly, and there are many different purposes for cutting. It is perfectly reasonable to conclude that a cut of type A is excellent for slicing soft tissue, type B works best for bashing skulls, and type C is only any use for stationary cutting (for example, for testing blade sharpness or the effect of different blade profiles).

In any case, cutting practice is vital for historical swordsmanship practitioners, and it can yield important feedback about the swords in question or a given cutting style. There is a world of difference, though, between unscientific "let's have a go at cutting stuff" practice and properly thought out cutting research and training. And above all, cutters should remember that targets don't avoid, parry, or hit back.

# CHAPTER FIVE
# Writing Swordfights

## ON WRITING SWORDFIGHTS

> "It makes me so happy. To be at the beginning again, knowing almost nothing.... A door like this has cracked open five or six times since we got up on our hind legs. It's the best possible time of being alive, when almost everything you thought you knew is wrong."
>
> — Tom Stoppard, Arcadia

They say "write what you know," so here goes. As you have probably gathered by now, I have spent the last 20 years of my life researching and recreating medieval, Renaissance, and 18th century swordsmanship. There is an abundance of written and illustrated sources that – with a decade or so of full-time work, much of it with sword in hand – yields a clear and unambiguous picture of how a sword fight should go down. It shows what works reliably, what doesn't work at all, and what sneaky tricks work just once.

In contrast to my own experience, most of what goes on in someone's head when they picture a swordfight is drawn from the movies. Here's the rub: a film duel must be visible (the audience must see what's happening), and nobody should die (actors might be replaceable, but then you have to re-shoot all their scenes). So the motions are big, slow, and (relatively) harmless. In a real fight the last thing you want is for your actions to be visible, and your opponent should die. So the motions should be small, fast, and deadly.

The huge advantages that fiction writers have over all other producers of imaginary swordfights is that they can kill as many people as they like without going to jail. They can also take as long as they like, pages even, to describe an action that might be so small and quick that it's invisible to the untrained eye. So there is no story-telling medium better adapted for getting the fights right.

This section is intended as a guide to fiction writers, in any genre, who want their fights to be believable to the growing number of us that know something about swordsmanship. I will describe the main different fighting contexts (duel, melee, and self-defense) and how they affect what you should do to win; the different weapons and how they work; I'll survey the main styles as practiced in Europe, for which we have written sources; I will speculate a little regarding the styles for which we have inadequate evidence for a proper reconstruction; and I'll offer some examples of good and not-so-good written fights.

Before we get on with that there are a couple of characters I need you to meet, because I will be relying on their opinions.

The first is a master of knightly combat. He was so well known in his time that the main street in his home town is still named after him. I am talking, of course, about Fiore de' Liberi, who wrote a complete and detailed treatise on the Art of Arms in the early 1400s. His legacy has been the main focus of my research for the last decade. This medieval badass and winner of five duels is who I am referring to when I write "Fiore says." He claims some of the most famous knights of his time as his students; one of whom, Galeazzo da Mantoa, beat the legendary Marshal Boucicaut (the French commander at Agincourt) in a duel on August 22nd 1395.

Next up we have the elusive figure of Ridolfo Capoferro (as Inigo Montoya says in *The Princess Bride*: "naturally, you must expect me to attack with Capoferro"). Not much is known of Capoferro's life, but his book *The Great Representation of the Art and Practice of Fencing* is one of the most influential swordsmanship treatises ever written. Published in 1610, it has been copied, plagiarized, referred to, and respected ever since. Ironically, it is one of the worst *written* books I've ever studied. He was born in Cagli, a town in central Italy, in about 1558.

I would expect that any serious historical novelist would research the details of clothing, food, religion, and culture of the period in which they are setting their tale. It is in many ways much harder to do similar research into the combat systems, because they leave much less trace behind. There are no surviving objects to copy, no easily-followed recipes written down, and no gargantuan scholarly literature. How a specific blow is done may only be hinted at in an obscure manuscript, long overlooked by mainstream academia because it is "just about fighting" or "has little artistic merit." So one of the services this book will render is to provide a list of the most useful and influential sources that are currently available. It will by no means be a complete bibliography but a starting point, emphasizing those works that have been translated into English and/or interpreted in print. With this book in hand you should find the more technical and academic works more useful, because I have abstracted the general rules for you.

Of course, there are several distinct skills that go into a good written fight. They are:

- visualising the fight accurately, to avoid describing impossible actions;

- maintaining dramatic tension and pacing the fight to be exciting;
- maintaining characterisation: making sure that the characters' actions in the fight give the reader the sense of their personalities that you want; and
- serving the plot, so that the fight meets the needs of the story and is not just shoehorned in.

## General Admonitions

The core message of this section is summed up here, and can be reduced to the following:

- Understand the context of the fight.
- Separate instruction from action. Avoid describing the fencing theory and actions you are using during the fight itself.
- Instil a sense of danger with accidents and reversals, not the specific risks of a given technique.
- Follow historical examples, not modern opinions.

Let me expand a little on these.

### Understand the Context of the Fight

What works depends entirely on context. A brilliant solution to get your sword-wielding, armored, anthropomorphic hero out of an alley populated by two unarmored thugs holding daggers may fail in an open field against a centaur with a bow and arrow. Leaving fantasy aside for a moment, the primary contexts for which we have documented solutions are either prearranged, with the weapons, time, and place agreed in advance; or they are spontaneous, where at least one party was not expecting to fight. They are also either mortal, so death is expected or desired, or agonistic, in which both parties expect to survive. They are either between individuals (there may be several fights happening, but each action is one-on-one) or between groups (or a group ganging up on an individual). Lastly, they are either for training or for real.

Note that, with the exception of the group/individual distinction, all of these differences are mental: they truly exist only in the minds of the combatants. And of course the two (or more!) sides may be engaged in different types of fight. A classic trope of historical and fantasy fiction is the dastardly murder of an unsuspecting victim who turned up to a duel thinking it was a fencing match. Likewise what works for the ambushers does not work for the ambushed.

A prearranged mortal fight between groups is a battle; a prearranged mortal fight between individuals is a duel; and a fight that comes as a surprise to an individual but not to the thugs that have ambushed her is, you guessed it, an ambush. There are of course all sorts of shades of grey between these contexts, but we have to start somewhere.

The most common scenarios are

battle,
ambush,
tournament,
training, and
duel.

Let's take them in order.

**Battles** have (usually) two groups who have manoeuvred themselves until the battleground is chosen and the fight begins. The fight will normally start between two well-formed groups. Unit cohesion, advantage of ground, advantage of numbers, level of training, level of troop morale, advantage of weaponry, and tactical superiority are perhaps the best predictors of success. It is axiomatic that people fighting for their homes and way of life fight harder than those simply expanding an empire. That said, thanks usually to tactical superiority and training, empires certainly did expand; think of disciplined Roman legions slaughtering the less organized tribes of Europe. But recall also Darius I's invasion of Scythia, in 514–512 BC, in which his large army was useless against the long-range bows and guerrilla tactics of the Scythians. The Scythians would have almost certainly lost if they had stood and fought so they changed the context from battle, at which Darius' army excelled, to ambush. The Romans succeeded so well largely because the tribes had fixed settlements that they wished to defend, but no long-range weaponry with which to strike and retreat. The tribes had no cohesion, and they were up against the most cohesive force on the planet.

There is a fundamental difference between mercenary forces who are by definition in it for the money, professional soldiers in their nation's armed services, farmers who take up arms to defend their homes, and levies or conscripts fighting because they have to. In fourteenth century Italy, for example, the city states hired mercenary troops to fight for them. Since nobody was in it for love, patriotism, or a higher cause, this meant that the armies would vie for position, and that when one had a significant advantage the other would sue for terms. Famously, "in 1439 in a battle, begun in the time-honoured *condottiere* manner of move and counter-move and no real fighting, between the mercenary forces of Bologna and Venice, the Bolognese used handgunmen and actually killed some Venetian men-at-arms. This was infuriating; the Venetians dispensed with the rule-book and went to it in earnest, defeated the Bolognese and massacred every gunman, for they said if people continued to use this devilish innovation, war would become really dangerous." (Oakeshott, page 29.)

Battles are won through organization, generalship, and luck. The specific fighting techniques of soldiers in the line of battle are invariably simple, repetitive, and require little space to work in. Likewise, while the fortunes of war might bring a footsoldier riches his fighting kit – even if beautifully decorated – will usually be functionally similar to those of his fellows. Individuality is largely counter-productive on the battlefield.

**Ambushes** are won by surprise, which depends on timing. Defense against ambushes is mostly a matter of spotting them before they occur, or of the levels of training in the two groups. It is very hard to draw weapons and make an organized defense against a well-laid ambush, especially if the ambushers have projectiles (arrows, javelins, etc.).

**Tournaments** (or any kind of organised competition) are defined by their rule-sets, and most dramatic tension comes from one or other competitor breaking the rules. It's common that the good guy follows the rules and the bad guy breaks them.

**Training** offers a rich vein of drama and characterization; just think of how many books and movies include training scenes. Luke and Yoda on Dagobah, Syrio Forel and Arya in *Game of Thrones*, and about half the scenes in *The Fencing Master*. With the master you have the opportunity to describe the harsh-but-fair, or sadistic, or ineffectual, or brilliant, or gnomic figure; meanwhile the student will tend to show their true colors, their innermost character, when under the right kind of tutelage.

**The Duel** is the most rarefied environment, producing the most sophisticated and interesting techniques and tactics. Basically a prearranged fight between two individuals, the duel could take place in public, as part of a legal or moral dispute, or in private, as an illegal settling of scores. As legal action, it is way better than a courtroom drama, and it could be found in most European

165

cultures until it died out in the mid-1500s. The last such duel on record was between two French noblemen, and I cannot resist giving you the full story. This is from John Cockburn's *The History of Duels*, 1888, cited in Robert Baldick's 1965 work *The Duel: A History of Duelling.*

"The persons were the Lords of Chastaigneraye and of Jarnac, who were both neighbours and kinsmen. The first had said to Francis I that the other was maintained so plentifully by his mother-in-law, with whom he had unlawful conversation. The King told this to Jarnac, for whom he had a great affection. Upon which Jarnac said to the King that Chastaigneraye had lied to him: but he not only maintaining what he had said, but adding that Jarnac had divers times owned it to himself, Jarnac did earnestly supplicate the King that the truth might be tried by combat; which Francis I granted, but afterwards recalled.

Upon his death, an earnest supplication was made to his successor, Henry II who, with the advice of his council, not only allowed, but appointed it at Saint-Germain-en-Laye, on July 10, 1541, when the King, the whole court, the constable, admiral, and marshals of France being present, the two parties were brought before the King, attended by their several friends and trumpets, when each took the usual oaths. After this they were led to their several pavilions, where they were dressed for the combat, each having a friend and confidant in the other's pavilion while this was doing. It is said that Jarnac was but newly recovered of a sickness, and that he whispered to a friend, if he did not trust to the goodness of his cause, he should fear the acting of the part of a poltroon. When all the usual preamble of the ceremonies was over, they were called out by the King's trumpet, and by his herald commanded to end their difference by combat. Chastaigneraye was observed to brave it with some insolence; but Jarnac carried it modestly and humbly.

Each attacked the other with great vigour; and, after several strokes and trifling wounds on both sides, while Chastaigneraye was making a pass at Jarnac, he fetched a stroke which cut the ham of Chastaigneraye's left leg, and presently redoubling his stroke, cut also the ham of the right; upon which Chastaigneraye fell to the ground, and the other ran up to him, telling him that now his life was at his discretion, yet he would spare it *if would restore him his honour, and acknowledge his offence to God and the King.* Chastaigneraye answering nothing, Jarnac turned to the King, and, kneeling down, prayed that now he might be so happy as to be esteemed by him a man of honour; and, seeing his honour was restored, he would make his majesty a present of the other's life, desiring his offence might be pardoned, and never more imputed to him or his, being the inconsiderate act of youth: to which the King made no answer. The former returned to his antagonist, and finding him still on the ground, lifted up his face and hands to Heaven, and said: *Lord, I am not worthy: not to me, but unto Thy name be thanks!*

Having said this, he prayed Chastaigneraye to confess his error: but, instead of this, the latter raised himself on his knee, and, having a sword and buckler in his hand, offered a pass at Jarnac, who told him that if he offered to resist any more he would kill him, and the other bid him to do it; without, however, doing him any harm, Jarnac made a second humble address to the King to accept Chastaigneraye's life, to which the King made no manner of reply.

Whereupon Jarnac coming back to his antagonist, who was lying stretched out upon the ground, his sword out of his hand and his dagger out of its sheath, he accosted him with the fair words of *old friend and companion*, entreated him to remember his Creator, and to let them become friends again. But he attempting to turn himself without the signs of repentance and submission, Jarnac took away his sword and dagger, and laid them at the King's feet, with repeated supplication to inter-pose for Chastaigneraye's life; which the King at last *was advised to do*, and ordered some of the officers to go to him, and surgeons to take care of his life; but he would not suffer his wounds to be dressed, being wearied of life because of his disgrace, and so died in a little time through the loss of blood. It being told the King that, according to custom, Jarnac should be carried in triumph, Jarnac protested against it, saying that he affected no ostentation or vain glory, that he had been only desirous to have his honour restored, and was contented with that; upon which the King made him this compliment, that he *fought like Caesar and spoke like Aristotle*. Yet the King's inclinations were towards Chastaigneraye. The poor lady, Jarnac's mother-in-law, whose honour was at stake too, was all the while at Saint-Cloud, fasting and praying, and waiting impatiently the issue of this purgation of her innocency."

(Italics original).

Legend has it that Jarnac, being the less arrogant of the two, hired an Italian fencing master, one Captain Caizo, to train him in the month's grace between the combat being permitted and the actual duel. There's a novel here, I think. Note that Chastaigneraye might have survived had he been less pig-headed. Indeed, as Fiore says about fighting in the lists (which in his day was invariably done in armor):

"I, Fiore, said to my students who had to fight in the lists, that fighting in the lists is far less dangerous than fighting with an edged and pointed sword in a *zuparello d'armare* [a type of padded jacket that provided some protection] because for those that play with edged swords, one parry that fails, in that blow it gives death. And one who fights in the lists is well armoured and blows can do little against him. He can win the battle [despite being hit]. Also another thing: it is rare that anyone dies as they are taken for ransom.

So I say I would rather fight three times in the lists than one time with edged swords as said above."

This after stating that he had fought five duels in a gambeson (a type of padded jacket that provided some protection) and "By the grace of God I, Fiore, came away with my honour, and without injuries on my body."

So the unofficial duel clearly existed side by side with the formal duel, and by the late 1500s it was the dominant form of interpersonal combat; at least, it's the context for which most books on swordfighting were written.

One rapier and dagger duel, of the many for which we have accounts, was described by Thomas Carlyle in his article "Duelling two hundred and fifty years ago," published in *The International Monthly Magazine* vol. 3 (1851). It's worth reading the whole thing so I have included it in an Appendix to this book, which you can download free from guywindsor.net/blog, but the critical point now is here:

"And so, on Calais sands, on a winter morning of the year 1609, this is what we see most authentically, through the lapse of dim Time. Two gentlemen stript to the shirt and waistband; in two hands of each a rapier and dagger clutched; their looks sufficiently serious! The seconds, having stript, equipt, and fairly overhauled and certified them, are just about retiring from the measured fate-circle, not without indignation that *they* are forbidden to fight. Two gentlemen in this alarming posture; of whom the Universe knows, has known, and will know nothing, except that they were of choleric humor, and assisted in the Netherlands wars! They are evidently English human creatures, in the height of silent fury and measured circuit of fate; whom we here audibly name once more, Sir Hatton Cheek, Sir Thomas Dutton, knights both, soldadoes both. Ill-fated English human creatures, what horrible confusion of the pit is this?

Dutton, though in suppressed rage, the seconds about to withdraw, will explain some things if a word were granted, "No words," says the other; "stand on your guard!" brandishing his rapier, grasping harder his dagger. Dutton, now silent too, is on his guard. Good heavens! after some brief flourishing and flashing,—the gleam of the swift clear steel playing madly in one's eyes,—they, at the first pass, plunge home on one another; home, with beak and claws; home to the very heart! Cheek's rapier is through Dutton's throat from before, and his dagger is through it from behind,—the windpipe miraculously missed; and, in the same instant, Dutton's rapier is through Cheek's body from before, his dagger through his back from behind,—lungs and life *not* missed; and the seconds have to advance, "pull out the four bloody weapons," disengage that hell-embrace of theirs. This is serious enough! Cheek reels, his life fast-flowing; but still rushes rabid on Dutton, who merely parries, skips, till Cheek reels down, dead in his rage. "He had a bloody burial there that morning," says my ancient friend. He will assist no more in the Netherlands or other wars."

## Separate Instruction from Action

Your reader does not know the rules of your fictional world like you do, nor does he have the same sense of its culture. So at some point you may need to describe or explain how swordfights work in your world: what equipment is used and why, which techniques are preferred and why, what constitutes victory and its rewards, and what the price of defeat is and why. It is in these areas that the details of this book may be most helpful to you. But the place to explain all this is not the fight itself! It will only slow things down and bump readers out of their immersion in the action.

You can either explain it all beforehand in your scene-building sections of the novel, or, if necessary, use witnesses to the action to explain what happened. The purpose of all this is to provide a sense of danger in the fight that will not be present during your lecture on the relative merits of straight swords versus curved, which was essential when the villain selected his from the sword shop right before he abducted the princess – curse him – but has no place in the action. We should know that his sword is curved, why he prefers that style, what it is good for, and what it says about his character *before the fight starts.*

## Instil a Sense of Danger

Instil a sense of danger in the fight by putting someone we care about at risk. What those risks are can vary hugely: losing might be fatal, or just embarrassing; might entail failure to rescue said princess, which will lead to civil war; or may be failure to win a one dollar bet. Whatever it is, the hero's subjective experience of the risk is what keeps us reading. We have to truly care about the outcome for the fight to be gripping.

Tom Hanks was not an obvious choice when we think of his role as an heroic astronaut in *Apollo 13*, but he's a shoo-in when we ask the question, "if all the A-list stars were stuck out in space, which one would Americans most want to get back? Who do they *like* the most?"

The classic tools for creating this tension are accidents and reversals. The fight itself is not interesting if we have a villain effortlessly dispatching a weaker opponent whom we or the hero have come to love (e.g. The hero's little brother); it's just the fight's place in the plot. When hero and villain meet for the final showdown it is all this history, the things that are riding on the outcome, that really matter. The harder the victory, the better the fight. Accidents include anything not intrinsic to the characters: the villain slips on a patch of mud (accident) while the hero foolishly, nobly, refrains from taking advantage (intrinsic). A fight without accidents is not only undramatic: it's also unrealistic.

Reversals of fortune (peripeteia) are critical, too. A fight that goes all one way is not gripping. It is the hero's struggles that make him interesting. Perhaps the most famous reversals in on-screen duelling are in the cliff-top duel between Inigo Montoya and the Man in Black. They start out left-handed, and Inigo is having difficulty. Then Inigo reveals that he is not really left-handed and switches to right-handed, beating back the Man in Black... who then reveals that he is not left-handed either. From there the outcome is a foregone conclusion.

Whatever the reversals or accidents are they must be easily grasped by a reader who has forgotten or skipped your careful groundwork. Slips, falls, dropping a sword, blades breaking, and distractions all work. But all drama is gone if the reader has to think or – worse – flip back to check your explanations, in order to figure out what is happening.

## On the uselessness of modern sports fencing.

Sport fencers in general know less than nothing about real swordfighting.

If your scene is set in a modern fencing salle then the actions, skills, insights, and culture of sport fencing are critically important. But they are utterly unrelated to the core skills and tactics of to-the-death swordfighting. When I pick up a swordfighting novel for the first time I usually check the acknowledgements section, and I brace myself for bullshit if I find a reference to a sport fencing club.

172

To put this in some perspective, think of the difference in training, weapons, and tactics in the modern infantry versus those of paintball. Both of them involve running around outside shooting people, but that's where the similarities begin and end. Success in one field does not predict success in the other. So beware: sport fencers in my experience like to think their art is related to real swordsmanship, because it descended from it. But it is so exquisitely adapted to the environment of the modern sport that it encourages behavior that would prove literally suicidal if the swords were real. To give one example: in events with the epee, the weapon most closely related (they think) to a real duel because the entire body can be hit and there are no rules of priority (no "right of way" awarding hits to one fencer in the event of a double hit), there is a 40 *millisecond* tolerance. This means that my action is invalid if you hit me 50 milliseconds before I hit you. So top fencers prioritize hitting first over hitting safely, and so win medals for actions that would get them killed. It can take a person *weeks* to die from a sword blow, but a touch to the shoulder with the force required to score in fencing – 750 g (7.5 N) – may do no damage at all. So, while I may have to see my tailor about mending my shirt *you* might have a foot of steel stuck in your lung. Or vice versa. The sport is a million miles removed from the fight. There are abundant contemporary descriptions of real swordfights that you may draw on, and there are a set of basic rules in this book to guide you. Just do yourself and your readers a favor and do not ask a sport fencer to fact-check your fights.

Terminology is one thing that sport fencing is good for. A legacy from its classical fencing roots (classical fencing is the term given to fencing with foil, epee, or saber after duelling with the sword became outmoded and before the development of modern electronic scoring methods, which began in the 1930s. It was termed "classical" by its 19th-century practitioners), sport fencing has an excellent and consistent terminology which allows you to clearly state who is doing what to whom. The important bits are as follows.

- Phrase: a series of actions, done without a break.
- Attack: the first offensive action in a phrase.
- Parry: a movement of the sword that defends against the attack, and does not strike the opponent.
- Riposte: an offensive action following on from a successful parry.
- Counter-attack: a defensive action that combines defense and offense in one motion, either by parrying and striking simultaneously, or by striking and avoiding. (So you would not parry and counter-attack; you'd parry and riposte, OR counter-attack.)
- Feint: an offensive action intended to draw a parry from your opponent.

Your reader always knows what is going on if you use these terms consistently. For instance, I might write this sequence if I was writing an hommage to the Princess Bride fight:

Inigo attacked with a flurry of feints and thrusts. The Man in Black retreated, parrying swiftly, looking for the chance to riposte. Finally it came; he parried a thrust, catching Inigo's blade near his hilt, and riposted with vigor and elan. He ducked away and, as the Man in Black followed up with another thrust, Inigo counter-attacked, forcing the Man in Black to parry again...

## An example fight
This example is all about describing specific actions in a way that makes sense to the general reader but includes just the right details, so that those who actually study these arts will recognize specific techniques from the historical sources; in this case, Fiore de'

Liberi's *Armizare*. Can you spot the *rompere di punta*, the *punta falsa*, and the eighteenth play of the *zogho stretto* from the Getty manuscript? Using jargon in the story would, I think, diminish the realism as it would jerk most readers out of the flow. I first wrote this as the beginnings of a possible side-story in the *Foreworld* universe, hence the mystic stuff, but it never went anywhere. It remains useful, though, as an example of very technical fencing told without terminology.

"A man of Earth and water, solid, but never predictable – at least in combat. Long ago our differences led us to test each other on the field, in harness. We had no intent to deny the order a valued knight, but at the same time his "stop fucking about with fairies and just hit the bastard" remarks had been said in my hearing once too often to ignore. I may have made some remark about mud-creatures versus angels that would have breathed some air into the fire between us. There was no cause for a judicial hearing, or any kind of formal censure, but we knew, for the good of all, we had to settle this; come into some kind of balance. So on a quiet morning, in a field out of view of our main encampment, we met sword in hand.

He glowed. The Earth loved him and sent tendrils up his legs to anchor him, yet let him move like the wind over her face. There was no break, no cracks even, in the connection I could see from the tip of his sword to the soles of his feet and down. His anger crackled, fire rising up his back, and though these sights were hidden to him I knew he would be reading me in his own way. He would read my resolve, and we had trained together enough before to know that there was no real difference in skill or power.

My aim was simple. Teach the arrogant bog-Irish bastard that the Sight worked by using it to beat him. His was the reverse: to make me admit that all this energy work was so

175

much wasted time, better spent with the weights or hitting the pell.

I could feel my anger, fire rising, and knew it would overwhelm me if I let it. I relaxed into it and allowed the cooling flow of watery reason to calm it, focus it into a ball, and shoot it down my blade. My point slammed forwards, taking me to the edge of balance and forcing him to meet my sword. As his weapon rose I redirected to bind him, angling my point to his visor, but he was already inside it and passing in under cover to grapple me. He was very strong so I avoided him, grabbing the middle of my blade with my left hand and slipping my sword arm away from his grasp. There was no opening to strike, but I got contact with the tip of my sword against his right wrist and linked us together. Now I could read him, or so I thought. Without changing the contact he got hold of his blade with his left hand and let go with his right, and got a grip on my point. I had thought that kind of masking is just not possible without intensive inner training, the kind he had always mocked. Either he was a fraud, which just didn't feel true, or he was accessing the same skills through a different path. None of this helped the fact that he now had hold of my point, obliging me to smash in using my superior leverage on the sword to aim a blow with the hilt at his visor. All well and good, but essentially forcing me to enter into his preferred measure.

He seamlessly redirected my strike with his left forearm, letting go of my point, grabbing his hilt with his right hand, and leaving him on top of my sword with his point about to hook into my neck and his leg behind mine. I don't know how I managed to get my left hand under his arm and turn him away enough that his throw failed, but the spirits were with me and we ended up separated, moving apart to gain some space. I felt a presence around us and risked a glance to the side. There was a silent rank of our brethren, watching. None made a move to interfere.

This time he attacked, a strong horizontal blow to my helm, fast enough and tight enough to force a parry. I went to beat his sword aside but his just grazed mine, and he came down inside my counter-blow. I had seen this attack before, of course, but again he had managed to hide his intentions. I converted my strike into a second parry just in time, and struck at him. He lifted his weapon enough that my flat glanced harmlessly off his helm, and we were again separated.

My blow took me into a low guard on the left side from whence I thrust, angling the blow up under his jaw. He caught it and beat it down to his left, flicking his point up towards my neck. Exactly as I'd hoped. My sword rose with his and drove into his flat, smashing in towards his face. The only counter was to yield around it, to my right, which he did, converting the action into a pommel strike, which raked harmlessly along my shoulder as we passed each other. I was slightly quicker in the turn, spun around on my left foot and presenting my point to his back, but before I could strike he had moved away. I wasn't angry any more, and neither was he. We were having fun. And we both realized it at the same moment. From there, the fight changed altogether. We kept going, landing blows that should have broken bones, each of us being thrown by the other until we were both covered in bits of grass and mud. It was glorious. By the end we were howling with laughter, unable to breathe, leaning on our swords.'Breakfast?' he suggested through his panting laughter.'Oh yes,' I replied. And we staggered off the field to find some."

## An inside view of a normal lesson

One type of character that is very hard for non-specialists to get right is the martial arts teacher. In general, they get depicted as either gnomic (Yoda), despotic (take your pick, from *Kill Bill's* Pai Mei, to Syrio Forel from *Game of Thrones*), or bafflingly incompetent (most others). In short, the problem is that the writer thinks that to be seen as a good teacher, one worth studying with, the master must demonstrate their own skills over and over again, in one way or another. That is exactly analogous to the Olympic gymnastics medals being give out to the athlete whose *coach* did the best routine. The only measure of a teacher is their students.

It has been shown time and again that the worst thing a teacher can do, especially one teaching combat, is to generate the experience of defeat in their student. Most training happens in the brain; conditioning the student to lose will indeed develop in them the habit of losing.

In a normal lesson given by a competent teacher, the student hits the teacher every time he gets something right, and gets hit every time he gets something wrong. This creates a natural learning environment in which the student will rapidly progress. If the aim is to establish the skill of the teacher as a fighter then show him fighting a worthy opponent. If the goal is to show his skill as a teacher then show the student getting better. If you want to establish him as an asshole, and a bully, then show him beating his student to establish his dominance. In fiction it is usually the student who is the main character; their training is to help them accomplish their aims in the story (e.g. revenge).

I rate martial arts movies according to the excellence of their training montages, and indeed as a child I based most of my practice on those montages. If only you could see what my boarding school looked like at bedtime on the evening they let us watch *Karate Kid.* Two hundred kids with dressing gown belts round their heads, doing that swoopy-jump-kick thing. It was mayhem, and no doubt contributed to my choice of career. Anyway.

I have written here a little story about how a lesson should feel *to the student.* This is written from the perspective of a relative beginner. The lesson should feel like a series of waves getting more and more challenging, then relaxing a bit, and ending on a triumph. I've deliberately left the weapon-specific detail out to make this more easily adaptable.

The instructor was kitted up in his full padded teaching rig, so I knew the lesson would be intense enough to push me into error.

"When the line is open, hit me," he said, his voice a little muffled by the steel over his face.

We started out quite gently. He kept moving, so I had to shift about to get in range. The difficulty was increasing bit by bit until I was working pretty hard. Sometimes the opening would be there while I was just out of reach; other times it would close just too soon. Whenever I struck him I heard a happy "Yes!" from him, and every time I went for an opening that wasn't there I felt and heard a tap on my own protective gear.

He gave me the signal to pause, and we put our heads together so I would hear the next instruction.

"Same drill, but if I try to hit you, parry and strike."

We separated and he immediately threw a blow at my head, which clanged off my mask. Bugger. I knew better than to stop though and parried the next one, but I couldn't quite manage to hit back. I was off balance and ill-placed to strike. I backed off a little, and I had time to parry and strike the next time he came in. Result! He in turn backed off a little, leaving an opening I could hit into – so I did. Got him again! Then bang! His sword connected. He paused us to say:

"Keep your attention where it belongs: the threat and the opportunity."

And we were back at it. How did he know that I had been

thinking about my successes instead of the threat of his sword?

A busy minute-or-so later we paused again.

"You have difficulty covering yourself after striking. Let's work on that. First drill. You attack."

We squared off for the set drill, and sure enough I noticed that I was a bit off balance after my attack, due to over-commitment, which left me open and vulnerable...

The lesson would continue from here by taking that one basic flaw, easily seen in a familiar context, and improving it there before applying the same skill (fully committing without over-commitment) in more challenging circumstances. At the end of the lesson the student has hit the master perhaps 300 times, the master has hit the student perhaps 30 times, and the student can clearly feel an improvement has been made.

## *Writing about Swords*

Swords have a magic all their own. What other tool has attained the same place in mythology, history, and fantasy? What else comes in such an incredible array of shapes and sizes? Even the most cursory glance over the breadth of sword types and designs that have actually been employed in earnest would make you despair at the stunted imagination of the average fantasy sword creator.

This of course gives rise to a simply staggering breadth of jargon, which poor writers will use in place of description. Most people know what a rapier is, more or less. But a makhaira? Yes, well done you Greek scholars or weapon nuts. This sword is *famous* but nobody has heard of it. Alexander the Great fought at Gaugamela with the makhaira given him by Kition, King of Cyprus. When the Apostle Peter used a sword to cut the ear off of one of the servants of the high priest (John 18:10) in the Bible it was, in the original Greek, μάχαιρα: makhaira. When it is written in the mighty King James version of the Bible that Jesus said, "think not that I am come to send peace on earth: I came not to send peace, but a sword," (Matthew 10:34) it is again a makhaira. But put that into a novel and you are flat guaranteed to send 99% of readers out of the zone and off to a dictionary or the web, where they will end up sucked into a whirlpool of meaningless chatter and free porn. Hopefully so only after they discover that the makhaira was popular from about 400 BC, and was a longish-for-the-period-but-short-by-our-standards forward-curving sword, good for cutting, that Xenophon recommended for use by cavalry in place of the straight-bladed *xiphos*.

See the difference:

"Peter drew his makhaira and cut off Malchus' ear."

Versus

"Peter drew his cavalry sword, and struck at Malchus, the forward-curving blade effortlessly slicing his ear off before Jesus intervened. He wiped the blood off the makhaira's blade and resheathed it"

Of course there is no guarantee that the original author had any idea what type of sword Peter carried, nor whether he meant makhaira as a specific morphology rather than a generic word for sword. These days we expect writers to be specific but, to get back to rapiers for a moment, "rapier" *was never used by the Italian authors who described its use in its period.* Capoferro and others just used the word *spada*: sword. We all know that the rapier is long and pointy with a complicated hilt, but long and pointy was just what swords were like to Ridolfo and his colleagues.

So how should swords be described? Other than the culturally specific matter of decoration, the key elements of sword design are as follows:

- length
- weight
- mass distribution
- blade shape
- and hilt type.

A longer sword allows you to reach further at the expense of manoeuvrability. It requires more skill to be accurate when thrusting, and it will tend to be slower to make disengages (where you take your point to the other side of your opponent's blade). You can hit harder when cutting, but the action takes more time. A longer sword offers your opponent a longer lever to work with when the blades are in contact. It also requires more space in which to work, and is harder to draw or conceal.

A heavier sword hits harder, energy being equal to mass times the square of speed, but it is slower to move because it offers more resistance to acceleration. A heavier blow is harder to parry, and a heavier blade is less likely to be deflected by clothing or other impediments.

How the mass is distributed in a sword is more important than its overall weight. A lot of mass near the tip makes it hit like an axe, but also makes it handle like one. The point of balance is the best simple predictor of handling: too close to the handle and the blade is dead in the hand, too close to the point and the sword is unwieldy. Most swords, in my experience, balance about three to eight fingers down from the crossguard. Three fingers down for a light, fast, thrust-y sword; eight for a war-like engine of doom.

The shape of the blade has a significant impact on its use. In general, curved swords cut more efficiently than straight ones.

The backwards curve of a saber or katana is optimal for slicing cuts. The forwards curve of a kukri, or indeed a makhaira, is superb for hacking with. Straight swords are easier to make and are generally easier to thrust with accurately. Most swords are wider than they are thick, and can cut and thrust very well. The exceptions are blades with a triangular cross-section such as the medieval estoc and the late 17th-century smallsword, both of which can only really thrust effectively. Headsman's swords, such as that used on Ann Boleyn, were traditionally point-less, being used only for cutting. (The idea of a "cut and thrust sword" is equivalent to the idea of a "go forwards *and* turn corners car." Sure we have drag racers that don't corner and electric cars that don't go, but in general cars all do both.)

Hilt design is usually classed as either "open" or "closed." In other words, are there bits of metal protecting the fingers or not? The classic knightly sword with a cross hilt is open; the aforementioned rapier is closed. This is, of course, a matter of degree, with a sword-stick having no hilt at all and a Scottish broadsword having a completely enclosed hilt.

We should also be clear at the outset that sword design is never just pragmatic. Until the notoriously ineffective designed-by-committee sabers of the early 20th-century (I'm thinking of the thrust-only 1908 British cavalry saber) nobody ever started from first principles and figured out the "best" general sword design for killing people. It is *always* as much about fashion, money, status, and culture as it is about creating a working tool. Even the gloriously excellent 1796 Pattern Light Cavalry Sabre, designed by (it is said) the famous cavalry commander Major-General John le Marchant, is fit for a specific purpose (slaughtering French infantry from horseback). I use mine for opening champagne, but it would not fare well against a man in armor. When we come across an innovation in sword design, such as the widespread adoption of the knuckle-bow in the 16th century (which has saved many a modern finger from being broken), we wonder why it was not developed earlier, but there is no simple answer. People just didn't want them, fingers be damned! There are technological innovations, of course; however, while they may have a great effect on sword production costs and quality, they don't generally drive design.

The main differences, I think, between fantastical weapons developed for actual use and those made purely for entertainment are the robustness of construction and the general understanding of the use to which the weapon will be put. Human ingenuity will find solutions to all sorts of problems, from how to stab someone and *not* kill them (see *point d'arret*) to how to do maximum damage with a single thrust (see the *cinquedea* shortsword). The range out there is truly vast.

We need some kind of classification system to bring order to the galaxy of sword designs. To start with, when is a big knife a small sword? There is no generally accepted guideline so I have my own. As a blade gets longer leverage becomes more important when defending against it. There comes a point where it makes practical sense to distinguish in your opponent's sword between the half closest to the handle, which is strong, and the half closest to the point, which is weak. This is because the length of blade provides you with a lever with which to work . All swordsmanship systems I have trained in divide the blade into at least two parts: strong (fort, forte, etc.) and weak (foible, debole, etc.). Some systems divide it into three, some four, and one even divides it into twelve! (That would be Thibault, of course.) This is relevant where the sword is being used for both attack *and* defense; the distinction is moot where defense is primarily taken care of by a big shield. This is because the shield can passively absorb the energy of the blow and does not necessarily have to move the sword out of its original path.

In my experience, strong/weak becomes a useful distinction somewhere around the 20 inches (50 cm) mark. Blades this long or longer behave like swords: those shorter behave like knives. Think of the Roman legions standing in line behind their shields with short stabbing swords (such as the Pompeii gladius): this iconic sword is, in my terms, a dagger. Alternatively, think of the medieval German *grosse messer* (big knife), which its users thought of (evidently) as a knife, with its 36" blade and two-handed grip: I'd call it a sword.

## Brust's sword

Let's look at an example of a fictional sword. I love the works of Steven Brust, especially the *Khaavren Romances*. It's a beautifully written homage to the works of Dumas. He is the only author I have read who breaks the rules and gets away with it, for instance by having characters in the midst of a duel think long and complex thoughts complete with witty asides and acts of memory. He even manages to get the characters to *talk to each other* during a fight, using flowery language, in spaces of fencing time that would not really be big enough for a grunt. But in the matter of sword design, oh dear. In chapter four of *The Phoenix Guards* he has Aerich order a sword of the following dimensions from a smith: blade length 47 cm, blade width "a uniform three-and-one-half centimeters," weight three-and-three-quarter pounds, and the point of balance "within one centimeter of the guard." Leaving aside the mish-mash of metric and imperial units, what we have here is a heavy, unwieldy spade. The uniform width alone is huge. It's fully 7.4% of the length, which makes this a machete. That would be fine, but a heavy machete weighs about 24 oz, so 1.5 lb. Less than half this monster. The blade being parallel-edged will have a heavy point and so will cut okay; except it is straight and so is not optimal for cutting. The thrusting capability is also compromised by the blade shape, because we must assume a pretty obtuse point. I guess this is closest to the form of a gladius, which should be a maximum of about 2.2 lb, or 1 kg.

The weight is about right for a knightly longsword, 3 ¾ lb being about 1.7 kg, which would have a blade length about 38–40 inches.

So there might be a unit error here (no doubt the fault of the editor), but if it had a blade width in the proportion here it would still be a monster with a blade as wide as my hand all the way to the point: 3.5" is almost 9 cm. I don't see any way to make that shape at this weight.

And that point of balance – oh dear. A sword needs for some of the weight to be forward of the hand, so that actions can be done using momentum imparted by gravity. Many knives, especially smaller ones, balance at or near the hilt, which gives a measure of fine control. A sword that balances this close to the hand, especially one of this weight, will be exhausting to wield, and subsequently imprecise. No swordsman would ever order such a thing.

Aerich specifies the type of forging, which most swordsmen know nothing about, but does not specify what type the guard should be; in this world, though, swords seem to come as more or less rapiers or longswords. This is neither, and so surely the guard should be a simple cross or rapier-like. He uses the terms "hilt" and "handle" apparently interchangeably, unless the guard is to be made of oak. A contradictory and nonsensical set of requirements, all in all, using a hodgepodge of terminology and units, and leaving us thinking that perhaps this Aerich has never handled a blade.

Am I a sword geek? Clearly. Even allowing for the possibility that this passage is deliberately wrong to highlight the unreliability of the narrator, this passage bounced me right out of Dragaera and into WTF territory. Not the inestimable Mr Brust's intention, I'm sure.

## Carrying the Sword

Swords were generally suspended from a waist belt and housed in a scabbard on the non-dominant side (so, on the left for right handers). Daggers, and swords short enough to be called such, are usually worn the same side as the hand that will use them.

The reason for this is blade length. If you snag a tape measure by your right hip and see how far you can pull it out with your right hand, then snag it by your left hip and try the same thing (with your right hand), you will find that drawing across your body allows you to draw a much longer weapon. On me the difference is 90 cm (35") to 130 cm (51").

A favorite fantasy weirdness is the back-carry, with the blade jutting over your shoulder. Using the same tape measure trick, on me this allows a puny 70 cm (28"). So you are either constrained to use a short sword or an incomplete scabbard, or to take the sword off the shoulder before drawing. I'm sure that for simply lugging a sword long-distance, or perhaps for climbing up a wall, folk could and did sling the sword belt over their shoulder, but it has never been the norm because it is impractical for normal use.

There is one notable exception to this in *The Steel Remains* (2008), a fantasy novel by Richard K. Morgan. In this story there is a special back-carry scabbard that the hero keeps his longsword in. It opens like a zipper to let the blade out. (It was made by a race of super-engineers called Kiriath. We are in fantasy territory here, so Morgan gets away with it, but at least he bothered to find a solution to the drawing the sword problem.) You can tell from reading this that he *knows* that back-carrying is silly, but cool, and so he has created a technical work-around.

"Movement again, whoever it was hadn't scared off. Ringil whirled, hand up and reaching past his head for the Ravensfriend's jutting pommel. The sword rasped at his ear as he drew, nine inches of the murderous alloy dragging up from the battle scabbard and over his shoulder before the rest of the clasp-lipped sheath on his back split apart along the side, just as it was made to. The rest of the blade rang clear, widthways. It made a cold, clean sound in the pre-dawn air. His left hand joined his right on the long, worn hilt, the scabbard fell back emptied, swung a little on its ties, Ringil came to rest on the turn.

It was a neat trick, all Kiriath elegance, and an unlooked for turn of speed that had cheated unwary attackers more times than he could easily recall. All part of the Ravensfriend mystique, the package he'd bought into when Grashgal gifted him with the weapon. Better yet, it put him directly into a side-on, overhead guard, the bluish alloy blade up there for all to see and know for what it was. Their move — up to them to decide if they really did want to take on the owner of a Kiriath weapon after all. There'd been more than a handful of backings down in the last ten years when that blue glinting edge came out. Ringil faced back along the path, hoping wolfishly that this wouldn't be one of them."

(*The Steel Remains*, Richard K. Morgan, chapter 7.)

Oddly, there is very little material in the historical sources regarding drawing the sword. Capoferro, for instance, gives us this image:

Under the title "Way to Place the Hand on the Sword" (as I would translate it) he simply tells us to step back with the right foot, and extend your arm (presumably with the sword attached) in prima (above the shoulder); unless you have your left foot forwards, in which case you can unsheathe the sword without moving your feet. If you have other weapons (cape or dagger) then draw your left foot back while presenting the sword in quarta (on your left), to keep the opponent away while you sort out your weapons.

That's it. Nothing at all on how exactly to pull it out of the sheathe, or when it's reasonable to do so. Nothing.

Fiore (bless him) does give us five plays of the sword in the scabbard against the dagger, but in each of them the scabbarded sword is being carried in the hands, either point up or point down. You can see my take on how to do these plays in *The Medieval Dagger*, pp. 148–154.

The original images are pretty clear:

With the sword held point up you parry the dagger attack by striking downwards:

And with the sword held point down...

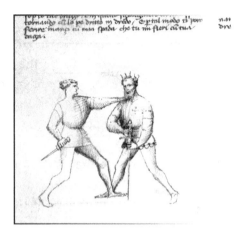

...you can either parry downwards as before or upwards, like so:

Vadi at least does show us one sword-drawing technique, here, again against a dagger attack (what is with these suicidal dagger people?):

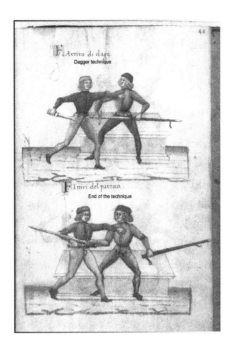

Unlike Fiore's actions, this can be done with the scabbard attached to the belt – as one would expect – but it is not shown that way here.

Domenico Angelo covers the draw briefly, in *l'Ecole des Armes* (1763). This is from the English translation, *The School of Fencing*, produced by his son Harry in 1787, pages 4–5.

"The First Position to Draw a Sword

You must stand straight on you legs, with your body sideways; keep your head upright and easy, look your adversary in the face, let your right arm hang down your right thigh, and your left arm bend towards your left hip; your left heel should be near the point of your right foot, the point of your right foot in a line with your knee, and directed towards your adversary; and, holding your sword towards the dook of your scabbard, you must present yourself in order to draw."

This is clearly not a quick-draw method! He is describing the formal draw at the beginning of an academy bout, perhaps, or a real duel, in which all the punctilios are being observed. He continues as follows:

"In this position, fixing your eyes on your adversary, bend your right arm and raise it to the height of your shoulder, and carrying your hand the to the grip of your sword, which hold tight and firm, turning your nails toward the belt, draw your sword, raising your hand in a line with your left shoulder, and make a half circle, with vivacity, over your head, presenting the point in a line to your adversary, but no higher than his face, nor lower than the last rib, holding your arm straight, without stiffness in the elbow, or the wrist; in presenting thus the point, you must raise the left arm in a semi-circle, to the height of your ear, and single your left shoulder well, that the whole body may be in a profile; which instruction cannot be too closely attended to."

Got that? Good.

The most detailed discussion of this that I can find is in Girard Thibault's glorious *Academy of the Sword* (translated by John Michael Greer in 2006 and published by Chivalry Bookshelf). He devotes chapter 3 to "The Correct Way of Drawing the Sword and Entering Into Measure." Most interesting to me is his instruction to advance on the enemy while drawing, "meeting him with a spirited resolve."

I will paraphrase the instructions for the sake of brevity:

A.   After a few paces forwards, grab your hanger and scabbard with your left hand; step with your left foot and, as it lands, grip your sword with your right hand with your forefinger over the outside arm of the hilt.

B.   Keep stepping forwards; grip the scabbard hard as your right foot lifts. Lift your right foot higher than usual and draw the sword while opening your right hand [yes, he really says that]; pause, your right foot in the air.

C.   Close your right hand, turn the wrist, and pick up your point in a half-circle until level with your shoulder with your point back. Keep your arm slightly bent.

D.   Bring the sword down in an overhand blow as you place your right foot. Step with your left foot and, while it is moving, let the sword carry on down to your hip while you turn the sword in your hand and put your thumb on the inside arm of the hilt. [Thibault has a very non-standard way to hold a sword.]

This goes on for another paragraph and, even with all these steps, you are still not yet in measure!

He also includes instruction on drawing while retreating, captured in images E, F, G, and H.

Note that the draw is always done while out of measure; there are no sources I can find to tell us how to draw quickly when surprised. Perhaps this is because there is nothing to it – you just pull the damn thing out as fast as you can.

I think this is because fast-draw techniques were not traditionally part of the fight: you draw out of measure, and then the duel begins. It was thought cowardly to strike while your opponent's weapon is still in its scabbard. This is in marked contrast to both the Wild West and pre-Meiji Japan, where duels were often begun with the weapons in their holsters or scabbards and speed on the draw was a major component of victory.

## Damage

There are three ways in which the sword does damage: it destroys the body's mechanics, hydraulics, and/or electrics. So the opponent stops working because he cannot move a missing or broken limb, or because he has bled out, or because his brain has shut down thanks to a steel spike being rammed through it.

An opponent's ability to keep fighting is hugely dependent on their psychological state. There are abundant examples of historical duels in which ghastly wounds are given and received, yet the fight goes on. We have this idea that without modern medicine the wounded usually died of infection, but that is exaggerated. There are abundant examples of duellists surviving even multiple stab wounds to the body and head. My two favorite examples of survival despite injury are the Duel of the Hat, between La Garde and Bazanez, and the second duel between the poet Richard Brinsley Sheridan and the dastardly Captain Mathews, in August 1772.

### The Duel of the Hat: La Garde vs. Bazanez

La Garde de Valon was a famous swordsman. He was enough so that a Monsieur de Bazanez sought out a pretext for a duel, found one in some verses that La Garde had written, and presented his challenge by offering his hat to a friend of La Garde's, the Baron de Merville, saying, "take this to your poet, and tell him that I will not take it back again unless I take his life with it." The hat was a magnificent thing, with a huge plume and a beautiful gold cord. When finally they met, Bazanez had his cousin Fermontez with him, and La Garde was accompanied by his younger brother, Mirabel. Alfred Hutton has the story, in *The Sword and the Centuries*, no doubt via Audiguier:

"La Garde is waiting for them. As soon as they appear in sight the two principals salute each other smiling, approach with their hats in their hands, and embrace one another with as many compliments and courtesies as if they had been the best friends in the world. Then they lock up their servants in a barn, and carry away the keys to the ground which they have selected for their field of fight.

La Garde, having told Mirabel to keep Fermontez amused with a bout of rapier and dagger, withdraws some fifty paces to arrange matters with his principal. They engage. La Garde is a splendid swordsman, and lands a thrust right in the centre of Bazanez's forehead; but the skull is a strong one, and the point does not penetrate. Presently he is more successful, for the second takes effect in the body, and he exclaims: "There, that is for the hat!" They begin again, and he lands the third also in the body, adding: " And that is for the plume." They charge each other a fourth time, La Garde crying out: "And now to pay for the beautiful gold cord. Really, sir, your hat fits me to perfection;" and he promptly pays for the said cord in precisely similar coin. Bazanez, badly wounded and thinking of anything rather than hats, shrieks out: "Look to it, or you are a dead man!" then, actuated more by despair than by judgment, throws away his sword, and, taking his dagger in his right hand, rushes upon La Garde and stabs him in the neck. In the struggle they both fall, but Bazanez, being uppermost, redoubles his energy and gives him no less than fourteen wounds from his neck to his waist; but in his death agony La Garde bites off a good half of Bazanez's chin.

While all this is going on, Master Mirabel, the young brother, is amusing himself at rapier and dagger with Bazanez's cousin, and receives from him several thrusts which pass between his shirt and his body without hurting him, but at last sends him back a real one. Fermontez stops, calls out to him: "Are you wounded?" and at the same instant rushes at him, closes, and attempts to wrestle; but the unwounded Mirabel, fresh and vigorous, holds him tight, when the injured lad shrieks out to his principal, who is busy finishing off La Garde: "Cousin. cousin! look to yourself: I am killed." On this Mirabel relaxes his hold, and poor young Fermontez sinks down dead on the ground. Mirabel is a brave boy, and he is excited, too; he calls to Bazanez, who is retiring from the scene: ' Ho, you! you have killed my brother, and I your cousin; let us finish the affair together." But Bazanez, who has regained his sword and also the famous hat, though minus that large piece of his chin which his enemy has swallowed, is already on horseback, and, bowing, says: "My dear boy, your brother was such a splendid swordsman that he has not left anything in me for a fresh fight; I am going to see my doctor;" and away he canters."

## Sheridan versus Mathews

The Sheridan and Mathews affair revolved around Mathews paying inappropriate attentions to Sheridan's fiancée. This account of the duel is from an eye witness, Mr Barnett, and was written shortly after the affair. It is quoted in *Memoirs of the Life of the Rt. Hon. Richard Brinsley Sheridan,* by Thomas Moore.

"... Mr. Sheridan immediately drew his sword, and, in a vaunting manner, desired Mr. Mathews to draw (their ground was very uneven, and near the post-chaises).--Mr. Mathews drew; Mr. Sheridan advanced on him at first; Mr. Mathews in turn advanced fast on Mr. Sheridan; upon which he retreated, till he very suddenly ran in upon Mr. Mathews, laying himself exceedingly open, and endeavoring to get hold of Mr. Mathews's sword; Mr. Mathews received him on his point, and, I believe, disengaged his sword from Mr. Sheridan's body, and gave him another wound; which, I suppose, must have been either against one of his ribs, or his breast-bone, as his sword broke, which I imagine happened from the resistance it met with from one of those parts; but whether it was broke by that, or on the closing, I cannot aver.

Mr. Mathews, I think, on finding his sword broke, laid hold of Mr.Sheridan's sword-arm, and tripped up his heels: they both fell; Mr. Mathews was uppermost, with the hilt of his sword in his hand, having about six or seven inches of the blade to it, with which I saw him give Mr. Sheridan, as I imagined, a skin-wound or two in the neck; for it could be no more,--the remaining part of the sword being broad and blunt; he also beat him in the face either with his fist or the hilt of his sword. Upon this I turned from them, and asked Captain Paumier if we should not take them up; but I cannot say whether he heard me or not, as there was a good deal of noise; however, he made no reply. I again turned to the combatants, who were much in the same situation: I found Mr. Sheridan's sword was bent, and he slipped his hand up the small part of it, and gave Mr. Mathews a slight wound in the left part of his belly: I that instant turned again to Captain Paumier, and proposed again our taking them up. He in the same moment called out, 'Oh! he is killed, he is killed!'--I as quick as possible turned again, and found Mr. Mathews had recovered the point of his sword, that was before on the ground, with which he had wounded Mr. Sheridan in the belly: I saw him drawing the point out of the wound. By this time Mr. Sheridan's sword was broke, which he told us.--Captain Paumier called out to him, 'My dear Sheridan, beg your life, and I will be yours for ever.' I also desired him to ask his life: he replied, 'No, by God, I won't.' I then told Captain Paumier it would not do to wait for those punctilios (or words to that effect), and desired he would assist me in taking them up. Mr. Mathews most readily acquiesced first, desiring me to see Mr. Sheridan was disarmed. I desired him to give me the tuck, which he readily did, as did Mr. Sheridan the broken part of his sword to Captain Paumier. Mr. Sheridan and Mr. Mathews both got up; the former was helped into one of the chaises, and drove off for Bath, and Mr. Mathews made the best of his way for London."

Sheridan made a full recovery and lived another 44 years. Ironically, he had won the first duel and could easily have killed Mathews. But mercy is its own reward.

My point is that our impression of a sword blow being instantly lethal is generally wrong, unless the sword removes, or goes right through, the head. Then, usually, the recipient immediately loses consciousness. But even that may not be fatal as the case of Phineas Gage, perhaps the famous head-wound victim, proves. On September 13, 1848, Gage was foreman of a work gang blasting rock while preparing the roadbed for the Rutland & Burlington Railroad outside the town of Cavendish, Vermont. Setting a blast involved boring a hole deep into a body of rock; adding blasting powder, a fuse, and sand; and then compacting this charge into the hole using a tamping iron. This time the iron struck a spark against the rock and the powder exploded, carrying the tamping iron through Gage's head. The iron entered on the side of his face behind the left eye, and went out at the top of the skull. This steel spike was an inch-and-a-quarter thick, three feet and seven inches long, and weighed 13 ¼ pounds. According to the records, Gage spoke within a few minutes, walked with little or no assistance, and sat upright in a cart for the ¾ mile (1.2 km) ride to his lodgings in town. It did way more damage than a simple sword thrust could, and yet there is no doubt that had this been combat he could have, at the very least, got up again and struck back. He lived another 12 years.

Deaths from a sword blow are, then, rarely immediately fatal, unless they result in decapitation (and if you'll forgive a gory aside: we know that the brain can remain conscious far about 20 seconds after decapitation, thanks to the astonishingly committed scientist Lavoisier. When he went to the guillotine on May 8th 1794, he had arranged with his assistant that after his head came off he would keep blinking as long as he could. He kept it up for about 20 seconds). Even running a sword through a heart might have only a delayed effect. According to a pathologist who came to teach a class on the effects of blades and bullets on bodies at a knife seminar I attended, much depends on the stage of contraction the heart is in at the moment of penetration. If it is contracting, squeezing out blood, then the hole is partly sealed, especially if the blade stays in. But if it is expanding, sucking blood in, then it may basically explode in the chest; leading to catastrophic loss of blood pressure, unconsciousness, and death.

Quick deaths in swordfights usually occurred through decapitation, puncturing the heart, or the severing of a major artery. The body can bleed out in about 30 seconds. Slow deaths were usually the result of punctured lungs collapsing or septicemia setting in. Severed arms and legs were not common, but they could occur. Survival was quite likely if the patient did not bleed out. Bear in mind that until the late 19th century the *only* medical solution to a compound fracture or a seriously infected limb was amputation, which was often survived by the patient.

The mental state of the combatants is usually maximum arousal expressed as rage, especially when wounded. The records abound with tales of men continuing to fight long after a sensible modern person would have stopped and called an ambulance. We see the same thing today when people who ought to lie down and die, given the damage they have taken, just keep going.

There is no pain in the midst of combat. That comes later. Both combatants are likely to be hugely aroused if the fight is mortal, and pain signals from damage just don't register. They have a lack of response to pain similar to that of junkies and lunatics. In my own experience, even in friendly bouts, I will sometimes end up with a huge bruise or a bleeding wound and yet have no idea how it got there. This is why there are no pain controls in combat-oriented martial arts. A come-along hold that works on a not-too-angry drunk has no effect on a seriously aroused person. So techniques usually focus on doing major structural damage (such as Jarnac's slicing through Chastagneraye's hamstring) or being immediately fatal (such as thrusting through the head).

So, when writing a fight, make sure that cause and effect are working properly. Would that damage get that reaction at the time it was delivered?

# CHAPTER SIX

# Gaming

## GUY IS NOT A GAMER. YET.

First up, a confession. I know almost nothing about game design. What I do know I learned either from the book *Characteristics of Games*, by George Skaff Elias, Richard Garfield, and K. Robert Gutschera, or from *Audatia's* designer, Samuli Raninen. Also, the questions posed by the designers of the *Clang* project when I consulted for it lent useful insight into how games work. But I am not, by any stretch of the imagination, a gamer. I play games with my kids, but the last computer game I played enough to get good at was *Chuckie Egg* on a 128KB Amstrad (that's late 1980s, for you young'uns who don't remember Amstrads). I only occasionally play card games: usually poker, at which I suck, or *Audatia*, at which I'll kick your skinny butt. I played some *Dungeons and Dragons*, again in the 1980s but not since, and I've never taken part in a LARP. The closest I've come to that is some battle re-enactment in the late 1990s. So I don't know gaming well. How on earth did I end up creating *Audatia*, the medieval combat card game?

On a Wednesday evening in October 2012 Rami Laaksonen, who has been a keen though irregular swordsmanship student since 2001, came to a rapier class. Rapier is his favorite weapon by a mile. After class, we got talking about how hard it is for some swordsmanship students to remember the basic terminology and theory of Fiore's *Art of Arms*. Sure, it doesn't help that it's all in Italian. Medieval Italian. With funny spelling. I don't recall why we were discussing Fiore rather than Capoferro.

Rami suggested putting the terms on flashcards. After all, the average kid can remember about a trillion Pokémon characters so why not sword moves? This brought to mind the enemy recognition cards used by the Armed Forces. In WWII it was German planes and ships; in Afghanistan these days it's pictures of wanted terrorists. G.I. Joe is constantly being reminded of what the enemy looks like while he is playing poker. So why not make swordsmanship playing cards?

Then Rami said, "why not a game?"

And a student passing by chipped in: "I'd buy it."

Rami said, "but I can't design games." I said, "I can't draw. So we'll have to hire people who can."

But we had no money. Fortunately Rami was enrolled at Haaga-Helia college doing a business degree, and they had a start-up grants program. It would be enough to get us started, if we could persuade them to part with some cash. We went there together; with my background in running my own company and a fairly large international following, they handed over €5,000, which could only be used to hire expertise. No quick trip to the Apple store for us.

I then put Facebook to work and, having posted that I was looking for a game designer, about a dozen game designers popped up out of the woodwork. One student of mine has a brother-in-law who is a massively successful game designer. He met with me a couple of times; in the end he was too busy to take the game on, but he gave us some good advice. (That's the problem with successful folk. People keep asking them to do stuff. And paying them properly.

Damn.) Then Samuli Raninen, from a small company called *Games and Tales* based in Oulu in the north of Finland, got in touch. I explained what we needed. For about four thousand euros, we wanted a game prototype with which we could raise money on Indiegogo. I had a short track-record on crowdfunding at that point: one "failed" project that nonetheless delivered and one "successful" project, which I had also delivered on. But I had no track record with games, and neither did Rami. Nobody would believe for one second that we could create a game together, and rightly so. To convince people to part with their hard-earned, we would have to show them that the game was done. So, a working prototype was essential. We would also need sample artwork, which would sell the game more than any other single thing.

Samuli's interest was piqued, and he came down to Helsinki for a meeting. He knew nothing about swords except that they are cool, and so he listened carefully and asked questions. In less than half an hour, the basic idea of how the game would work was there. It was astonishing to watch.

Fortunately, *Games and Tales* had not one but two geniuses on staff. Jussi Alarauhio produced glorious prototypes, and for tiny money (in game design terms) we launched our campaign to coincide with the biggest gaming convention in Finland: Ropecon. We were very careful about timing our campaign. Ropecon, an event at which I had been doing swordsmanship demos and giving well-recieved lectures ("Realities of Steel") for a dozen years, happened at the start of our campaign; GenCon was right in the middle, and just before the end was WMAW, which is a very popular swordsmanship event where – again – I am well known. So we had lots of opportunities to plug our campaign and many, many people stepped up to help. They thought the game idea was cool and they knew, because we had our prototype ready, that it could actually work. For example, when I asked on Facebook if any of my friends would be going to GenCon, an event that we really wanted a presence at but had no money with which to send someone to, four people volunteered. We sent them prototypes and played the game with them over Skype, and off they went: our guerilla campaigners. One even played the prototype with the head of gaming at Kickstarter. A young man came up to me after my demo at Ropecon and said he was having trouble backing the game. I asked what the problem was, and he said:

"I can't decide between the €3,000 and €25,000 perks. What would I get for my €25k?"

"What do you want?" Was all I could think of to say.

Then I explained that, according to the rules of the campaign, we couldn't offer him equity in the company, but that he could have pretty much whatever he wanted so long as he didn't ask us to compromise the historical fidelity of our game.

In the end we agreed that his own company, *TK Creations*, would "present" the game like a movie producer, and he would be consulted on all major decisions; further, should the game do well, he would have an opportunity to invest in the company. All in addition to getting his own deck and, of course, copies of everything we do.

So Rami and I had the money, the designer, and the artist, and the game was a go. Now all we had to do was make it, and that's where the real challenge lay. Getting every nitty-gritty detail as accurate as possible and noting where we had to bite the bullet and compromise for the sake of playability was really, really hard.

For example, Fiore clearly and without ambiguity states that the guard *posta di donna* can make all seven blows of the sword. Allow that in the game, though, and nobody would ever use any other guard. So in the game *posta di donna* can't make all seven blows, but only the ones that I would normally do from there: the ones it's best at. Damn, that hurt.

And of course, we have delivered. Later than expected and with no extra cash for fripperies like, say, paying the founders any money at all, but the game is done. I can lay my hand on my heart and say that this game is the most accurate possible representation of Fiore dei Liberi's swordsmanship style within the constraints of a card game. My contribution to all this was just checking every single detail of interaction: determining from my research and experience what would happen when X meets Y. Our genius designer has managed to incorporate all the key elements of swordsmanship, including some degree of what happens when the blades meet. This is the key thing that every other game fails at. In a normal swordfight computer game you can strike and you can parry. There is no nuance at all. In real life the swords interact with each other when attack meets parry. Sometimes the attack is beaten wide. Sometimes you get stuck in the middle. You get to swing your arms about with platforms like the Wii, but if you are parried on the screen your arms don't just stop: they swing through. That doesn't usually happen in real life. Samuli incorporated this in *Audatia* by having icons on the top edge of each card that either line up, indicating that the swords are bound together, or don't, indicating that the parry has beaten the attack wide. He also introduced placing the cards on the table in such a way that the motion of the sword in space is tracked. Strength is a factor too: if the swords are bound together the stronger player can choose to let the weaker push his sword one way, or he can push his opponent's the other way. This is done by orienting the "Bind Side Card," and it determines what close-in techniques either player can play next.

Are your eyes glazing over yet? Yes, we sacrificed a lot of easy-entry playability for the larger goal, which was to model Fiore's art in a playable game. The most obvious aspect of this is that we have kept the Italian terminology. That was the first thing *everyone* said: lose the Italian or lose half your players. We kept the Italian because that's the original point of the game. We plan to produce easier-entry games using simplifications of the same core mechanics, but this is our flagship. Play the game and you will learn the terminology, tactics, and techniques of the *Art of Arms.*

So my experience in gaming is limited to helping game designers represent swordsmanship in their games. I tell them how it is; they represent it according to the needs of their game. Samuli was working for Rami and I so, at the end of the day, I could overrule him on points of accuracy versus playability. That was never needed, though, as he was as keen to make it authentic as I was. It was quite different at *Clang!*, where I was a hired expert with an opinion but no skin in the game. They were deeply keen to get it authentic, but I had no actual voting rights in the way the game was put together.

## DIGITAL V ANALOGUE

So how does swordsmanship track in a game? As I wrote on July 15th 2013:

Swordfights are resolutely, absolutely, analogue. It is random, chaotic, and non-linear to a degree. But for centuries – millennia even – man has been imposing order on the chaos, cataloguing the actions, naming the techniques, and systematizing the art and practice of combat. This begins with taxonomy, such as naming the positions swordsmen use or find themselves in, the blows that they strike, and the various ways in which they defend themselves. Understand this, though: there are really no hard and fast rules. If I am in position A and you are in position B, and I attack with a strike X and you are supposed to defend with action Y; you might do the right thing and win, do the right thing and lose, do the wrong thing and win, do the wrong thing and lose, do nothing and win, do nothing and lose, or do any of the above and come to no conclusion.

I have consulted for enough game designers to know that the only accurate answer to any of their questions is "it depends," but what they need and demand is a hard and fast instruction: if X do Y.

Games are, in their underlying mechanics, always digital and usually binary. So making a sword fight in a game model mirror a sword fight in reality is basically impossible. It can't even be done sword-in-hand at the salle, even if we were using sharp swords, because the critical stress of having someone actually trying to kill you is absent. (I go into this in detail on pages 186.) But we can make the game such that the action sequences in the game precisely model those in the source material. The game can represent the ideal of the Art in a way that cannot be replicated in messy reality. So, we cannot be accurate but we can be true.

Let's look at the blows of the sword. Fiore describes "seven blows:" six cuts – forehand and backhand blows that descend, rise, and go across the middle – and the thrust. The thrusts are "of five types" – forehand and backhand, rising and descending, and one up the middle. So a total of eleven defined blows. He even goes so far as to determine the paths of the blows: fendente (descending), for instance, "breaks the teeth, exits at the knee, leaving a sign of blood."

Fiore's lines for the descending blows.

There is our paintbox: the multiple possible strikes broken down into two main types (cut and thrust), further subdivided into forehand and backhand, and then again into seven lines. The rising thrust is neither forehand nor backhand. This is a gift to game design because we can just use these ready-made definitions. Our game has all of the cuts exactly as described. We reduced the thrusts to just forehand and backhand because we would otherwise be swamped with blow options, and in practice, sword-in-hand, the critical distinction to make when defending against a thrust is the side from which it originates.

Every now and then in freeplay someone will actually use one of the blows, just like in the book. It does happen. Every now and then. But usually the line is a little off, the exact path not quite as illustrated. So then what? When does a mandritto (forehand) become a roverso (backhand)? Where is zero? And how many people have perfect plumb and can see exactly where the line goes? And when does a fendente (descending blow) become a mezano (middle, horizontal blow)? At five degrees above the horizontal? 15? Of course, in real life experience and training tell you when you can treat a blow as if it were a fendente and when you must treat it as a mezano, taking into account a hundred extra details of which its path is just one. Beginners learn the rules and follow them precisely, or they fail. Advanced students break the rules successfully all the time. Swordsmanship is a spectrum phenomenon.

So let us think of the light spectrum. It is obvious that purple is not blue, green, yellow, orange, or red. But where exactly does blue become green? Only judgement can answer in this area, and it will vary from person to person without anyone being demonstrably right or wrong. But for the purposes of children playing with paints, or indeed an instructor teaching swordsmanship to beginners, the spectrum is useless. We take exemplar versions of the thing in question and treat it as the thing itself. The blue in the tube of paint, the line of fendente in the book before us, becomes the "correct" version, the only true one. And this is what happens when swordsmanship meets game design. Nuance is lost: the thousand, thousand subtle variations and shades are forced together under one lump heading. And that is fine. It's what we do for beginners every day in the salle.

The over-simplifications we use for communicating the Art to beginners are useful. So, while a game based on swordsmanship cannot ever truly replicate the Art there is no doubt in my mind that it is possible for such a thing to be a fair representation of the Art in another medium. Simulators for flight training are not flying, but they are very useful in pilot training. The difficulty we face when translating analogue swordsmanship to digital gaming is precisely where to draw those lines: how to chop up the spectrum into a paintbox.

The blows were an easy example. Flowcharts of move and counter-move are much, much harder. This is not least because they presuppose that every technique attempted will be a reasonable facsimile of the technique intended: something which anyone who has ever seen a fencing match, let alone a real swordfight, knows is pretty unlikely. Deriving general rules from the Art to the game is not hard. Most swordsmanship styles have at their base an "if he does this, do that" heuristic structure. But any decent game must allow a degree of uncertainty. As I mentioned above, when the imaginary attack and parry meet in *Audatia* there is a built-in randomizer that determines whether the attack was beaten wide or remains close; thus determining whether the defender can strike freely or must enter in. Neither player can control this; although, the defender is in a better position to affect it because he can see which side the icon is on and he can take the icon into account if he has options as to which parry to make.

We also introduce uncertainty by limiting the number of cards in the player's hands. This reduces the number of blows the players can make in a way that is not realistic, but it is a necessary condition of the game. There would be no gameplay if we allowed every player to make every blow whenever they felt like it. Instead, we would have an endless round of bish-bash-bosh, with no real structure or tactics. It would also be impossible to hold all those cards in your hand at once.

There are compromises that have to be made within the constraints of a card game, which are unnecessary when holding a sword. But, on the other hand, there are compromises we make in training to avoid killing our training partners that are rendered unnecessary by the non-lethal nature of the cards (we have killer art, but not killing cards).

## ADVICE TO GAME DESIGNERS

I hope it is clear from this book and others that I know my way around swordsmanship. However, I cannot possibly know anything about the game you are designing. So my best advice is this:

1.  Decide beforehand what you want the swordfights in your game to do. Are they the point of the game (such as in *Audatia*, where winning the swordfight wins the game); are they about character development (showing good and bad characteristics through behavior under stress); or are they about narrative (beat this swordsman to get to the next stage of the story or the next level in the game)?

2.  Decide how important authenticity and realism are to you. It may be the be-all and end-all, as it was for *Audatia*, or it may be utterly irrelevant. Or somewhere in between. If your game has Spartans fighting Samurai you *know* that it ain't historical, but you might want every detail of the Spartans' panoply to be period-correct.

3.  Decide on the optimum length of the fight. Is it over in a couple of blows so the character can grab the loot and run,

or is the narrative of the fight itself as important as the narrative of the game?

If the fights are supposed to have a narrative then follow the general guidelines I give here for writers. It's fundamentally the same. Find period examples. Work out the technical content you want to include. Create narratives of attack and defense.

If the fights are supposed to just work well enough to get the character to the next level then I can't really help you, because it doesn't really matter what the content is. But if the techniques and tactics are a key element of the game itself then there is an awful lot of real-world-tested swordsmanship out there for you to draw on.

# CHAPTER SEVEN
# Training

## HOW TO GET IT RIGHT FIRST TIME: PRACTICING FOR STATE OF MIND

This post addressed a key issue that most people encounter at some point. Performance deteriorates under pressure, but many things are a one-shot-only deal. This goes for swordsmen especially: one missed parry can be fatal. Here's how we do it.

Posted on 14th August, 2013

We had an interesting time in the "intermediates" class this week. (Those scare quotes are to point out that, after all these years, we should probably be calling it the Advanced class.) We started out to address the problem of freeplay devolving into tippy-tappy shit. You know the thing: right leg leading, no passing at all, sniping out with snappy little cuts from a middle guard position, and point in line. That sort of sport-fence-y, speedy stuff that has nothing to do with the Art as Fiore represented it in his book. But here's the thing; it is far and away the best approach when fencing for points, which is why sport fencers do it. And that is what fencers will do in any kind of competitive fencing environment, because it works. But we are not creating sport fencers here, we are training martial artists, so we had to come up with a way to make our free-fencing practice more useful.

We started with the usual set-up, which is one person taking on each member of the class in turn, but we did it in the following way: we only tried to create first drill, with a designated attacker and defender. When a blow was landed, at whichever step of the drill, the combatants had to maintain awareness of each other and retreat out of measure without dropping their guard.

- In round one the defender had to stand their ground, and the attacker had to approach from out of measure and attack with a committed *mandritto fendente*.
- In round two the defender could work from any guard.
- In round three the attacker could attack with any blow.

Needless to say, we almost never saw first drill in its basic form. All sorts of things went "wrong," and most of the fighting that ensued was done in the proper measure and with proper commitment. The idea of the set drill was enough to shoe-horn the students into a better approach. There was no tippy-tappy shit at all. Maintaining focus after a blow was struck and you were safely out of measure was perhaps the hardest thing for most, so we worked on that. (I made reference to the way Koryu students do their drills: bow out of measure, enter into measure, do the drill, retreat with total focus, and bow again. We need more of that in class, I think.) The drill was for both students to approach into measure simultaneously with agreed attacker and defender roles, do first drill without pause and, passing each other, retreat under cover until out of measure again. Change roles and repeat.

216

The first few rounds were not good. So we had a discussion on mindset, and suddenly it got a lot better.

This is a common problem in just about every advanced class I teach. The first round of anything is crap so we have a short chat, and then it gets much, much better right away. This means that students are entering the class in the wrong mindset. Obviously, in any martial art you only get the first opportunity to win because if you lose once you die. There are no practice runs, no rehearsals. State of mind is *everything*.

It can only be my fault if a whole class is doing something badly. I must not have trained them in the necessary skill. So we had a look at the key techniques for establishing a desired state of mind: visualization and focus. Naturally, we have drills for developing these skills!

We started with visualization, choosing images that generate a specific state. We started with injustice, to generate anger. Think of any injustice, and the state of rage begins to build. Then we thought of a rose, which calmed them down. Then the person(s) you love most in the world. Three different states of mind in as many minutes. So, then, how to focus? For this we used the "awareness of breathing" meditation. Breathing is usually so boring that normally you don't think of it at all. Requiring yourself to simply notice every breath is really hard: the mind naturally wanders. So the practice is to *gently return your attention to the intended object.*

We then chose images that represent the desired physical attributes of a swordsman. The class chose grounding, agility, relaxation, and balance. Each student chose something that symbolized these things to them, and then practiced keeping that image clearly in their mind's eye.

Then the mental attributes: the class chose calmness and relaxed, focused attention. Each student chose something that represented the desired state for them, and practiced keeping that image clearly in their mind's eye.

Then they combined these images, if applicable (there were some pretty funny mash-ups). The idea is to create a personal symbol that represents the ideal physical and mental virtues of the perfect swordsman, and to be able to meditate upon it for a few minutes to establish the optimum state of mind for training.

We then got up and did the same drill as before. It went much better, of course.

To finish up, I asked them to think about this practice, and to develop their own image to meditate upon to generate the correct state of mind before class. Every class.

## YOUR TRAINING TOOLBOX

November 19th 2013

It has been my experience that beginners feel they have learned something when they get to try a new technique, but experienced students of the art feel they have learned something when they have identified and corrected a flaw in their skills. This is normal and the student is correct in both cases. It can seem daunting to a beginner to look at our basic syllabus and realize just how much new material there is to learn, but it can also be frustrating to a more advanced student to feel that they have done it all before so there is nothing "new" to be learned. Both states of mind are unproductive, and both have at their root a lack of understanding as to what the syllabus is for. So I shall explain.

I guess most of my readers know that I used to work as a cabinet maker, and I still do woodwork as a hobby. So let me offer an analogy, based on woodwork, for the syllabus problem above.

The purpose of the syllabus, from breathing exercises to pair drills and from push-ups to freeplay, is simply this: it is a toolkit with which you can craft, from the raw material of yourself, the swordsman you aspire to become.

Once a drill or exercise is sufficiently well learned that it does not require effort to recall, it becomes available to you as a tool. So we equip our beginners with a very basic toolkit; just as someone taking up woodwork might buy a set square, a saw, a plane, and a chisel. The drill is effectively useless until it is in memory. We then apply these tools to the business of making swordsmen. The student will acquire new tools as they develop, either of a whole new type (hello, G-clamp) or a variation on one already owned (such as a plough plane). The process of learning new drills is analogous to the process of buying new tools; it's lots of fun and, for some people (tool collectors), is the whole point of the exercise. But owning tools is not craftsmanship. Knowing how to keep them sharp and put them to use is craftsmanship. I am an avid tool-collector in both fields: I have some woodworking tools I will probably never use, and I have some drills from other arts and from the early days of my career that I take out and polish every now and then, but will never actually apply to the business of my improvement as a swordsman.

One of the hallmarks of a craftsman is that they not only have the right tools, but that they will unerringly select the right tool from the rack for any given job. If the job requires a tool they don't have then they will buy it or make it, or change the job. Every cabinet maker has a stock of self-made jigs and tools that they knocked up to get a particular job done. So, in swordsmanship, understanding the problem you are trying to fix means you instinctively know what tool you need, and if you don't have it you either create it or buy it (which for my students equals "ask Guy").

It is also critical to understand your material. Just as a cabinet maker knows that ash is the best material for drawer sides, and that beech is stable and cheap but vulnerable to woodworm, so the student must know their own physical, mental, and spiritual strengths and weaknesses. These will determine what kind of swordsman you should create out of yourself and the tools you will need to do it. Swordsmen are fantastically lucky in that the Art does not require a specific body type. Sure, there are some obvious advantages to being tall and thin if you are a rapier fencer but the best rapierist I ever trained was neither. To ignore her height, in this example, would have been stupid. Instead we made her size an integral part of her style and I have watched her skewer tall, skinny blokes more than once.

A beginner who has a well-earned sense of satisfaction because they now "know" the exchange of thrust is in a similar position to the beginner woodworker who has saved up enough money to buy a shiny tool that they have no clue how to use properly. It is a necessary and laudable first step on the way to craftsmanship. If you were to come along to one of our advanced classes you would see that same drill being put to use, in various contexts, to expose flaws and correct them. One drill can have many uses, of course: it could be diagnostic, represent the tactical hierarchy of the system, be for power-generation, something else, or all of the above.

So, here are a couple of questions.

- Do you know the proper uses to all the tools you have?
- Do you have all the tools you need for your current craftsmanship needs?
- Do you keep them shiny, sharp, and accurate so they can be called on when needed?
- Do you deliberately select the best tool for the job in hand?

If your answer to any of these questions is "no" then see me after class and we will fix it!

## My top three stay-sane-and-healthy tips for modern living

This was first posted on July 22nd 2014. It was my first real foray into writing about lifestyle advice, which is something I spend a lot of time on at the salle given how most of my students' lifestyles are not well-adapted to martial arts training.

One of the great advantages of being a professional swordsman in the 21st century is that nobody can reasonably expect you to be normal. As you might imagine, I engage in all sorts of odd behavior in the name of good physical and mental health, above and beyond simply swinging swords around in a historical and martial manner. Of course I do meditation and breathing exercises – nothing unusual there – and all sorts of physical jerks, push-ups, and whatnot. That's not odd, really: millions of people do those. But these three habits are the ones that our current culture is most skewed against, and so by that standard count as weird.

My top three bizarro practices, from a 21st century perspective, are:

**1) Avoid sugar.**
Reading up on the effects of refined sugar has led me to believe that, after smoking, our addiction to the sugar high is probably the worst thing we do to ourselves. Why is it that we can control and tax alcohol and tobacco as legal, luxury drugs, and not do the same to sugar?* I have tightened my belt by two notches and, most importantly, I have stopped crashing in the afternoons since cutting the sugar high out of my daily routine and relegating it to occasional-treat status. It used to be so that when teaching all day I would have to dose up on sugar mid-afternoon to function. Now

that does not happen; nor do I need a sugar fix to teach in the evenings. We just got through the week-long Fiore Extravaganza, the most exhausting seminar of the year, and I went from start to finish without ever getting seriously physically tired. That's absence of sugar for you. It was my most serious cause of chronic fatigue. And it's in everything! Read the labels on your food. Maltodextrin is one of the very few chemicals with a higher glycemic index than glucose; high fructose corn syrup does not belong in the human body at all; sucrose; dextrose; and anything with -ose on the end: it's all poisonous shit.

And starch is sugar too, sort of.

About five years ago I found out that I am allergic to wheat, which lead me to naturally cut out a lot of starch (until I found all these excellent wheat-free breads, beers, pastas, etc.). It is very hard to eliminate wheat from the modern diet; our entire economy has been based on wheat for three thousand years or so (much like the USA's is based on corn). Simply cutting wheat did wonders for me, if not for the ease with which I can find food I can eat. Cutting out all other starch sources (pasta, rice, potatoes, etc.) has also been hugely helpful. I don't avoid them the way I have to with wheat. I just don't eat them that often – about once a week, or so. Starch breaks down very quickly into glucose, and thus behaves much like ordinary sugar. I eat enormous amounts of proper vegetables instead, usually fried in olive oil and garlic, often with bacon...

Recommended reading: Gary Taubes, and also Tim Ferriss on the Slow Carb Diet.

## 2) Squat.

Squatting on a rock. Note, not actually having a crap.

Really it's astonishing when you think about it: about half of all my beginners cannot squat on their haunches. In other words, they can't take a dump properly. Mankind has crapped in the woods and fields for millennia, and we squatted down to do it. Now we enthrone ourselves in porcelain splendor, and grunt and strain to do what should be easy.

Squatting should be a natural rest position. The human body is built to stand, lie down, and squat. I often squat down to play with my kids, read a book, wait for a bus, or whatever. I squat any time my legs or back are tired. People look at me funny. I don't care. Chairs are a recent, very welcome and excellent in their place, invention, but healthy they ain't. Inability to squat is a modern phenomenon with hard-to-measure consequences. I always find a bin or a block to prop my feet up on when having a crap; it puts my legs in a much more natural position. One of the advantages of having little kids is that there are standing blocks in our bathroom so the kids can reach the tap; these blocks do double duty as footstools in the bog.

Recommended reading: an amusing article in Slate magazine (http://www.slate.com/articles/health_and_science/science/2010/08/dont_just_sit_there.html).

On a related note, I have played around with flat-soled shoes for years. Heeled shoes are needed for riding with open stirrups but not otherwise. Though they can be gorgeous, modern heeled shoes are simply bad for most peoples' back, legs, and feet. Barefoot is better. I tried out my medieval shoes in the medieval town of Verona on a recent trip to see my friends fight in the Torneo del Cigno Bianco. I found them to be a perfect compromise between the ghastly (because very, very ugly) modern barefoot shoes, and decent leather ones. With thin flexible leather soles, they are now my normal footwear in all non-freezing weather. I have yet to find a good flat-soled winter boot and, this being Finland, WINTER IS COMING. Any advice?

**3) Unplug.**

Outside. You can't beat it.

When I was working as a cabinet maker – and more so now as a hobbyist – I used machines to do the grunt work, and hand tools for the interesting and enjoyable stuff. Machines get the job done; tools make the work a pleasure. Using an electric drill is a step too far towards mechanization for some people (see Tom Fidgen, for example); others love the roar as the planer starts up. I am making the distinction not on the grounds of the machine itself, but on the user's relationship with it. Machines to save labor: tools to enhance it. Can you imagine a woodworker who allowed remote access to his table saw to allow his customers, or friends even, to determine when it's on and when it's okay to turn it off? No, me neither. So why do we feel that our friends, co-workers, or clients should have any say in when our own personal pocket phones are to be on or off? Or how often we should check our emails? It's madness! I have my phone on when I feel like it is a tool, a pleasure to use, and a thing that is making it easier for me to achieve my ends. Otherwise I turn it off. I check my email when I feel like it: every hour or so when I am eagerly awaiting a message from an old friend on something I care about, or every day or so just to check in on whatever things other people might want from me; or sometimes not for a few days, or even a week. And you know what? Nobody has yet died for want of an email from me, because nobody's life depends on my work. Your situation may be different, but ask yourself this: what's the worst that could happen?

There are some people for whom I am always on call. My wife, my kids, my siblings and parents, and maybe five or six close friends. They can demand my immediate attention at any hour; with the exception of my kids, they all wield this power with commendable restraint. The rest of the world? Even those lovely people who buy my books, come to my classes, those on whom my livelihood depends (of which group I assume you, as a reader of this book, are likely a member)? Nope. Sorry. There is nothing truly urgent in the world of swordsmanship. By all means contact me: I'm happy to hear from you. Just don't expect me to reply immediately.

Recommended reading: none. Go outside and play instead, or pick up a real book.

So, there are my top three. Bear in mind, though, that these are habits, not laws. I don't expect hosts at a dinner party to cut sugar for me, I do sometimes wear my utterly fab and lovely heeled shoes, my favorite armchair has an imprint of my arse deeply worn into it, and I have been known to check email when I should not. Part of my approach to life is the idea that habits have deeper consequences than one-off or rare occurrences; in swordsmanship training, in health matters, and in general. One cigarette won't kill you, but smoking probably will. I never follow any training routine religiously. For some people, whatever behavioral changes they try need to be thought of as laws, or they find they slip back into bad habits too easily. Do what works for you, and let healthy habits be their own reward. I don't know who's reading this, but I'm pretty sure you're a decent person who deserves to be healthy.

You can't make a living by cutting sugar, squatting, and turning off your phone. You can just make your life much, much healthier. Which makes for a *better* living.

So, what are your top stay-sane-and-healthy tips?

*Sugar in candies is taxed as a luxury in Finland, but not in doughnuts, cookies, etc. It's taxed at the point of sale, not at the point where the food companies buy it. I'd like to see sugar-containing food of any kind sold separately and all of it taxed, like single malt or cigars. It would be too damned expensive for food manufacturers to get us hooked with the white stuff. We'd all be healthier for it, and the taxes would pay for the insulin, cardiac resuscitations, cancer wards, and other medical expenses that our illnesses from our sugar fixation require. Let sugar be the new nicotine!

## Throw off your Mental Chains

This post ties in with the earlier one "The Myth of Talent", on page 85. When I originally posted it on June 25th 2014, raised a few hackles; especially from those afflicted with the disease I am describing. Oh well.

One of the most destructive forces in the world we live in is the "talent" mindset. I mean that literally. It underlies not only millions of minor miseries, but also the core of human evil.

In short, if you believe in innate talent then you believe that some people are inherently better than others. It is a short step from there to believing that some people are therefore subhuman, and we all know where that leads. [This one statement lead to a lot of people getting cross. But it is fundamentally, and absolutely true. If you see character traits as inherent, it is natural and inevitable that you will start to classify people according to their most obvious visible traits. Like skin color, or gender.]

The stimulus for this blogpost was reading Carol Dweck's book *Mindset: The New Psychology of Success,* on the recommendation of my friend Devon Boorman. In short, her work in psychology has demonstrated that belief in fixed traits leads to the "fixed mindset," which creates all sorts of problems. These are solvable by switching to a "growth mindset:" a belief that things can be learned. Go read the book. The bit that struck a chord in me, and literally woke me up to what went wrong when I was growing up, was where she wrote that, for "talented" kids, *effort equals failure.* And that is exactly the problem I had. I could not work hard at anything, anything at all, because if it did not come easily then it threatened my fundamental identity; only duffers have to try. So I only ever did the things that came easy, and I shied away from anything that demanded actual work.

I hope the utter foolishness of this is apparent to all my readers.

I was a star pupil at school. Clever, and everyone knew it. I got all the way up to University entrance without ever once revising for an exam or doing a stroke of work beyond the essays or homework set by the teachers. I was a shoo-in for Cambridge, and I had been told so from the beginning. My younger sister (every bit as clever as me but actually industrious with it; a year younger, but in the same academic year) and I both applied. She got in. I didn't. I was absolutely furious. I had been betrayed. I was supposed to be super-talented. But Cambridge, I imagine, could spot a dilettante when they saw one and didn't need one more arrogant and entitled little shit clogging up their colleges. I got into all my other University choices and chose Edinburgh ('cos it's the best). I then managed to get all the way through University on a combination of luck and blather but, by then, I actually had no choice: *I did not know how to study.*

Yup, I had no idea of what people actually did in libraries across the campus. I read a lot and wrote essays when asked (never more than one draft), but I had no idea how to actually work through difficult problems or come up with solutions and test them against the evidence – all that sort of thing. Rhetoric, logic, and grammar, yes; I could write a decent argument. But nobody had ever taught me how to work things out, how to wrestle a body of knowledge down from *unattainably complex* to *I know this.* It wasn't thought necessary to teach me this because I was "clever." I would have resisted it anyway, because it was equivalent to failure.

Please note that I don't blame my teachers or parents for this. It was genuinely believed back in those dark ages that praising kids for their attributes was good for them. It wasn't until Dweck and others started running actual studies that it was discovered to be so counter-productive. Remember: as late as the sixties, some doctors thought *smoking was good for you.* In years to come people will say with similar disbelief, "they used to praise *attributes* not *effort!!!* How dumb must they have been!" (And yes, they will attribute the mistake to an inherent trait: that is how deep this cancer of the mind runs.)

One advantage of all this not-studying was that it left me with lots of time for training martial arts; I was doing Tai Chi, fencing, Karate and Kobudo in my first year, and it was through fencing that I got into looking at historical fencing sources. Even then my interpretations of historical sources were all about making it fit with what I already knew (parry *quarte* with a longsword, anyone?), and were not a true interpretation of the source.

So how did I escape from this quagmire?

Swordsmanship.

In the year 2000, thanks to some crazy-ass training shit that I am still not ready to write about, I came to realize that *the truth of the art* was more important to me than my own identity as a "talented" person. Suddenly, being wrong was not such a problem (see page 95). My inflated ego got out of the way enough that it didn't feel like I was risking my very self to admit "I don't know this" and "this is hard," and I gradually learned how to study. I learned how to break problems down, how to enjoy a challenge, and how to embrace failure as a necessary step on the way towards mastering my field. Now, I am elated by the learning opportunity when someone hits me in the face with a sword despite my best efforts to stop them. Really. The result was a massive increase in the speed of my improvement.

I could dwell on the decades of wasted opportunities, created by my stuck-ness in the quicksand of the talent mindset, but that would lead to bitterness, not growth. Instead, I relish the feeling of my feet being free to run, trip and sprawl, and to get up again.

As a teacher, then, I have no interest at all in the apparent level of talent in my beginners. None. I am not looking for someone who will win tournaments for me in a year or two: I am looking for students who will grow in their study of the art, from whatever their starting point. In some respects, those who have most trouble learning in the beginning are the most rewarding to teach because their development is that much easier to see. I sometimes catch myself giving fixed-mindset-inducing praise and stab myself in the eye to make it stop (that may be a slight exaggeration). I try instead to praise effort over attainment, and whenever students find the things I give them to do difficult I tell them that I would not waste their time on something easy. The message: easy *is a waste of your valuable time.* Effort *is what matters.*

This is also why I dislike most sports and other physical pursuits. They tend to require a particular body shape to get to the top, such as in ballet. Got stumpy legs and heavy bones? You will never be a top-level ballerina. Sorry. It makes me furious that someone with short legs will never be picked for the solo, just because of the aesthetic of the art. Fuck that for a load of fixed-mindset arsery. Likewise combat sports with their weight requirements, and so on. In these fields some fixed attributes (like height in basketball, weight in judo, and so on) actually matter. This is so utterly stupid and anti-growth it makes me boil, and in my eyes it makes these pursuits fundamentally less worthy.

Swordsmanship is perfect in this regard. There is no ideal body type. Whatever yours is, you can fight on equal terms so long as you take your relative sizes into account. Sure, tall people can reach further but their arms break easier. Wrestling with people who are bigger and stronger than you is really hard (and is therefore a great learning environment). But if you can gouge out their eyes, as Fiore would have us do, then the strength difference is less critical. Think little folk can't take giants apart? I give you the Gurkhas.

It is true that "natural" talent in certain fields appears to exist. In some sports, there are people who do astoundingly well for a short while and with little effort. But, actually, if we were to plot performance over time between the plodder (someone with no actual handicaps, just an apparent lack of talent but who is willing to work hard) and the natural, the graphs look like this:

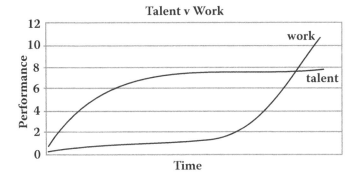

Depending on the activity and the degree to which genetics play a part, the point at which the lines cross can be at the beginners' course or world championship levels. But cross they will. Early performance is simply no predictor of long-term achievement in any worthwhile field. This has been demonstrated over and over in books like Malcolm Gladwell's *Outliers*, Matthew Sayed's *Bounce*, and Anders Ericsson's work studying violinists (which spawned the much misunderstood 10,000 hour rule. 10,000 hours of practice it not sufficient unless it is mindful practice. Plus you also need luck: no career-ending accidents, for example).

That by itself should be enough to get people to drop this talent nonsense, but it goes deeper than that. For some reason, probably related to saber-toothed tigers and an evolutionary quirk in human cognition, we prefer to believe in inherent traits over learned skills. Think of the utter nonsense of inherited power, which is based on the idea that the inherent trait of being descended from the current ruler makes you the best candidate for being the next one. (Don't get me wrong: I'm a monarchist through and through – there is just no fun in the republican way – but there is no good reason for monarchy to be hereditary.)

So why do people continue to believe in talent? It's for two fundamental reasons:

1.  We tend to praise attributes over effort, and to attribute results to innate factors rather than processes. It's the outcome over process problem all over again. So kids grow up believing that some people are just naturally gifted. This is partly true, but it's also wholly inaccurate and wildly counter-productive.
2.  Attributing success to talent gives us an excuse to fail. He did well because he's a natural; therefore, my failure is not my fault. I am just not naturally good at it.

Make no mistake about it, this is toxic thinking.

Praising talent makes less glamorous kids feel like failures before they even try. And it makes the stars associate effort with failure. It is disastrous for both groups. One gives up and the other *cannot* work systematically to improve. I know this because it happened to me.

As a parent I have had many, many moments of heart-swelling pride in my kids, and a very few moments where I felt I was a good-enough parent. One such moment came while watching a really good ballerina on TV with my younger daughter, who was then four years old. She loves ballet, and she was in awe of this ballerina. And she said in tones of wonder:

"She must have practiced *really a lot!*"

## Forms, Intervals, and Skill Progression

This article was written and posted online way back in March 2008, long before the blog existed. Much of it remains current, though.

Martial arts, by and large, are systems for applying a theory of what should work best in combat when under the extreme duress of the combat environment. Those of us working with research-based arts (as compared to living traditions, where the source is the instructor) often lack training in that most vital component of taking the art from the page to the duelling ground: training methodology. There is not much use in knowing how an action should be done to save your life and take your opponent's if the command to do it gets stuck between brain and body, leaving you standing by helplessly as your opponent applies what he can actually do. This article is meant as a guide to my students that are taking classes or running branches, and is perhaps of interest to other martial artists as well. In it, I outline some basic components of training: solo form, pair drills, skill progression, and interval training. Conditioning – preparing the body to execute all of the above – is taken for granted (as I trust all my students are working from the conditioning guidelines in the syllabus). For specifics of individual drills, or forms, readers should refer to the syllabus as published online.

### Form and Function: using solo forms for martial training.

If you have ever been working on a martial technique with a partner, had trouble getting it, and taken a break to work through the motion required on your own in the hopes that it would help you do it in the partner drill, then you intuitively understand the main point of using set forms to practice martial arts. There are arts that do nothing but form and others that have abandoned form practice as useless. Most lie somewhere in between. It has been my experience that forms are a training tool and, like any other tool, if used correctly they are very useful; if used wrong they are a waste of time.

Form practice is often shrouded in a great deal of pointless mystique: "practice this form diligently, grasshopper, at 7 a.m. and

7 p.m. for seven years, and you will become unbeatable," saith the master. Grasshopper duly does this and is then thoroughly annoyed when he gets pasted in his first fight. This article is intended to describe the underlying theory of the forms practice we do at my school in the hopes that my students will better understand why we do things the way we do. It is also intended to give those outside the school some useful ideas about training the forms they know, or about writing forms to help themselves practice whatever art they are interested in.

Well-constructed forms are comprised of techniques, connective steps, and conditioning exercises, assembled according to an aesthetic typical of the art to which they belong.

The techniques are applications, and are supposed to work against specific attacks in specific directions. If you don't know the applications, in detail, you're just doing choreography.

The connective steps allow the techniques to be put together into some kind of pattern, which is usually determined by the presence or absence of multiple opponents, the size of the training space, and, in some cases, aesthetics.

Conditioning exercises such as jumps, rolls, and spins may be part of the fighting techniques, but they are more usually included to build strength, agility, and power. Some forms are adapted purely as conditioning exercises, the primary purpose of the form being to improve health and strength rather than to convey martial skill.

Whatever form you practice it is vital to understand not only every application of every step, but also what is included for the sake of the pattern and what is for health or conditioning. Practicing forms without that knowledge is like practicing a language phonetically, with no idea of what the sounds actually mean. You may make some fatally embarrassing mistakes when finally using the language in conversation.

Forms are usually written to encapsulate one aspect of a style, or the whole style. You can usually tell which by seeing how many forms you are expected to learn. The form(s) provide a zip-file – if you will – that, when practiced, drills the artist in the most important actions of the style and serves as a notepad or table of contents for the rest.

There is some evidence to suggest that forms have been used in European martial arts since their inception, but very few descriptions survive. The Bolognese tradition (from 16th century Italy) has the richest vein of forms detailed in the surviving treatises: Marozzo's "Assaults" and Dall'Agocchie's "way that one must follow when stepping in the said guards" (page 11 verso) spring to mind as obvious examples. As Dall'Agocchie says, "this stepping is one of the chief things you must practice if you want to have grace with weapons in hand." (12 recto, translation courtesy of Jherek Swanger.)

There are, in my experience, only two types of student: those that practice and those that don't. Those that practice invariably spend at least as much time training on their own as they do with a partner, simply because partners are hard to find at home, at the office, waiting at bus-stops, and so on. Solo training is a vital part of learning any skill, and form is uniquely adapted to making solo training effective. We can't always have a partner available, nor necessarily much space or time to train in. Knowing a few forms allows a student to get the most out of even a short practice; it provides a clear structure to follow and a source of ideas for further training. While doing a form the student might notice that their thrusts lack power, and so is inspired to go spend some time thrusting at targets. Or they may notice that their stance is weak and go do their dedicated stance work, etc. Even if all they practice is the form then, if that form is well conceived, they will cover all the main points of their style, and will have spent their time profitably. Nothing can replace partner work in set drills or sparring, but nothing can replace solo technical practice either.

I usually teach our forms as a sequence of applications that are drilled with a partner before adding to the form. So, we would start with the application of step 1 and practice that in pairs, and then practice solo. We then cover step 2 as a partner drill, then solo, and then as part of the form (steps 1 and 2 together, plus any connective steps necessary). When writing a form I try to keep connective steps to a minimum and have at least 5 or 6 applications strung together without them, to start with. This process continues (often over several practice sessions, especially for a longer form) until the form is complete. If we are talking about normal human beings, the students will by now have forgotten or elided at least some of the steps, and so it is vital to keep the applications fresh by periodically practicing them in isolation.

Once the form is learned the student can start working on polishing the details: where exactly should the left foot be and why, what guard position does this blow finish in, how extended are the arms at this stage of the attack, etc.

We introduce repetitions at different speeds when the form is reasonably fluent:

1. "Treacle speed." Very slow, as if wading through treacle. This builds stability and strength, and gives the student time to notice as many details as possible.
2. "Walking speed." A comfortable pace at which the form remains accurate. This gives a sense of the flow of the form and its rhythm, and should be quite relaxing.
3. "Fast." As fast as possible. This builds speed, obviously, but also highlights the slippage-away from clean technique that speed inevitably brings.

As an idea of the speeds involved: our longsword syllabus form at treacle speed takes me about 1 minute, 30 seconds at walking speed about, and about 25 seconds at fast speed. Most seniors have a walking speed about 30–38 seconds. With long practice treacle speed gets very, very slow and walking speed gets faster; fast gets quicker too, but, most importantly, gets more precise.

All this focus on the form in isolation can lead to the applications falling by the wayside. So once the student can go through the form at a reasonable pace, cleanly and quickly, we introduce partners who will give the correct attack or other stimulus at the correct measure and correct time, while the person in the middle goes through the form. The form goes in several directions so multiple partners are needed to save time on the partner running around to the right place for the next technique. Ideally the flow of the form, and its content, is identical with and without these assistants, but in real life there is always some slippage.

So we introduce the time element. Let's say we have four students, A, B, C, and D, all wearing light protective gear. A starts and goes through the form at walking speed, which is timed. A takes 32 seconds from start to finish. We add a 5 second margin, and allow him 37 seconds with partners. B, C, and D, if they know the form well, will know exactly which line each attack should come in and at what distance, and which steps are attacks themselves. So they should in theory be in the right place at the right time, and doing the right thing. Ha. The form with its applications is then timed, and everyone does one push-up for every second over the 37 allowed. This eliminates a lot of faffing about on the second run through, which is usually better. Next we time B, and A, C, and D are the assistants. And so round we go. By the time everyone has been in the middle they should all have a very clear idea of which applications they had forgotten, and which of their partners caused them the most push-ups through forgetfulness. It creates an element of stress, which helps the students concentrate on the essentials: making the applications work.

This exercise is invariably followed by several rounds of slow form, which allows the students time to include the things they learned from the timed rounds into their solo work. I find this greatly improves the students' ability to practice the form effectively; the applications are drummed in under pressure, and form becomes associated indelibly with function. It also gives a very clear idea whether the assistants know the form properly or not. If they do the right place to stand and the right thing to do for the next step are obvious, and require no real thought. Students caught not knowing where they should be have only a superficial understanding of the form; exercising it this way does more than any number of solo repetitions to help the student internalize what each step is for.

Once the students really know the form it becomes a mnemonic aid: not only for the specific applications, but also the general principles and classes of technique in the system. For instance, step 2 of the syllabus form is a roverso fendente blow. This acts as a chapter heading "cutting practice," under which the student can write "pell practice," "tatami cutting," "tyre striking," "cutting drills x, y, and z," etc. This serves primarily to remind the student to go and do all those things, but also to remind the student that the blow in the form is the end product of all that training; and so it must represent the edge alignment learned on the tatami, the power generation learned on the tyre, the ability to move directly into other blows learned in the cutting drills, etc. Step 1 has even more potential depth: the defense of the sword in the scabbard against a dagger strike. This serves as the chapter heading "dagger plays," and/or "drawing the sword," and/or "segue sections" (those parts of the treatise that connect one section to another, including the Bastoncello plays: dagger against sword, sword against dagger, sticks and dagger against spear, etc. See my article "A Swordsman's Introduction to Fior Battaglia" for more details); a huge body of material worthy of a whole set of other forms. This provides a useful class tool in that we can go through the form and then split the class into groups: each group working on variations, alternative applications, and related material, for a given step. We can work through the form step-by-step this way, or allocate a different step to each group. We call this process "unzipping the form."

Learning forms is a skill in itself. Students who come with an extensive background in form-based martial arts can usually pick up the syllabus form from start to finish in 15 minutes (provided they have enough basic training that the actions themselves are familiar). Those learning their first form usually take many hours spread over many days – even months. There is an intrinsic advantage to learning forms in that it trains the memory for other things, and develops the mind's ability to notice and record patterns. This is one of the reasons that I incorporate forms of varying lengths and types across the syllabus.

Lastly, we move beyond form by creating spontaneous, free-flowing technical sequences, using the form as a starting point. Our syllabus form has three techniques done from tutta porta di ferro: rompere di punta, rebattere, and the colpo di villano play. When going through the form any one of those techniques can be done any time you find yourself in that guard; likewise there are a range of actions done from posta di donna la sinestra, any one of which can be done whenever we arrive in that guard. So the individual applications, variations, and alternative actions from particular guards – indeed any action within the Fiore syllabus – can be blended into a seamless, endless progression of techniques using the form as a base, a starting point, and an end.

## Interval training

Form practice is also one of the simplest venues in which to introduce the idea of interval training, in which the intensity or complexity of the practice increases and decreases with an overall increase over the course of the session. This is standard practice in most training environments, both within a given session and between sessions. In short, start easy and get harder. Ease off when it is becoming too hard, but not all the way back to the starting level. Increase the intensity again from there, and get past the previous hardest level. Then go back a bit, but not as far as before, etc, etc. This is most easily illustrated in a graph: the Y axis shows intensity level (however it may be measured; examples include heart rate, weight lifted, number of repetitions, speed of repetitions, complexity of material, etc.), and the X axis shows time.

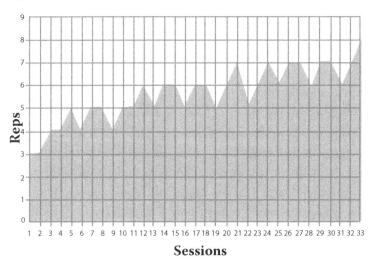

**Sessions**

The bottom line (0–24) can be read as units of 5 minutes for a 2 hour class, 24 consecutive classes on different nights, 2 years counted in months. Note that the peak at x=15 is flattened. This shows a training plateau, which is broken through on the next run-up. These figures are not exact, obviously, but represent the idea of interval training. My own training tends to go in waves of about 6 weeks of increasing intensity followed by a relaxation period of light training, and then a further 6 week build-up starting higher up the scale than the previous. I also run every class in this way, with gradual build-ups and slow-downs.

240

So, when using the form for this you can, for instance, do 5 repetitions of increasing speed from treacle to fast; then a 1 minute break; then 5 repetitions from walking to fast; 1 minute break; then 5 fast; 1 minute break; then 6 repetitions from treacle to fast; and so on. See how far you get. If you make it to 10 start the next session with 6 reps, and build up to 11, etc. Replace the breaks with super-slow repetitions once you're starting with 10 reps per set. This becomes viciously hard fitness training with built-in technical and tactical training. Sometimes it's fun to end up as a quivering wreck when you finish training.

If you find you hit a plateau, from which you cannot improve to the next target, the trick is to fall back a couple of paces and take another run at it. Let's say you're doing push-ups; you want to be able to do 50, but at the moment 20 is the limit. So, start at 16 for a couple of days and then add one per day until you hit 19 (just short of the present limit). Then reduce back to 17, build up to 21 (hurrah! One limit gone!), and then back down to 18, etc. You keep this up until you hit 32, where you get stuck. After a couple of days of trying, drop back down: not to the previous starting point (probably 28), but to the one before (27), or even further. Then take another run up at it. With luck and hard work, you should pass 32 the next time you get there. This principle applies equally to form training and swordsmanship training in general: when you hit a plateau, go back down a few steps (this is the only solution I know to the perennial problem of the intermediate's plateau, where a relatively senior student gets stuck at the same level for months, feels he cannot improve, and quits in frustration because he does not know to take a couple of steps back). The solution to the problem you are working on is rarely in the problem itself, but is more usually in the steps that lead up to it. Cross-reference with the compound counter-riposte drill (see below) shows the principle at work in a technical drill context.

*Freedom by Degrees: developing core skills into freeplay.*
All serious martial arts have set drills as part of their training curriculum. Most also include sparring at some point earlier or later in the student's progression towards mastery. How any given art views freeplay, sparring, or whatever you choose to call it, determines its nature. Some view it as basically unnecessary (for them, the art is the drills), some view it as the single best indicator of a student's progress, and some view it as the sole measure of success. In my opinion, freeplay is essential in the same way that having spontaneous, unstructured conversation is eventually necessary when learning a foreign language. But how many native speakers understand the structure of their own language?Sparring is always at least somewhat unrealistic when it comes to European swordsmanship arts. The arts are usually intended to ensure victory in mortal combat, but we cannot have fatalities in training. So, while sparring is the closest we ever come to duelling it is not, and cannot be, a truly accurate simulation of the duel. We have our historical sources to tell us what works when losing is death; we cannot know, without breaking several laws and abandoning common sense, whether what we are practicing is equally effective. However, sparring will tell us something about how well we can execute the techniques we practice in a more random context. Perhaps the most important indicator of whether a school practices a martial art or a combat sport is whether the students train to become good at sparring, or spar to become better at training. Modern sparring contexts are pretty far removed from historical duelling reality (which had its own rules of engagement, like all combat scenarios), and so a club or school that emphasizes success in sparring as the primary goal of training has developed a sport out of an art. There is absolutely nothing wrong with that, nor anything particularly modern about it: combat sports are as old as martial arts and have always been closely related.

Things change somewhat when we consider the interpretive

nature of the current state of western martial arts. The process goes like this:

1.  find a source to work with,
2.  develop canonical physical interpretations of the plays and techniques in it,
3.  extrapolate the cardinal principles (if they are not directly discussed),
4.  compare and contrast the source with others of the same lineage and others of the same period, and
5.  develop a training regime for becoming proficient in the system.

For most of the medieval sources, and many of the later ones, we are still at the stage where the canonical interpretations of the core plays are changing, sometimes quite radically. As new information comes to light, or we simply begin to understand something that was obscure, we have to go back and re-evaluate our previous ways of doing things. Sparring is useful in this context only because it can sometimes bring to light mechanical or tactical errors in our working interpretation. If we are truly interested in finding out what the masters of old were doing then the phrase "it works in sparring" can be abandoned altogether as irrelevant. They, by and large, were not concerned with what works in sparring, but what works in the duel. However, if an interpretation follows the text, looks like the pictures (where available), follows the core principles of the system as discussed or discovered, makes tactical and mechanical sense, and after drilling it extensively it works in the context it was supposed to when that spontaneously occurs in freeplay, then it's probably right.

So, assuming we have a canonical interpretation and basic set drills to practice it in, what then? Going directly into sparring is like taking someone learning English as a foreign language and entering them for the debate team at the point where they can say "Hello, my name is Henri." Instead, we must gradually introduce levels of complexity. I will use two systems, from sources 200 years apart, to demonstrate the process: Fiore's *Fior Battaglia* and Capoferro's *Gran Simulacro*.

Let's take them chronologically, and begin with a set drill developed from each book.

## Il Fior di Battaglia (1409)

Fiore gives us a clear tactical structure for his system, defined by the four masters of battle. First is the attacker; second, the remedy master who defends against the attack; third, the counter-remedy master who, having attacked, beats the remedy; and fourth, the counter-counter-remedy master who beats the attacker's counter. The plays usually show just the remedy master (who defends against an attack with a cover); he is followed by his scholars who, after a successful cover, do nasty things to the "player" who has attacked. Every now and then we see a counter-remedy master, and he beats either the remedy master himself or one (or more) of his scholars. (Some counter-remedies work only against a specific play; others work against the cover itself and so prevent all the plays that would otherwise follow it.) Let's take some concrete examples and build a set drill that encapsulates the system.

The set-up: Attacker stands in posta di donna, and the defender in posta di dente di zenghiaro.

1. Attacker attacks with mandritto fendente.
2. Defender covers with a roverso sottano (stepping offline to his right with his right foot), beating the attacker's sword up and to the right, and then cuts down mandritto fendente to his head (folio 33 recto).
3. Attacker allows his sword to be beaten aside, keeps the hilt

244

forward, and enters underneath the defender's fendente; he extends his left arm forward, wrapps the defender's arms in his left, and executes a pommel strike to the face.

4. As the attacker wraps, the defender takes another step off the line with the front foot and collects the attacker's wrapping arm in a ligadura sottana.

So now we have a four-step drill with every action predetermined. This must then be trained until it is fluent. No variations, no alternatives. The most common error in set drill is thinking past the technique you're actually doing: if going through to step 4, the defender's fendente gets forgotten or the attacker's pommel strike becomes a vague nudge. The best cure for this is twofold. Firstly, step the drill so that every time you go through it you start with just step one. Reset, and go steps one-two. Reset, and one-two-three. Reset, and one-two-three-four. Then back to the beginning again. One, one-two, one-two-three, etc. This sets up the logic for every action clearly, before you have to do it. Secondly, pay attention, and if you feel that your partner is not properly executing his action because he is anticipating your counter then leave the counter out. I often stand still when my partner expects me to cover and watch his blade hover a meter away from me, out of measure, and ask him when he is actually going to attack.

Then we add a degree of freedom at one step in the drill. The nearer the beginning you allow the freedom, the more the drill will change. We usually start at the remedy: at step two, the defender can either do the basic form, strike to the attacker's hands after the cover, strike with the point to the face, enter with a pass and a pommel strike, enter with a half-sword thrust, or step away and cut to the attacker's arms instead of covering. This should be practiced with no counter-remedy on the attacker's part to begin with. So we now have five new little set drills. The attacker can counter when both partners are comfortable with the options available. This counter will of course vary, depending on the remedy. If you find that the counter-remedy for any given remedy is not working then create a new set drill and take your counter-remedy from whatever part of Fiore's system offers the closest context. At this stage, the counter-remedy must occur after the cover (except against the cut to the hands, which replaces the cover).

Now the fun begins, and the remedier can counter the counter-remedy; indeed he should choose his remedy so that if it fails he can pull off the counter to the most likely set of counter-remedies. This is the beginning of learning to apply tactics to your decision-making.

So, with one degree of freedom we already have an incredibly complex and varied drill. The attacker's counter-remedy will vary, but not freely; he has to wait for the cover, and can only attack in one line. This is already a good test of how well you understand the system you are studying. Can you, as an attacker, cope with all the sensible remedies from that position? Can you, as a defender, cope with all the counter-remedies that the attacker may pull off? If at any stage you find a combination where one of you reliably fails (for example: I attack, you cover and enter with half-sword, and my counter-remedy doesn't work), take it out of this context and drill it on its own as a set drill. Re-evaluate your choice of counter if neither of you can make the technique work in a set drill.

Now apply this process to each step of the drill in turn: the set-up (donna to zenghiaro); the attack (mandritto fendente); the remedy; counter-remedy; and counter-counter-remedy. Allow only one step to be free, though. We can add another degree of freedom once that has been drilled in. For example: the attacker can come in with any blow, and the remedy can be any of those discussed above (cover and cut, cover and thrust, attack the arms, etc.). Make sure that in this process every technique is recognisably Fiorean as best you understand them: using his guards, his tactical approach, and his actions and plays.

After each step up in complexity return for a while to the basic, set form of the drill, and create new set drills to fix any technical problems that may occur. Don't forget to allow a degree of freedom at the end (i.e. in the basic form that would be the attacker's counter to the ligadura sottana, if he can think of a sensible way to do it). So neither partner knows how long the drill is: four steps, or five? This establishes the idea that choreography is not to be too heavily relied on.

Notice that the tactical logic to each action is very clear, and that both parties are holding at least two steps in their head. This is the beginning of learning tactics.

This process culminates in a drill where each party can choose their own guard position, either one can attack however they like, the remedy can be whatever the defender chooses, the counter-remedy is likewise open, and there is no set length to the drill. You keep going with counters and counter-counters until either you separate with no conclusive blow struck or there is a clear, finishing action on one side. That's called freeplay. Or sparring.

## Gran Simulacro (1610)

The usual set-up in this system is one fencer standing in guard (let's call him the patient); the other approaches with a stringering (let's call him the agent); the patient responds, usually with an attack by disengage; and the agent parries and ripostes. The next level is the patient disengaging with a feint, which the agent falls for, tries his parry, and gets stabbed.

We begin with a set drill that exemplifies the system: the first play of the book, shown on plate seven.

The set-up: patient and agent out of measure and standing on guard in terza.

1.  Agent steps into measure, stringering the patient on the inside in quarta.

247

2.   Patient disengages and attacks, lunging in seconda.
3.   Agent counter-attacks, turning his hand to seconda and striking the patient as he comes forward (parrying and striking in a single motion, also with a lunge).

So far so good. The next step should be to allow the patient to disengage with a feint, because Capoferro says so, holding his body back as shown in the book. The agent goes to parry and strike, and the patient parries and ripostes. As with the previous drill, this should be practiced until both parties can execute both sides of the drill. I would also recommend stepping the drill (one, one-two, one-two-three, etc.).

Now we introduce one degree of freedom: the patient can disengage and attack, or disengage and feint. The agent will get hit if he falls for the feint: if he doesn't, he can just step back. We can enlarge that degree by allowing alternative responses to the stringering: the patient can attack with a disengage-beat, with a disengage-beat-feint combination, etc.; all of which the agent has to deal with.

The second degree of freedom would probably be the choice of guard in which the patient waits. Capoferro makes frequent reference to specific waiting-guards determining the choice of stringering, and hence what happens next.

One particularly useful set drill I developed for use in my school is what we call the compound-counter-riposte drill (the term comes from classical fencing. It means a riposte with at least one feint made after your attack has been parried and you have parried the defender's riposte).

It is fairly long but, when set up and running, it makes an excellent base for adding degrees of freedom.

The set-up: patient stands on guard in terza, and agent stands out of measure in terza.

Step 1:
1.  agent steps into measure, stringering the patient on the inside in quarta. Patient does nothing, and the agent extends and lunges.

Step 2:
1.  agent steps into measure, stringering the patient on the inside in quarta; and
2.  patient disengages and attacks, lunging in seconda.

Step 3:
1.  agent steps into measure, stringering the patient on the inside in quarta;
2.  patient disengages and attacks, lunging in seconda.; and
3.  agent parries in seconda and ripostes.

Step 4:
1.  Agent steps into measure, stringering the patient on the inside in quarta;
2.  patient disengages and feints, extending in seconda;
3.  agent parries in seconda; and
4.  patient disengages to quarta and lunges, striking the agent.

Step 5:
1.  agent steps into measure, stringering the patient on the inside in quarta;
2.  patient disengages and feints, extending in seconda;
3.  agent parries in seconda;
4.  patient disengages to quarta and lunges; and
5.  agent parries in quarta and ripostes.

Step 6:

1. agent steps into measure, stringering the patient on the inside in quarta;
2. patient disengages and feints, extending in seconda;
3. agent parries in seconda;
4. patient disengages to quarta and lunges;
5. agent parries in quarta and ripostes; and
6. patient recovers and parries in quarta, and ripostes.

Step 7:

1. agent steps into measure, stringering the patient on the inside in quarta;
2. patient disengages and feints, extending in seconda;
3. agent parries in seconda;
4. patient disengages to quarta and lunges;
5. agent parries in quarta and feints;
6. patient recovers and parries in quarta; and
7. agent disengages and strikes.

Step 8:

1. agent steps into measure, stringering the patient on the inside in quarta;
2. patient disengages and feints, extending in seconda;
3. agent parries in seconda;
4. patient disengages to quarta and lunges;
5. agent parries in quarta and feints;
6. patient recovers and parries in quarta;
7. agent disengages and strikes; and
8. patient parries in seconda and ripostes.

Step 9:

1. agent steps into measure, stringering the patient on the inside in quarta;

2. patient disengages and feints, extending in seconda;
3. agent parries in seconda;
4. patient disengages to quarta and lunges;
5. agent parries in quarta and feints;
6. patient recovers and parries in quarta;
7. agent disengages and strikes in seconda;
8. patient parries in seconda and ripostes; and
9. agent recovers, parries in seconda, and ripostes.

Step 10:
1. agent steps into measure, stringering the patient on the inside in quarta;
2. patient disengages and feints, extending in seconda;
3. agent parries in seconda;
4. patient disengages to quarta and lunges;
5. agent parries in quarta and feints;
6. patient recovers and parries in quarta;
7. agent disengages and strikes in seconda;
8. patient parries in seconda and feints;
9. agent recovers, parries in seconda; and
10. patient disengages and strikes in quarta (the compound counter riposte).

It looks like a lot when written out like this, but this is actually a pretty simple drill requiring only the following techniques: the stringering, disengage in both directions, lunging in seconda and quarta, parries of seconda and quarta, and a feint in both lines (an extension followed by a disengage, change of hand position, and lunge). In my experience students that cannot follow the logical progression of this drill (attack with a feint, parried; riposte with a feint, also parried; counter-riposte with a feint) are not yet ready for even light freeplay because they cannot follow the actions as they occur, nor plan their attacks.

The first degree of freedom to insert is at the beginning: by stringering on the other side, the whole drill repeats itself with quarta and seconda reversed. Then perhaps allow an action in contratempo at a given step, instead of a parry-riposte.

This drill also lends itself well to creating a flow drill, in which there is an endless round of riposte and counter riposte: each with a feint (feint, disengage, lunge, parry, parry, feint, disengage, lunge, parry, parry, etc.). This serves as an excellent test of a student's ability to remain technically accurate after multiple actions. It can then be used to create opportunities for the more advanced actions (parry and riposte in a single time, avoidances, etc.) to be drilled, which brings me on to the question of skill progression.

## Skill progression: how do we develop our core skills?

Everything begins with set drills. He does this, I do that, and he does the other. This is the best vehicle for acquiring a basic competence in the mechanical actions of the system you are training in and an idea of the tactical choices that the system emphasizes.

We usually begin with the basic mechanical action done on its own to the air (for example, cutting from frontale to longa, lunging in quarta, or whatever). We then put this in the context of a target, either inanimate (a pell, the wall target, etc.) or a live partner. We then demand the same action as a response to a given stimulus: in these cases, the partner attacks on the inside line and we parry (frontale or quarta) and riposte (cut to head, lunge in quarta). We then increase the complexity of the situation in which the action is to be performed, be that as part of a longer drill, as an option at a given stage, or in freeplay.

Perhaps the single most useful tool for developing the skill to execute a particular action is the flow drill. Every action sets up the conditions for the next one so we can either choose a context where the actions should remain identical, or choose one where we are expected to adapt our actions according to the changing circumstances. I will take two specific drills in use at my salle to illustrate these two approaches. They are the rapier flow drill based on the riposte with a feint as described above, and the dagger disarm flow drill built up from three of Fiore's dagger disarms.

Let's take the more mechanically conservative first.

Here's the compound riposte flow drill:

1.  set up the compound-counter-riposte drill as above;
2.  at step 10, agent parries and feints;
3.  patient parries;
4.  agent disengages and attacks;
5.  patient parries and feints;
6.  agent parries;
7.  patient disengages and attacks;
8.  agent parries and feints; and
9.  repeat from step 3.

So now we have a continual round of parry, feint, disengage, lunge, recover, parry, parry, feint, disengage, lunge, etc. On its own this presents quite advanced technical challenges to most students: maintaining proper measure, proper parrying technique, the correct execution of the lunge, and so on; not to mention disengaging without fouling your point on your partner's hilt. Only when you can maintain the flow for at least half a dozen rounds, without losing your form, should you break it.

Breaking the flow: once the flow is established, choose one of you to break it with an action that prevents the drill from continuing by resulting in a successful strike. The usual first choice for a break is an action in contratempo in place of the second parry. For example, parry your partner's feint but, as he attacks, parry and riposte in one tempo, preventing him from recovering and parrying. Once both partners can do that at will on both sides try breaking with a contracavazione: when he feints, parry and, as he goes around your parry with a cavazione, follow his blade with a contracavazione; striking him, again in contratempo. If that's easy, try pulling off a scanso della vita, scannatura, or any other play you are working on.

Counter the break: when you are working on a technique used to counter an action (like the scanso della vita, for example), using the flow drill gives you a venue for finding out whether you can see the action coming in time to counter. First drill the action in its normal context (for example: agent stringers on the outside; patient attacks by cavazione; and agent counters with a scanso della vita) and then in its counter (agent stringers on the outside; patient feints by cavazione; agent does a scanso; and patient parries and enters), again as a set drill. Then add one degree of freedom. Patient can attack or feint, and agent does the scanso only if he believes it will work (i.e. he has fallen for the feint). When that is working nicely set up the flow drill, which agent will break with a scanso. Patient counters if he sees the scanso coming: otherwise he gets hit. Patient should try to set agent up to fail.

So, we have a formula for training. Set drill leads to flow drill, which leads to breaking the flow, which leads to countering the break. Every action is drilled in isolation and tested in the flow.

So, let's apply this to the dagger disarm flow drill (which is described in detail on page 125 of *The Medieval Dagger*).

1.  Agent attacks mandritto;
2.  patient disarms using first play of first master of dagger (same in Getty and Novati);
3.  patient attacks roverso;
4.  agent disarms with the first and second plays of the third master of dagger (shown in Novati only);

5.  agent attacks with sotto;
6.  patient disarms using cover of the ninth master (same in Getty and Novati);
7.  patient attacks mandritto; and
8.  go back to step 2.

With practice this becomes a seamless, unbroken motion of disarms and strikes, with no pauses to reset. If you do get hit then just keep going. Stop only if the drill starts to break down. Of course, these three techniques must be drilled in isolation before being put together into the flow drill. The drill should also be stepped through a few times (1, 1-2, 1-2-3, 1-2-3-4, etc.) before establishing the flow.

You will notice that, after a round or two, the starting position (usually left foot forward for both parties, in measure for the pass) is long gone, and you are executing techniques with the "wrong" foot forward, moving in the "wrong" directions, and so on. If, though, your core interpretation is correct you'll find that the principles that make the techniques work are simple and easily applied in different contexts: break his structure on contact, control the weapon, leverage to disarm, and strike immediately.

Fiore tells us (on page 11v) that there are five things we must know to do with the dagger: disarm, strike, break his arms, lock and counter-lock, and throw him to the ground. The flow drill has plenty of disarms so break it with a lock, an arm break, or a takedown; whichever you are working on. If you know the counter to that technique then set up the flow, set up one partner to break it with whatever remedy you are working on, and see if you can pull off the counter.

Then begin adding degrees of freedom, such as you can attack in any line after each disarm; you can use alternative disarms; you can break with the attacker's counter-remedies, as well as the variations on the remedy; you can switch hands; and so on. You have the entire contents of the dagger and abrazare sections to play with.

Pretty soon this begins to look like freeplay, which it can become. Given that we are using the dagger it is important to distinguish between freeplay and preparation for street defense. In street defense work we are usually looking at surprise attacks, in which case it is vital to have a single, simple response to the threat (often referred to as the flinch). In Fiore's system, and even more so in Capoferro's, the core system is not designed as a street defense flinch but as training for some kind of arranged combat. Surprise is not the primary threat that these systems deal with. So, while it is absolutely fine to adapt our historical systems to modern contexts, we should be careful about mistaking freeplay as I am describing it for street-fight preparation.

The last step in the process of skill progression, adding degrees of freedom to freeplay, is to return to the beginning. Always finish up with slow, careful, and technically precise iterations of simple drills. It is your proficiency at the simple actions that determines your ability to use them in complex situations, so always return to the source and repair any damage to your form that the more free-form training may have done.

## STRIKING BY THE NUMBERS

Posted on March 12th 2013, this article addresses the core idea of finding ways to measure progress. "That which is measured gets managed" (as Peter Drucker famously remarked). What is less well known is the next bit: "whether it should be or not". In swordsmanship it is very hard to find measureable variables though, so we measure what we can.

One of the difficulties of training in any art is the lack of measurable feedback. Every body is different, and there is little we can do to provide objective goals. Enter the tape measure.

Readers familiar with my *Max Your Lunge* approach (you can download the article free from guywindsor.net/blog) to developing a good rapier lunge will see where this is going…

In the intermediate longsword class last night we had a small turn-out, which lent itself to some serious measuring. We started by measuring our maximum possible reach, from the tip of the sword to the edge of the back foot.

We then struck at the pell and measured the linear distance on the floor between the back foot and the base of the pell. This gave us a ratio between actual, comfortable striking range and our natural reach. We marked the position of the base of the pell on the floor, to provide a quick reference point. To eliminate the effect of blade length on the proportions, we subtracted the length of the blade (crossguard to point) from both figures. The spread of ranges was huge: including the blade, our tallest could reach 342 cm, our shortest, 288 cm. But the proportions were strikingly consistent.

I then had the class work for 10 minutes on range, doing whatever exercises they thought might help (this is not a basic class). Then we went back to the pell, and the average improvement was about 10%! Clearly, these students did not warm up properly before class.

This gave us a sense of their maximum reach, but what proportion of that would we actually use? So next up we hit the tyres, and when that was working well I went round and measured their reach. An average reduction of 42%. We want to get closer to hit hard.

But what about the threat? So next they did the same blow (mandritto fendente) against a partner who would counter-attack (step 2 of the stretto form of first drill). Out came the tape again.

Now they increased their range from 58% of maximum to 79% of maximum.

So, the *correct* measure to strike from depends on what you want the strike to do, and the tactical circumstances in which it is to be done. There is value in being able to strike comfortably to the maximum reach of your skeleton, but more value in always being in the right place to strike according to tactical circumstances.

The initial lessons from this are as follows:

- Targeted warm-up increased range by about 10%.
- Warm range minus blade length was between 48% and 66% of the foot-to-fingertip length.
- You should be able to reach about 60% of your foot-to fingertip-length, plus blade length.
- Your maximum power range is proportionally about half of your warm maximum reach. This was the most variable measurement.
- When striking against a resisting opponent you will tend to compromise power and reach, using about 80% of your warm maximum range.

So, following are the things to check and work towards systematically:

- Being able to comfortably reach to about 60% of your foot-to-fingertip length.
- Reducing the difference between warm and cold: keeping your body such that warming up is eventually unnecessary to strike at your maximum range.
- Extending the range at which you can strike with power, from wherever it is towards your maximum warm reach.
- Understand the relationship between measure and tactical circumstances: more range = less power, but more time to react

to the opponent's response. Your ideal striking range will depend, among other things, on what you expect your opponent to do. The perfect starting point for the attacker in the basic form of first drill is about 70% of maximum range, but that should be increased to about 80% if you expect a counter-attack. Good luck making that kind of calculation on the fly!

I don't mean to suggest that we should reduce the *Art of Arms* to a set of statistics. But this kind of practice can provide a measurable, objective set of targets to aim towards in certain specific aspects of your skill at arms.

## Bullshit

This was my most viewed blog post ever, with double the hits of the next-most popular, for over a year. It's still #2. Go figure.

8th October 2013

The real thing is the only bullshit-free scenario in martial arts. If you're an MMA fighter it's the ring on fight night, if you're a soldier it's being in the presence of the enemy, and if you're a swordsman it's someone trying to kill you with a blade. But the real thing must be prepared for, so we have drills, exercises, and training. Problems only arise when we mistake one scenario (a training drill) for another (the real thing). To properly understand any drill you must have a clear idea of exactly how it deviates from reality. I call this "spotting the bullshit."

Let us take a simple example of a drill that is usually included in day one of our Fiore beginners' course: the basic execution of Fiore's first play of the dagger. This technique is a disarm done against the common overhand blow.

In its basic set-up, the drill goes like this:

"Both players start left foot forwards, hands down, in a proper guard position. This is very artificial, and is intended only to create a consistent starting point for beginners.

**Disarm and counter**

1. Attacker and defender both in porta di ferro, left foot forwards.
2. Attacker passes to strike with a fendente.
3. Defender intercepts attacker's wrist with his left hand and turns it to the left, creating a leverage disarm with the dagger against the back of his wrist.
4. Defender collects dagger, and strikes.

(You can find it on pages 51 and 52 of *Mastering the Art of Arms Vol. 1: The Medieval Dagger.*)

There is nothing wrong with this as a starting point. But it has, at least, the following dollops of bullshit in it:

1. The attacker is not trying to kill you.
2. The weapon is not sharp.
3. The roles are pre-set: attacker and defender.
4. You can't run away or call the cops.
5. You have to wait for the attack.
6. You are wearing protective gear that will allow the attacker to make contact, but would not work against a real dagger (we tried this with a mask on a dummy).
7. Your defense is pre-selected.
8. The line of the attack is pre-selected.
9. The attacker is not allowed to counter or continue.
10. The attack is done with little force.
11. The attack is done slowly.

I am sure that you can think of other dollops, but 11 is enough to be going on with. So, how do we deal with this? How can we eliminate the bullshit without killing students?

To start with, problem number 1 cannot be trained outside of the real scenario. Don't even try. It is the one element that really makes the difference between those that have done it for real and those that haven't. (I haven't, and I don't intend to.) Regarding combat sports, you haven't done it until you've been in the ring or competed in a serious tournament. Fortunately, those are much more survivable environments so anybody who trains seriously enough can get there and do that art "for real." This is one of the big attractions of combat sports, I think: the real environment is available. I will never forget my first fencing competition. It was an eye-opener, to say the least!

So, if my drill above is so full of bullshit, why do we do it?

It does teach core mechanical principles, such as grounding, finding lines of weakness, and so on; and it teaches core tactical principles, such as controlling the weapon before you strike, timing, and control of distance. It gives beginners a chance to reconstruct a technique from the book, given the source of our art; and it acts as a perfectly good starting point. (Just as a child learning to read by sounding out the individual letters and creating the words is not really reading yet, we don't say that they should just recognize the words straight away. This level of practice is a necessary step on the way to expertise.)

Be aware that this drill does NOT teach a survival skill, or situational awareness,or decision making, or judgement, or the ability to execute the action under pressure.

But, given our list of eleven dollops of bullshit, we can map a route through training to systematically eliminate each of them in turn (except for the first). By applying the "who moves first" multiplier, for instance, we can eliminate point 5; so, the "defender" is not required to wait but can enter or move away, gaining some control over the timing. We can eliminate 7, 8, and/or 9 by allowing degrees of freedom for one or other student. By applying the rule of Cs* you can increase the intensity in a systematic way, and so eliminate 10 and 11.

It is very important not to eliminate all the bullshit all at once; especially when eliminating number 2, by practicing with sharps, you should absolutely keep all sorts of other bullshit present to avoid serious injury.

So, by carefully considering all the ways in which a set drill is not a real fight, you can design variations to the basic version to systematically clean up some of the bullshit. You will need lots of different drills, each with a different bullshit profile, to make sure that you are training in all of the attributes of the "real" technique.

**The "Rule of Cs"** every drill is first worked through with the players:

Cooperating in creating correct choreography.

This means exactly what it says: the students are just cooperating in going through the motions of the technique.

Once that is easy increase the difficulty by increasing intensity or introducing a degree of freedom (e.g. the attacker might vary the line of attack), with one player adjusting the difficulty for the other to learn at their most efficient rate. Ramp it up if it works all the time; ease off a bit if it fails more than twice in ten reps. This is called:

Coaching correct actions

Finally, the players each try within reason to make the drill work for them. When coaching, the attacker would try to make sure the defender can usually counter him; when competing, you just try to make your action work. This can be dangerous if it gets out of hand so be careful, and wear full protection just in case. In practice, the more experienced

scholar should get most of the hits without departing from the drill. This is fine, and it gives a good indication of whether your training regime is working. So,
Compete.

\* (Abridged from *Mastering the Art of Arms Vol. 1: The Medieval Dagger* p. 136)

# Acknowlegements

(Part of this was written as a blog post on 20th September 2012, when my kids were 5 and 3.)

One of the many joys of having kids is their charming misconceptions about how the world really works. For example, both my daughters love driving my car. When bringing them home from daycare, as we get off the public road and onto our parking area, I often take them one at a time onto my lap where they can steer the car while I work the pedals and the gear stick. It causes howls of outrage when I interfere with their steering, but more often than not it is necessary to avoid collision with a tree or someone's parked car. And when the car is finally parked in our spot, whichever little angel was last in command will proudly boast "I did it ALL BY MYSELF!" – blithely oblivious of my input. In a three-year-old, it's charming. In a grown-up, it's obnoxious.

If I chose to edit out a whole lot of data, I could tell you this story about how I'm a self-made man. The company I founded and run operates on three continents, my school was built up from nothing by the sweat of my brow, and, dammit, I did it ALL BY MYSELF.

Um, no. Strictly speaking, the first two statements are true: my company, my school, does operate on three continents, and there was a lot of my sweat involved in getting the school off the ground. But my role was actually not so different to my three-year-old deciding that she wants to drive the car, being allowed to do it, and actually working pretty hard to steer the thing.

Yes, founding the school was my idea. Yes, I am solely responsible for the quality of training, the syllabus, and the development of the art. But I was getting an awful lot of help from before the school was even thought of. My parents, of course, didn't just keep me from starving or dying of exposure. They also went to enormous lengths to have me (and my siblings) educated. My country paid most of the costs of my higher education up to degree level (I got an MA from Edinburgh back when tuition was free so long as you passed all your exams). This education was, of course, critically important for developing research skills and giving me the freedom to train martial arts seven days a week. My interest in swordsmanship was supported and enhanced by the company of like-minded souls in the Dawn Duellists' Society, which I helped found back in 1994. The first treatise I ever discovered and made publicly available, Donald Mcbane's *The Expert Sword-man's Companion*, I found in the State-owned and paid-for National Library of Scotland, which had looked after the treatise for a couple of centuries.

So, all by myself, right?

Then I decided to move to Finland and open a school. I borrowed £10,000 from my bank, which my parents guaranteed. My girlfriend managed to find affordable training space for our first classes through the Helsinki city sports facilities. A friend of mine in England created a website for me for free (thanks again, Andrew). Two of my best friends in Finland at the time (and still today, thankfully) were the best martial artists I had ever met, and one was the best blade-maker in the world (at least I think so. He would disagree). So there was little real risk in setting up the school because if it failed I would still have learned something, and I would have the rest of my life to pay back my parents.

But I did it on my own, yes?

Then, on day one, there were students. Lots of them. People who gave me the benefit of the considerable doubt and enthusiastically supported the school with their presence, their money, and their time. Some of them are still training today. A few months after opening the school I felt the need to go to the USA to teach and train. My friends at ISMAC gave me a teaching spot to begin building my international reputation; my newfound colleagues welcomed me with open arms and a ready blade, and back home a student who happened to have extensive, prior martial arts training took on the responsibility of keeping classes running while I was away. There were students who arranged to host and maintain the website, students who helped find our permanent training space, and students who arranged demonstrations and other events.

But, dammit, all by myself, no?

As the school developed and as my books were written (yes, mostly by myself, but if you compared the first drafts to the finished products and could see the editorial work done by my peers you'd realise how much of the books' success is owed to other people's work), students from far and wide came to me for training, and for help setting up their own local branches. I have never yet deliberately created any branch outside Helsinki: I don't have the time or the inclination. Yet the widespread international character of the school, and its spread within Finland, is beyond doubt, and is entirely due to the efforts of the local students.

Students have been pouring time and effort and skill into the school since it started. Henri created our current website. Ilkka took the photos for, and laid out, my second and third books. Jari

267

took the photos for the *Mastering the Art of Arms* series. At the insistence of my students, I created a formal syllabus. I didn't really want to because it is a ton of work, but I am so glad they demanded it because it has spawned one of the best projects yet: the syllabus wiki. I did not create the wiki: that was Jaana. I did not even buy the video camera. Dozens of people from around the world contributed to an Indiegogo campaign to raise funds for equipment and other costs.

The associations that the school's students have created, and which are essential to the wellbeing of the school, require management and entail legal responsibilities that the serving board members willingly take on. Much of the grant money the school has benefited from wouldn't be coming in without those associations.

But I did this ALL BY MYSELF!

I could go on in this vein indefinitely. But my point is: I and my school have benefited hugely from political and economic factors that we have done nothing to create, and since its inception the school has inspired hundreds of students to support the Art, and the school itself, in all sorts of ways. My job as I see it is to provide the environment in which training can happen, and to lead the research and development side of things. I take enormous pride in the school and its success, but let me be clear: I can't take all the credit. I didn't do it all by myself. I just happen to be the most visible element, the tip of an iceberg of good luck, goodwill, and hard work.

This particular book came from an original suggestion by Neal Stephenson, who also very kindly provided the foreword, and it has been madly improved by the input from dozens of students and friends, too numerous to name here. Denís Fernández Cabrera came up with the original cover design, and Bek Pickard at Zebedee Design did the layout and overall book design. This is the third book she's made for me, and it makes my life very much easier to not have to worry about the layout. Rebecca Judd, editor sans pareil, found and fixed approximately a gagillion typos and other non-standard uses of English (I put the "gadgillion" in here to tease her. And spelled it two different ways just to rub it in).

The costs of producing this mighty tome were covered by a crowdfunding campaign, as is becoming my habit! So thanks are due to the following kind and supportive souls:

Aaron Glimme

Aaron Jones

Adam Surber

Alberto Dainese

Aleksi Airaksinen

Alex Clark

Alexander Foster

Alexander Hollinger

Alexander Sandosham

Allan Stevns

Anders Malmsten

Andrea Morini

Andreas Kammel

Andrew Gilmartin

Andrew J Lackovic

Andrew Malloy

Andrew Mizener

Andrew Moore

Andrew Rozycki

Andrew Somlyo

Andrew South

Andrzej Kuszell

Andy Gibson

Andy Groom

Anette Säkö

Anthony Hurst

Antti Jauhiainen

Arnar Hafsteinsson

Artis Aboltins

Arttu Junnila

Arturo Banda

Ashe Richards

Bastian Busch-Garbe

Ben Holman

Ben Schreiber

Benjamin Ford

Benjamin House

Benjamin Szymanel

Benjamin Vonarx

bidoof

Bittmann, G.

Brian Stewart

Brian W Batronis

Bruce Harlick

Carey Martell

Carter Bush

Cathy Spencer

Cay Blomqvist

Cecilia Äijälä

Charles Deily

Charles Taylor
Charlotte Villa
Chris Bartus
Chris Hare
Chris Lauricella
Christian Engelund
Christoph Busche
Christopher Cooke
Christopher Halpin-Durband
Claire Bodanis
Cody Hartley
Cody Kerr
Culann Farrell
Daniel Blay
Daniel Cadenbach
Daniel Gerszewski
Darko Andreas Zuercher
Dave Kroncke
Dave Wayne
David Britten
David Empey
David Harrison
David Rudd
Dawfydd Kelly
Denís Fernández Cabrera
Dierk Hagedorn
Dietrich Dellinger
Doug Hulick
Dougg Joness
Elizabeth Beyreis
Eneko Villanueva Verdejo
Eoin Brennan
Eric Artzt

Erica Stark
Erik White
Ernesto Maldonado
Evan Ringo
Federico Dall'Olio
Federico Griggio
Florian Cesic
Franklin Walther
Garrett Harper
Gemac – Esgrima Medieval – Porto
George Lewis
Gindi Wauchope
Görner, Michael
Grégoire Dubois
Haris Dimitriou
Harry den Ouden
Heikki Hallamaa
Henry Vilhunen
Ian Tustin
Ilpo Luhtala
Ioannis Papadopoulos
Irene Amoruso
Jaakko Tahkokallio
James Fisher
James Piesse
James Wran
Jan Kukkamaki
Jan Stals
Janne Hurskainen
Jarkko Hietaniemi
Jason McBrayer
Javier Andrés Chamorro Bernal

— Acknowlegements —

Jean-Rémy Gallapont
Jeffry Larson
Jennifer L Corrigan
Jennifer Landels
Jeremy Bornstein
Jeremy Coyle
Jeremy Tavan
Jessica Burley
Jim Steiner
Joakim Westerberg
Joel Norman
Johanus Haidner
John McLaughlin
John Patterson
John Rothe
John Sugden
John Van Lennep
Jonas Schiött
Jonathan Besler
Joni Karjalainen
Joonas Iivonen
Joonas Lahtiharju
Jouni Alanärä
Juhani Gradistanac
Juho Hännikäinen
Jukka Heinänen
Jukka Varjovuori
Jussi Hytönen
Jussi Laasonen
Justin Snyder
Justin Weaver
Juuso Koivunen
Karin Levenstein

Kary "Realm Master K" Williams
Katrin Wendland
Keith Nelson
Kenric Lee
Kevin Inouye
Kevin Murakoshi
Kevin O'Brien
Kliment Yanev
Konstantin Tsvetkov
Lars Olsen
Lesley Mitchell
Lloyd Eldred
Lorna Winn
Louise Mann
Lukas Lehmann
Luke Ireland
Mackenzie Cosens
Marc Auger
Marco A Assfalk de Oliveira
Marcus Vencel
Mark Allen
Mark Bottomley
Mark Cogan
Mark Davidson
Mark Jolliff
Mark Nelson
Mark Teppo
Markku Mulari
Markku Rontu
Marko Saari
Markus Schoenlau
Martin Noack
Martin Sanders

Martin Wilkinson
Mathieu Glachant
Matthew Mole
Matthew Schmid
Matthew Stewart-Fulton
Merja Polvinen
Michael Baker
Michael Jarvis
Michael Payne
Michael Prendergast
Michael T. Stokes
Michal Barcikowski
Mikko Behm
Mikko Hänninen
Mikko Korhonen
Mikko Parviainen
Mikko Sillanpää
Mira Aaltio
N. Eddiford
Neal Stephenson
Neil Muller
Neufeld Tamás
Nicholas Barton
Nico Möller
Niko Tanhuanpää
Nikodemus Siivola
Noah Bacon
Noora Kumpulainen
Nuutti Vertanen
Olli-Pekka Korpela
Otto Kopra
Oula Kitti
Patrick Shirley

Patrik Olterman
Paul Mullins
Paul Wagner
Perttu Hämäläinen
Peter Törlind
Petri Ihatsu
Petri Wessman
Philip Kramm
Philipp Jaindl
Phillip Pierce-Savoie
Phoebus Ferratus
Pier Antonio Bianchi
Ralph Hempel
Ralph Miller
Rami Laaksonen
Randy Holte
René Kriek
Richard Crabtree
Richard Cullinan
Richard Jurgens
Richard Lowry
Robert Charrette
Robert Fisher
Robert Mauler
Robert Sayers
Robert Sulentic
Robin D. Toll
Roger Svalberg
Roland Cooper
Roland Fuhrmann
Ronny Kilén
Royce Calverley
Ryan Wolf

— ACKNOWLEGEMENTS —

Samuel Munilla
Scott Aldinger
Scott Nimmo
Sean Hastings
Sébastien Jubeau
Sergei Terjajev
Shannon Walker
Simone Zarbin
Stacy Stocki
Stefano Salvadori
Stephen Hobson
Steve Planchin
Steven Danielson
Susanna Sorvali
Suvi Ylioja
Szymon Szymanski
Taneli Pirinen
Tapio Pellinen
Teemu Kari
Tero Alanko
Terry Olson
Thomas Belloma
Thomas Griffiths
Tia Kiesiläinen
Tiago Ferreira
Tim Owens
Tim Trant
Timon Pike
Timothy Carroll
Tina Aspiala

Titta Tolvanen
Tom Hudson
Tom McKinnell
Tomas Suazo
Tome Loh
Tony C Nelson
Tony Stewart
Topi Mikkola
Tracy Mellow
Tuomas Lempiäinen
Tuomo Aimonen
Tuukka Pääkkönen
Tuuli Salmi
Valeri Saltikoff
Ville Henell
Ville Kankainen
Ville Kastari
Ville Vihikangas
Ville Vuorela
Ville-Hermanni Kilpiä
Walter Neubauer
Walter Vasquez
Warhorse Studios
Wesley Arnold
William Brickman
Wolfgang Pretl
Yancy Orchard
Younghwan Choo
Zoë Chandler

# Further reading

If you've enjoyed this book you might like my blog (guywindsor. net/blog), and please consider buying one or more of the following:

*The Swordsman's Companion*, a training manual for medieval longsword, 2004. http://guywindsor.net/blog/tsc

*The Duellist's Companion*, a training manual for 17th century Italian rapier, 2006. http://guywindsor.net/blog/tdcbook

*The Little Book of Push-ups*, 2009. The title says it all. http://guywindsor.net/blog/pushups

*The Armizare Vade Mecum,* mnemonic verses for remembering Fiore's Art, 2011. http://guywindsor.net/blog/avm

*Mastering the Art of Arms vol 1: The Medieval Dagger,* a training manual for Fiore's dagger material, 2012. http://guywindsor.net/blog/dagger

*Veni VADI Vici,* a transcription and translation of Filippo Vadi's *De Arte Gladiatoria Dimicandi,* with commentary and analysis, 2013. http://guywindsor.net/blog/vvv

*Mastering the Art of Arms, vol 3: Longsword, Advanced Techniques*

*and Concepts* (forthcoming in 2016). http://guywindsor.net/blog/maav3

If you already have them all, thank you for your generous support of my work!

Finally, let me ask you now to review this book, for better or worse, wherever is convenient for you. If I've done something right I need to know to do it again; moreover, I need to know what could be improved. As Vadi wrote: "And if this my little work finds its way into the hands of anyone versed in the art and appears to him to have anything superfluous or wrong, please adjust, reduce or add to it as he pleases. Because in the end I place myself under his correction and censure." Thank you!

# Bibliography

This bibliography is much larger than the book strictly needs; it is adapted from a separate and more academic publication I am working on. However, it is complete (in that it has the reference details for every work I cite in this book), and I thought it might be useful to writers, game designers, and martial artists, to get some useful ideas about further reading.

Not every citation is a recommendation, so I have added an asterisk to every secondary source that I consider recommended reading *for this subject,* and added a short note as to why you might want to read it. Note then that if I have mentioned it in passing in the text, and so cited it here, I might not be recommending it because it's probably not useful to you, even if it might be entertaining or otherwise interesting.

## MANUSCRIPT SOURCES:

Anonymous. *Royal Armouries Manuscript I.33*. Royal Armouries, Leeds.

Fiore dei Liberi. *Il Fior di Battaglia* (MS Ludwig XV13). J. P. Getty museum, Los Angeles.

Fiore dei Liberi. *Flos Duellatorum*. Pisani-Dossi Library, Corbetta, Italy.

Fiore dei Liberi. *Il Fior di Battaglia*. (Morgan MS M 383). Pierpont Morgan Museum, New York

Fiore dei Liberi. *Florius de Arte Luctandi* (MSS LATIN 11269), Bibliotheque Nationale Francaise, Paris.

Monte, Pietro. *Exercitiorum Atque Artis Militaris Collectanea*. Escorial MS A.IV.23, El Escorial, San Lorenzo de el Escorial, Spain.

Vadi, Philippo. *De Arte Gladiatoria Dimicandi*. Biblioteca Nazionale, Rome.

Silver, George. *Brief Instructions on my Paradoxes of Defence*. Additional MS 34192. British Library.

Vadi, Philippo. 2005. *L'arte cavalleresca del combattimento*. ed Marco Rubboli and Luca Cesari. Rimini. Il Cerchio

*Codex Döbringer*. Ms. 3227a. Germanisches Nationalmuseum, Nuremberg, Germany

*Codex Ringeck*. MS Dresden C.487. Sächsische Landesbibliothek, Dresden, Germany

*Gladiatoria*, MS KK5013, Kunsthistorisches Museum in Vienna, Austria

*Talhoffer's Fechtbuch*. MS Chart.A.558. Universitäts- und Forschungsbibliothek Erfurt/Gotha. Gotha, Germany

*Codex Danzig*, Cod.44.A.8, Biblioteca dell'Accademia Nazionale dei Lincei e Corsiniana, Rome.

*Paulus Kal's Fechtbuch*, Cgm 1507 Bayerische Staatsbibliothek in Munich, Germany.

*Le Jeu de la Hache*, MS Francais 1996. Bibliotheque Nationale Francaise, Paris

## PUBLISHED SOURCES: FENCING PRIMARY SOURCES, ALSO MODERN EDITIONS AND TRANSLATIONS OF FENCING PRIMARY SOURCES.

Anonymous. I.G. 1594. *Giacomo di Grassi, His True Arte of Defence*, London: Thomas Churchyard.

l'Abbat. tr. Andrew Mahon. 1734. *Fencing, or the Use of the Small Sword*. Dublin.

Agrippa, Camillo.1553. *Trattato di Scientia d'Arme, con vn Dialogo di Filosofia*. Rome: Antonio Blado.

Alfieri, Francesco. 1640. *La Scherma*. Padua.

Angelo, Domenico. 1763. *l'Ecole des Armes*. Paris.

Angelo, Domenico. 1787. *The School of Fencing*. London.

Capoferro, Ridolfo. 1610. *Gran Simulacro del arte e del uso della scherma*. Siena, Italy: Silvestro Marchetti and Camillo Turi.

Fabris, Salvator. 1606. *Lo Schermo, overo Scienza d'Arme*. Copenhagen, Denmark: Henrico Waltkirch.

Forgeng, Jeffrey. 2003. *The Medieval Art of Swordsmanship: A Facsimile & Translation of Europe's Oldest Personal Combat Treatise, Royal Armouries MS I.33*. Benecia, CA. Chivalry Bookshelf.

Forgeng, Jeffrey. 2013. *The Illuminated Fightbook – Royal Armouries Manuscript I.33*. London: Extraordinary Editions.

Forgeng, Jeffrey. 2006. *The Art of Combat: A German Martial Arts Treatise of 1570*. New York: Palgrave Macmillan

di Grassi, Giacomo.1570. *Ragione di adoprar sicuramente l'Arme*. Venice: Giordano Ziletti.

Giganti, Nicoletto. 1606. *La Schola overo Teatro*. Venice: Giovanni Antonio and Giacomo de' Franceschi.

Girard, P. J. F. 1740. *Traite des Armes*. Paris.

Godfrey, John. 1747. *A Treatise Upon the Useful Science of Defence*. London.

Hope, Sir William. 1687. *The Scots Fencing Master*. Edinburgh.

Hope, Sir William. 1707. *The New, Short and Easy Method of Fencing*. Edinburgh.

Kirby, Jared. 2013. *A Gentleman's Guide to Duelling: Of Honour and Honourable Quarrels.* Barnsley, UK: Frontline Books. (This is an edition of Vincentio Saviolo's *His Practice*, from 1595.)

Leoni, Tom. 2005. *The Art of Dueling: Salvator Fabris' rapier fencing treatise of 1606).* Highland Village, TX.: Chivalry Bookshelf.

Leoni, Tom. 2009. *Fiore dei Liberi's Fior di Battaglia translation into English.* Wheaton, IL. Freelance Academy Press.

Leoni, Tom. 2010a. *The Complete Renaissance Swordsman.* Wheaton, IL. Freelance Academy Press. (This is a translation of Antonio Manciolino's *Opera Nova* from 1531.)

Leoni, Tom. 2010b. *Venetian Rapier: Nicoletto Giganti's 1606 Rapier Fencing Curriculum.* Wheaton, IL. Freelance Academy Press.

Leoni, Tom. 2011. *The Art and Practice of Fencing.* Wheaton IL. Freelance Academy Press.

Leoni, Tom. 2012. *Fiore de'Liberi Fior di Battaglia, Second English Edition.* Wheaton IL. Freelance Academy Press.

de Liancouer. 1692. *Le Maitre d'Armes.* Paris.

Malipiero, Massimo. 2006. *Il Fior di battaglia di Fiore dei Liberi da Cividale (Il Codice Ludwig XV 13 del J. Paul Getty Museum).* Udine, Italy: Ribis.

Manciolino, Antonio. 1531. *Opera Nova.* Venice.

Marozzo, Achille. 1536. *Opera Nova.* Modena.

McBane, Donald. 1728. *The Expert Sword-man's Companion.*

Meyer, Joachim. 1570. *Gründtliche Beschreibung der Kunst des Fechtens.* Strasburg.

Mondschein, Kenneth. 2009. *Fencing: A Renaissance Treatise.* New York: Italica Press

Monte, Pedro. 1509. *Exercitiorum Atque Artis Militaris Collectanea.* Milan.

Novati, Francesco. 1902. *Flos Duellatorum, Il Fior di Battaglia di Maestro Fiore dei Liberi da Premariacco.* Bergamo: Instituto Italiano d'Arte Grafiche.

Porzio, Luca, and Gregory Mele, 2002. *De Arte Gladiatoria Dimicandi.* San Fransisco, CA. Chivalry Bookshelf.

Rector, Mark. 2000. *Medieval Combat: A Fifteenth-Century Manual of Swordfighting and Close-Quarter Combat.* London: Greenhill Books.

Roworth, C. 1798. *The Art of Defence on Foot.*

Silver, George. 1599. *Paradoxes of Defence.* London. Edward Blount.

Silver, George. 1898. *The Works of George Silver.* Ed. Cyril G.R. Matthey. London. George Bell and Sons.

Terminiello, Piermarco. 2013. *The Lost Second Book of Nicoletto Giganti (1608).* United Kingdom: Fox Spirit Books.

Thomas, Nick S. 2007. *Rapier: The Art and Use of Fencing by Ridolfo Capo Ferro.* London: SwordWorks.

Tobler, Christian. 2002. *Secrets of German Medieval Swordsmanship.* Benecia, CA. Chivalry Bookshelf. (This is a translation and commentary on the Codex Ringeck.)

Tobler, Christian. 2004. *Fighting with the German Longsword.* Highland Village, TX. Chivalry Bookshelf.

Tobler, Christian. 2006. *In Service of the Duke (The 15th Century Fighting Treatise of Paulus Kal).* Highland Village, TX. Chivalry Bookshelf.

Viggiani, Angelo. 1575. *Lo schermo.* Venice: Giorgio Angelieri.

Viggiani, Angelo. 1575. *Lo Schermo.* Trans Jherek Swanger. Published online at http://mac9.ucc.nau.edu/manuscripts/LoSchermo.pdf

## SECONDARY SOURCES

*Amberger, J. Christoph. 1999. *The Secret History of the Sword.* Burbank CA.: Multi-Media Books. Lots of interesting articles and ideas.

*Anglo, Sydney. 2000. *The Martial Arts of Renaissance Europe.* New Haven and London. Yale University Press. Useful and interesting overview of early fencing treatises.

Augustine. 1931. *The City of God.* trans. John Healey. New York: Dutton.Brown, Terry. 1997. *English Martial Arts.* London: Anglo Saxon Press

Baldick, Robert. 1970. *The Duel: A History of Duelling.* Spring Books.

Bernstein, Peter. 2008. *Against the Gods: the Remarkable Story of Risk.* Wiley.

Capwell, Tobias. 2012. *The Noble Art of the Sword.* London: The Wallace Collection.

*Carruthers, Mary. 2008. *The Book of Memory: A Study of Memory in Medieval Culture.* Cambridge: Cambridge University Press. Really useful book on memory; helpful when reading any medieval treatise.

Castiglione, Baldassare. 1724. *The Courtier.* (Translator unknown). London: Bettesworth, Curll, Battley, Clarke and Payne.

*Castle, Egerton. 1892. *Schools and Masters of Fence.* London. George Bell and Sons.

Charette, Robert N. 2011. *Fiore dei Liberi's Armizare: The Chivalric Martial Arts System of Il Fior di Battaglia.* Wheaton, IL. Freelance Academy Press.

Chaucer, Geoffrey. 1987. "The Nun's Priest's Tale", in *The Riverside Chaucer,* ed. Larry D. Benson. Oxford: Oxford University Press.

Clark, G. 2007. *A farewell to alms: A brief economic history of the world.* Princeton, N.J.: Princeton University Press.

Clements, John. 1998. *Medieval Swordsmanship.* Boulder, CO. Paladin Press 1998

Cockburn, John. 1888. *The History of Duels.* Edinburgh (first published in 1720.)

Cohen, Richard. 2002. *By The Sword.* London. Random House.

Crystal, Ben and David Crystal. *You Say Potato: A Book about Accents.* 2014. Macmillan. London.

Curtius, E. R. 1990. *European Literature and the Latin Middle Ages.* Princeton, N.J.: Princeton University Press.

Ferguson, Niall. 2008. *The Ascent of Money: A Financial History of the World*. Penguin Books. London.

Ferriss, Timothy. 2011. *The 4-Hour Body: An Uncommon Guide to Rapid Fat-Loss, Incredible Sex and Becoming Superhuman*. Vermilion.

Friday, Karl. 1997. *Legacies of the Sword: The Kashima-Shinryu and Samurai Martial Culture*. University of Hawaii Press. Hawaii.

*Gallwey, Timothy. 1997. *The Inner Game of Tennis*. Random House Trade Paperbacks. Fascinating ideas on how skills are learned.

* de Gamez, Gutierre Diaz. tr. Joan Evans. 2004. *The Unconquered Knight: the Chronicle of Pero Niño*. Boydell Press. Great read, a contemporary's account of the life of a very successful knight in the early 1400s.

Gaugler, William. 1998. *The History of Fencing, foundations of modern swordplay*. Bangor, Maine: Laureate Press.

*Grossman, Dave. 1996. *On Killing*. Back Bay Books. Essential reading on the psychology of killing.

Hand, Stephen. 2006. *English Swordsmanship*. Highland Village, TX.: Chivalry Bookshelf.

*Hutton, Alfred. 1901. *The Sword and the Centuries*. London: Grant Richards. Great source for fencing stories.

Jacobs, A.J. 2009. *The Year of Living Biblically*. London:Arrow Books.

Kellett, Rachel E. . 2008. *Single Combat and Warfare in German Literature of the High Middle Ages: Stricker's* Karl der Grosse *and Daniel von dem Blühenden Tal* (PhD diss. Published by MHRA)

*Kirchner, Paul. 2004. *Dueling With The Sword And Pistol: 400 Years of One-on-One Combat*. Boulder CO.: Paladin Press. The best source for accounts of duels.

Lindholm, David. 2003. *Knightly Art of the Longsword*. Paladin Press.

Martin, George R.R. 1997. *A Game of Thrones (A Song of Ice and Fire, book 1)*. Bantam.

Mele, Gregory. 2013. *Captain of Fortune: Galeazzo da Montova*. Wheaton, IL.: Freelance Academy Press.

*Miller, Rory. 2008. *Meditations on Violence*. Ymaa Publication Center. Totally essential reading for anyone interested in how violence works at any level.

Mondschein, Kenneth. 2011.*The Knightly Art of Battle*. Los Angeles, CA. J. Paul Getty Trust.

Morgan, Richard K. 2008. *The Steel Remains*. Gollancz.

Nadi, Aldo. 1996. *The Living Sword*. Laureate Press.

Oakeshott, Ewart. 2012. *European Weapons and Armour: From the Renaissance to the Industrial Revolution*. Boydell Press. London.

Perez-Reverte, Arturo. 2004. *The Fencing Master*. Mariner Books.

*Pinker, Stephen. 2011. *The Better Angels of Our Nature*. London: Penguin. Really useful overview of how violence has declined since medieval times.

Richards, Colin. 2008. *Fiore dei Liberi 1409 Wrestling and Dagger*. Hamburg, Germany. Arts of Mars Books.

*Skaff Elias, George, Richard Garfield, and K. Robert Gutschera. 2012. *Characteristics of Games*. Cambridge, MA. The MIT Press. The fundamentals of how games work. Essential for all game designers. And players.

Syed, Matthew. 2011. *Bounce: The Myth of Talent and the Power of Practice*. Fourth Estate. London.

Taubes, Gary. 2007. *Good Calories, Bad Calories*. Knopf. New York.

Turner, Craig and Tony Soper. 1990. *Methods and Practice of Elizabethan Swordplay*. Carbonsdale and Edwardsville, IL.: Southern Illinois University Press.

Vail, Jason. 2006. *Medieval And Renaissance Dagger Combat*. Boulder, CO. Paladin Press.

Wagner, Paul. 2003. *Master of Defence.* Boulder CO. Paladin Press.

*Waitzkin, Josh. 2008. *The Art of Learning.* Free Press. Very useful and interesting book on how to master any field. Useful especially for martial artists.

Wilson, William. 2002. *The Arte of Defence.* Benecia, CA. Chivalry Bookshelf.

Windsor, Guy. 2004. *The Swordsman's Companion.* Highland Village, TX. Chivalry Bookshelf.

Windsor, Guy, 2006. *The Duellist's Companion.* Highland Village, TX. Chivalry Bookshelf.

Windsor, Guy. 2012. *Mastering the Art of Arms vol 1: The Medieval Dagger.* Wheaton, IL. Freelance Academy Press.

Windsor, Guy. 2013. *Veni Vadi Vici.* Helsinki, Finland: The School of European Swordsmanship.

Windsor, Guy. 2014. *Mastering the Art of Arms vol 2: The Medieval Longsword.* Helsinki, Finland: The School of European Swordsmanship.

Windsor, Guy. 2007. "The Elements of Test Cutting". *Western Martial Arts Illustrated* ed. Scott Baltic. Issue 2, Fall 2007.

Wolfthal, Diane. 2009. "La Donna alla finestra: Desiderio sessuale lecito e illecito nell'Italia rinascimentale," in *Sesso nel Rinascimento: pratica, perversione e punizione nell' Italia rinascimentale,* ed. Allison Levy. Florence: Le Lettere.

## Online sources and references

Many of the treatises I mention are available online at the amazing Wiktenauer. See www.wiktenauer.com

Aristotle, *Physics.* Translated by Hardie, R. P. and Gaye, R. K. online at: http://classics.mit.edu/Aristotle/physics.html

Capelli, A. 1912. *Dizionario di Abbreviature Latini ed Italiani.* Milan. online at: http://www.hist.msu.ru/Departments/ Medieval/ Cappelli/

Goldman, David P. 2012. "The Divine Music of Mathematics" online at http://www.firstthings.com/article/2012/03/the-divine-music-of-mathematics.

Viggiani, Angelo. 1575. *Lo Schermo.* Translation by Jherek Swanger. Published online at http://mac9.ucc.nau.edu/manuscripts/LoSchermo.pdf

Windsor, Guy. 2012. "Italian Longsword Guards". Online at: http://guywindsor.net/blog/guardsarticle

Zoe Claire, article on violence: http://unnecessarywisdom.wordpress.com/2013/05/02/boys-and-violence-its-not-the-problem-its-the-solution/

# About the Author

Guy Windsor has been researching historical Italian swordsmanship and knightly combat since the late nineties, and has been teaching the Art of Arms professionally since 2001. His books include *The Swordsman's Companion*, *The Duellist's Companion*, *Veni Vadi Vici*, and the *Mastering the Art of Arms* series. He also blogs on swordsmanship at guywindsor.net/blog

He lives in Helsinki, Finland, with his wife and daughters.

www.swordschool.com

Lightning Source UK Ltd.
Milton Keynes UK
UKOW06f1937180516

274543UK00006B/116/P

9 789526 793481